TRUE CRIME

Most Wanted

BY
THE EDITORS OF
TIME-LIFE BOOKS
Alexandria, Virginia

Most Wanted

COVER: CLAUDE DALLAS

Who Is Most Wanted?

The phrase *most wanted* conjures up thoughts of an FBI poster showing a grim-looking desperado whose face can be studied by post-office patrons while they wait in line to mail a package or buy a stamp. Whether they have won such an official designation or not, all of those whose stories appear in this book have been prime targets of authorities eager to bring them to justice. The kinds of acts such felons have committed—bombings, bank robberies, multiple murders, kidnappings, for instance—are deemed to pose especially serious threats to law and order and to society's well-being.

But it isn't just the nature of their crimes that defines the most wanted. To earn such a designation, a person must successfully avoid capture for a period of time, in spite of the most strenuous efforts of lawmen. In the classic scenario—as in most of the stories in this book—the authorities are a hunting party and the criminal is the quarry, the man on the run, and the action is spun out over weeks or months.

In some cases, however, it is by siege and not by chase that authorities bag their prey. Such an operation, which may involve hundreds of heavily armed men, along with planes, helicopters, tanks, and other military-style gear, brings the drama of capture to a quick conclusion.

I want to
meet and enjoy
the company of
a number of
women.

CHRIS WILDER

1

Driven to Kill

To the casual eye, Christopher Wilder seemed to have it all. A partner in a successful construction and electrical contracting company in Boynton Beach, Florida, up the coast from Miami, everything about him suggested that he was definitely doing all right for a fellow in his thirties. Fit, tanned, and tall at just under six feet, he wasn't bad looking despite a receding hairline, with bright blue eyes and a short, neatly trimmed blond-brown beard. He dressed carefully in faded designer jeans and silk shirts, sometimes slipping on a leather jacket for the occasional cool day. His casually expensive garb was set off by a gold bracelet and a gold Rolex wrist watch. There was one note, though, that was a little off key: what looked like a big diamond in his pinky ring was a fake.

Wilder loved expensive cars, and he loved driving them fast. He tooled around in a turbo-charged white Porsche 911 Carrera, and in his off-hours he occasionally drove another 911, a black one, in Florida sports-car meets, both as an amateur and as a professional. He was never a top racer or a big money winner, but he loved the macho aura of his fast-track hobby.

Married once and only briefly while he was still in his twenties, Wilder was very picky about women. He liked them young and beautiful — beautiful enough to be models. He wasn't shy about introducing himself to a stranger who'd caught his eye, and many of the women he approached were flattered when he said he was a fashion photographer looking for a model. When such encounters occurred, Chris Wilder ordinarily had a 35-mm. reflex camera swinging from his neck, as a sort of badge of authenticity.

His canalside house at 933 Mission Hill Road in Boynton Beach smacked of the playboy life. A Cadillac Eldorado and a fancy recreational vehicle sat in the driveway. Around back was a hot tub and a screened-in swimming pool, on whose bottom was painted a map of Wilder's native Australia along with a sprinkling of kangaroos and koala bears. A dock fingered out into the canal, with a speedboat for water-skiing on nearby Lake Ida.

Inside, Wilder had a photo studio, with track lights overhead and a big fan so he could give his subjects a sexy, windblown look. People who saw pictures Wilder took were surprised at their quality; they seemed quite ordinary, not what you'd expect from a published photographer. And he seemed oddly reluctant to take snapshots when he was with friends, often pleading that he was out of film.

Wilder seldom drank, and he didn't smoke or do drugs. He shunned the rough language of the construction trades. His harshest expletive was, "Oh, love a duck!" Nobody told off-color or ethnic jokes in his presence or poked cruel fun at others. Once, when an employee at Sawtel Construction and Electric made sport of an overweight coworker, Wilder called him to task sharply. He climbed all over another employee he heard speaking rudely to one of the women tellers at the local bank. "These are ladies," Wilder snapped, "and you will treat them as such." Not that he was an arrogant, overbearing boss. On the contrary, Wilder's employees appreciated his good manners and his easygoing ways on the job; he would even sing around the office. As cheery as he seemed, though, he chewed his fingernails down to the quick, so badly that they bled.

Wilder was fond of animals and ready to spend money on them. He owned three English setters — Turbo, April, and War. He contributed to Save the Whales, a fund set up to halt the decline in their numbers. On one occasion he took a wild raccoon with an injured paw to a veterinarian for treatment, which cost him $143. And Chris Wilder didn't simply steer clear and keep going when he saw a turtle crawling across a highway. He would stop and carry the creature to safety, lest another car run over it.

Women who found themselves in the animal lover's hands didn't enjoy such tenderness. Sometimes he didn't let up until they were dead.

Christopher Bernard Wilder was born on March 13, 1945, in Sydney, Australia. His father, Coley, was a U.S. Navy officer from Alabama, and June, his mother, was

The style of Christopher Wilder's spacious Boynton Beach, Florida, home suggests bachelorhood and success. An enormous sofa facing a stone fireplace is the focal point of the living room *(left)*. In the den, shown in the wraparound view above, mementos of automobile races in which Wilder competed cover the walls and fill the shelves around the giant-screen television. He kept his white Porsche 911 in the garage *(right)*.

an Australian. The infant almost died at birth. Indeed, the doctor suggested calling in a priest to administer last rites. But Coley Wilder would have none of that, and he told the doctor to forget the child's soul—just attend to his life. Christopher came close to death again a year or so later, when he was found floating facedown in a swimming pool. At about five, Chris inexplicably lapsed into a coma while the family was making a car trip across the United States. Six hours elapsed before he regained consciousness in a hospital, apparently without any ill effects, although Wilder would later claim to experience blackouts.

Throughout Wilder's boyhood his family, which eventually included three more sons, moved from one naval post to another: Sangley Point in the Philippines, San Francisco, Albuquerque, Norfolk, Las Vegas, the Philippines again. In 1959, when Chris was 14, Chief Warrant Officer Wilder retired, and the family settled in Sydney. As far as the boys were concerned, Coley Wilder ran a very tight ship, demanding that he be addressed as Sir and administering the belt for infractions of rules. "We were not a close family," said Stephen, the next brother. "There did not seem to be a great deal of love and affection between any of us although I do know my parents had a very active sexual life."

Chris was a poor student, and he dropped out of school at 16. He became an apprentice carpenter and did well at it. "All he cared about," said his boss, "was cars and work, cars and work." The boss had it only half-right: the youth cared about two other things—surfing, which he practiced passionately at the Sydney beaches, and girls, who came with the beaches. Edgy and nervous around most men, Chris seemed to relax in the presence of women—possibly because he was closer to his mother than to his father, or at least could wheedle things out of her. In any case, Wilder's American accent impressed the girls, and he played that for all it was worth.

When Chris Wilder was after a girl, it didn't matter to him if somebody got hurt, not even if it was his brother. "I once had a 16-year-old girlfriend," Stephen said. "Chris moved in. He ended up getting her in the bushes and taking nude pictures of her."

And there was something else Stephen noticed about his brother. He was, Stephen said later, "obsessed with having power over women." It was an ugly kind of power.

Exactly when Wilder started intimidating women into sex is not known. The first record of rape dates back to 1963,

when he was 17. Prowling an isolated stretch of Sydney beach with some like-minded youths one day, Wilder and his mates came upon an attractive young teenager and started to menace her. Then Chris stepped forward. He had a proposition: If she would submit to sex with him, he would protect her from the pack. And so she did—and of course he didn't. The others raped her too.

Wilder was arrested, jailed, and charged with gang rape. He pleaded guilty to "carnal knowledge," a legalism for rape by a juvenile. Because of his youth, a lenient judge sentenced him to one year's probation, provided that he undergo sex counseling. Wilder spent only a week or two behind bars in a detention center after his arrest, but it was long enough to mark him with an enduring terror of prison. His mandatory therapy included electroshock treatments: He was shown pictures of nude women, and electric shocks were applied as he became aroused. The notion, apparently, was to put the brakes on his libido. Instead, the treatment filled him with rage—and would give him some sadistic ideas to put into practice himself in the years ahead.

Why Suzanne Polanski* ever consented to marry Chris Wilder is one of those bafflements of male-female attraction. A 20-year-old schoolteacher when she met Wilder at the beach, she knew from the start that there was something off about him, at least sexually. He threatened forcible rape on an early date when Suzanne refused to pose nude for photographs. He eyed her 16-year-old sister and made an advance to her attractive mother that turned into an assault when he tried to rip off the mother's clothes and drag her down onto a bed. He gave up and sullenly left the house when she started screaming and threatening to call police.

The wedding took place in February 1968, and what followed was a debacle. Making love to his wife didn't satisfy Wilder sexually, and he often masturbated repeatedly in a single day. Wilder was so fixated on women that the only parts of the newspaper he looked at were the swimsuit and underwear ads. At the movies, the sight of a woman in bed or partly undressed got Wilder so worked up, breathing so heavily, that Suzanne was embarrassed. On one occasion, he appropriated her briefcase, and when she finally recovered the bag, it was stuffed with notes about women that included their names, addresses, measurements, and marital status. There were also numerous snapshots of nude women or of women draped in towels or wearing bikinis and dresses. Suzanne recognized many of the clothes. They were hers.

---

* Denotes pseudonym, used at the request of people who want their privacy protected.

There were other oddities: The apartment complex in which the couple lived was afflicted with a rash of what police called "snow dropping"—the theft of women's undergarments from clotheslines. Because of his record as a sex offender, the cops questioned Wilder closely in the matter. They let him go. But his wife found some of the lingerie in their apartment.

Suzanne soon learned to fear her husband's violent ways. Once, in a fury, he slammed his fist through the glass panel of a front door. There were times, too, when Wilder came home with mysterious scratches all over his neck and back. When his wife asked about them, Wilder shrugged and said that he'd been itching badly and had scratched himself. The explanation was hard to swallow because his chronic nail-biting left him nothing to scratch with.

An idea of how Wilder might have acquired the scratches came to Suzanne Wilder during their sexual relations. Chris would say to her, "I want you to hurt me. I want you to scratch me." Suzanne didn't care for that. Nor did she enjoy his insistence on frequent anal sex. But it was risky to deny him. When she refused his demands, he would slap her or shake her by the shoulders, then go into the bathroom and stay under the shower, sometimes for as long as an hour.

Suzanne Wilder eventually told police of frightening occurrences. Her husband, she said, was always tinkering with her car. After four months of marriage, her brakes failed one day, and the lines were found to be empty of fluid. Two weeks later the steering failed, and she ran off the road; a pin in the steering system was broken. Several months after that incident, she was lying in bed and smelled gas. She got up. All the windows were shut and Wilder was outside. In the kitchen, one of the stove's gas jets had been turned on to its highest setting.

Twice in her short marriage, Suzanne Wilder left her husband, then returned. Finally, after a miserable year, she couldn't take the abuse any longer and left him for good.

After the breakup, Chris Wilder began trolling for women more intensely than ever, often at Manly, a popular beach just outside Sydney. His bait was the camera. His quarry: young, slender, large-breasted girls and women. His technique was well-illustrated one November day in 1969 when he stretched out beside an 18-year-old nurse trainee at Manly. The smiling, blue-eyed young man engaged the girl in conversation. After a few minutes he politely inquired: Had she ever done any modeling? She was perfect for it. He should know because he was a professional photographer.

The young woman was flattered when he asked her to pose in a bathing suit he'd brought with him. The two of them went to a bathhouse, supposedly so she could change. Once there, however, he coerced her into posing nude; she was too frightened to say no. Afterward, he virtually blackmailed her into going to a hotel with him by threatening to send the photos to the hospital where she worked if she refused. Wilder raped the young woman. In the weeks following he wouldn't leave her alone, repeatedly calling her at the hospital and at home. She eventually told her mother what had happened, and they went together to the police. Picked up for questioning, Wilder confirmed what his accuser had said and added, "There is something wrong with me but I can't explain my actions." But the young woman wouldn't make a formal complaint against Wilder, so the police couldn't arrest him. The incident simply went into Chris Wilder's thickening dossier.

Nevertheless, the pressure was building, and Wilder responded in a way that he would later repeat. He ran. Selling a piece of property he owned on Queensland's popular Gold Coast, the 24-year-old Wilder bought a one-way ticket to the United States. Taking up residence there would be no problem, since as the child of an American serviceman he was a U.S. citizen. South Florida was his destination, and soon after his arrival in late 1969 he felt very much at home: it was warm, with great beaches, lots of pretty girls, and a construction boom. For a while he worked as a carpenter, then he struck out as a contractor with his own crew of workers. Back in Australia, his family was encouraged by the reports they got. "We were under the impression that he was a very successful person and that he had got himself all straightened out," his brother Stephen recalled.

The family was mistaken. Christopher Wilder was as possessed as ever by the desire to dominate women, so much so that he usually shied away from the assertive, self-confident ones. An exception was a bookkeeper at Sawtel, and the two of them dated for almost a year. But even in a relationship that appeared fairly normal, violence never was far beneath the surface with Wilder. When this woman one morning denied him sex, he flew into a rage and choked her to the point of death, then suddenly released her and headed for the shower.

The woman broke off the relationship, but months later Wilder still wanted to get even—in his mind, that meant having sex with her on his own terms. Wilder finally persuaded her to see him again, and when they met he gave her some strawberry shortcake he'd laced with LSD. He thought she'd lose control of herself, but the bookkeeper had taken LSD in the past and realized what he'd done. Instead of succumbing, she telephoned a friend she had met in a drug rehabilitation program and talked for a long time while Wilder simply sat and listened.

Another woman Wilder regularly dated, an Australian living in Florida, also got a terrible taste of his violence. On one occasion, he beat her so badly about the breasts and abdomen that she coughed up blood. Increasingly, it seemed that the only way Wilder could achieve sexual gratification was by brutalizing his partners. Watching pornographic films on cable TV one evening with another man, Wilder complained to his friend, "There's no violence. I sort of like a little violence."

Wilder didn't often photograph his more or less steady women friends. When he wanted someone to pose, he sometimes hired a prostitute at $100 or so an hour or arranged an engagement with a woman through an escort service. And at the same time, he avidly stalked the beaches and shopping malls for beautiful, impressionable young girls. Wilder once confided to a therapist that he might screen 50 potential victims before settling on one. His technique was to start slowly, handing out a phony modeling-agency business card, and proceed with a slick line, then gradually work up to dominance, coercion, and some sort of sexual contact. Wilder was very good at sensing whether a woman would fall for his act; he rarely got the cold shoulder. He claimed to score with 85 to 90 percent of his targets.

Now and again, things went a little wrong. Wilder had been in the United States only 14 months when Pompano Beach police arrested him for inviting young women on the beach to pose nude for him. He pleaded guilty to disturbing the peace and was fined $15 plus $10 in costs. Over the next five years, no one else came forward with an accusation against Wilder, not even the California woman who encountered Chris Wilder when he was visiting the West Coast in 1973. Fifty years old at the time, she and her 10-year-old twin boys had just left a movie theater when Wilder accosted them at gunpoint and drove them in his gray Cadillac to an isolated spot. He first attempted to have intercourse with the woman but desisted when she pleaded with him to stop because her children were there. He wasn't going to let her off the hook, however, so he forced her to perform oral sex on him. Afterward he made the children perform sex acts with one another and with their mother.

At last, Wilder drove them home. He was polite, even solicitous. Nevertheless, he warned his victim not to phone the police, and she didn't for 11 years. When she at last reported the crime, she told authorities that Wilder had been totally in command, as if he had done the same thing many times before. Dominance

Australia's Manly Beach was one of Christopher Wilder's favorite spots for finding naive young women he could coerce into posing for nude photographs.

and sex were his sole objectives, she thought. He didn't even look in her purse.

The odds finally caught up with Wilder in 1976. On a renovation job, he struck up a conversation with the home-owner's daughter, a pretty 16-year-old about to graduate from high school. When she told him she was looking for a secretarial job, Wilder said he knew about an opening and offered to take her to have an interview. He suggested that she dress seductively, so she changed into a blouse and didn't wear a bra. On the way, he suddenly pulled his pick-up truck to the side of the road and started pawing her. The girl screamed and tried to get away, but Wilder slapped her into submission and forced her to perform oral sex on him.

Then he said something unexpected and confusing to the girl. Claiming to be sorry about what he'd done, he asked her if she wanted to go to the police. She was afraid it might make him angry if she said yes, so she asked him to drive her to her boyfriend's house. As soon as her parents found out what Wilder had done, they called the police. When the cops picked him up, he appeared to be a broken man, sobbing and repentant.

The court-appointed psychologist, D. G. Boozer, concluded that Wilder was "tense, fearful, and apt to experience emotional upheavals which result in complete loss of intellectual controls." The psychologist also judged Wilder a danger to others in his present state of mind and recommended "a structured environment" for him—some kind of resident program where he'd receive treatment. A psychiatrist, however, arrived at the contrary finding that Wilder was *not* dangerous. The experts' opinions were academic in any case. On March 8, 1977, a West Palm Beach jury deliberated only 55 minutes before acquitting Wilder. One of the jurors coolly informed the victim's mother the panel had decided it would have been a physical impossibility for the girl to have performed oral sex on Wilder in the truck—the stick shift, they concluded, would have been in the way.

Wilder was ecstatic. He felt untouchable.

Three years passed before the law heard of Wilder again. Then, on June 21, 1980, a man approached two teenage girls at the Cross County Mall in West Palm Beach, introduced himself as David Pierce, representative of the Barbizon School of Modeling, and said he was seeking models for a pizza ad. Giggling with excitement, the girls tried on shorts and spike-heeled shoes that he bought at a nearby store. "My eyes are the cameras," he told them, evaluating their poise before singling out one, aged 17, for special attention. He bought pizza so she could show him how nicely she could chew. Something in the pizza made her feel disoriented, and when the man invited her outside for a private conversation in his El Camino pickup, she woozily went along. He drove her to a nearby warehouse area and told her to undress. Dreamily, she protested. He said, "You want to be a Barbizon model, don't you?" She recalled later that she felt as if she were detached from her body, floating to the roof of the truck and looking down at herself. The man had sex with her on the front seat, after which he drove her back to the mall.

The girl's grandmother called the Palm Beach County Sheriff, and both girls identified Wilder from a photo lineup put together by police. Detective Arthur Newcomb arrested Wilder at a construction job in Boca Raton. He seemed to be expecting it, and he tacitly admitted to the rape, saying that he was sorry for what had happened. He told Newcomb that he knew he needed help, that he had been seeing a therapist, but that he had discontinued the weekly sessions recently. His job kept him busy during the week, but when the weekend rolled around, he got lonely, something came over him, and he headed for a mall with his camera.

The girl remembered that Wilder had tossed the remains of the pizza slice into a Dumpster, and Newcomb retrieved it. Wilder clammed up when the detective asked what kind of drug he'd dabbed on the pizza; he was smart enough to know that if he admitted drugging the girl, he couldn't claim that she had consented to sex. A urine test of the victim might have revealed traces of LSD, but for some reason she got only a blood test, which showed nothing.

With no physical evidence and no corroborating witnesses, prosecutors had a slim case. Wilder was allowed to plead guilty to reduced charges of attempted sexual battery; the judge sentenced him to five years of probation on condition that he undergo sex therapy. It was the best they could get, thought Detective Newcomb. He felt sure that Wilder would be watched carefully for any probation violation.

Over the next few years Wilder to all outward appearances was a man on the mend, and there were no complaints against him. He seemed to focus his energies on the Sawtel contracting companies, and he went back to his therapist, Ginger Bush, whom he saw at least once a week. But he was a walking time bomb. From 1981 on, the sexual fantasies he reported in his sessions with Bush grew increas-

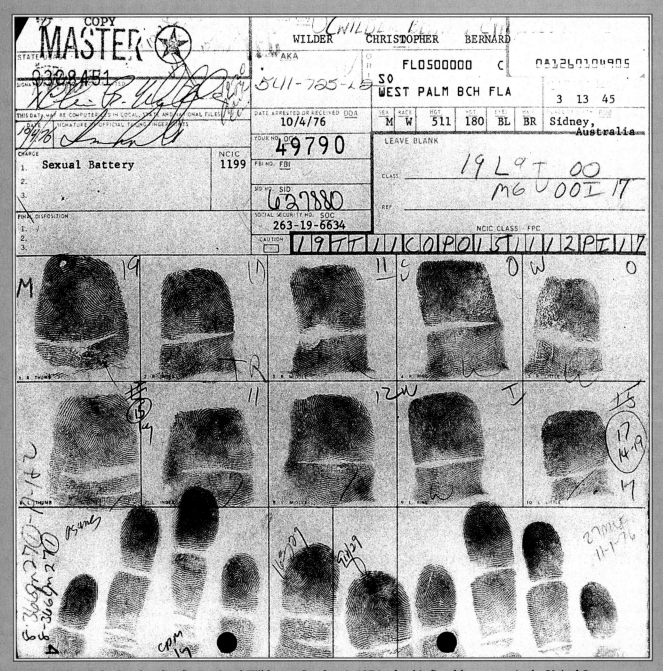

West Palm Beach police fingerprinted Wilder on October 4, 1976, after his first felony arrest in the United States. Accused of forcing a 16-year-old girl to perform oral sex, Wilder was acquitted at his trial five months later.

ingly savage and degrading; he daydreamed of enslaving women for sale in the flesh markets of Asia and Africa, of bondage, beatings, torture, and every brutalizing form of sodomy. He told Bush that one of his favorite novels was John Fowles's *The Collector,* in which a lonely butterfly collector kidnaps a beautiful young woman and eventually poisons her. A second therapist, psychiatrist Richard Zazzi, who saw Wilder a number of times in 1980 and 1981, confirmed that the fantasies were becoming more and more malignant. They now went far beyond pornographic photography and sexual coercion. To Zazzi, Wilder spoke of kidnapping women and cutting them up.

But fantasies were simply fantasies, and not actionable. In December 1982, in consequence of his good behavior, Wilder got permission from his parole officer to visit Australia. It was summer there, and the warm, sunny sands of Sydney called forth familiar habits. Within days of Wilder's arrival, police began receiving complaints about a bearded photographer soliciting girls at Wilder's old hunting ground of Manly beach.

On the 28th of the month, Wilder picked up two 15-year-olds at Manly by handing out bogus business cards and telling them he was an American modeling agent. Once in his car, he blindfolded the girls and drove to a park where he stripped them and took pornographic photos, some with the girls wearing sexy stockings and spike-heeled shoes he supplied. Wilder next drove them to the Top of the Town Motel, where he threatened them, kissed them, sucked their breasts, masturbated while they massaged him, and snapped more nude photos. At last, in late afternoon, Wilder set them free with the usual threats to send the pictures to their parents if they said anything. But the parents of one of the obviously terrorized girls finally pried out the story.

The police arrested Wilder the next day for kidnapping and sexual assault against minors. The crime was a grave one, demanding a bond of $350,000 — $50,000 of which he put up himself, with the balance from deeds to the homes of his parents and an uncle. A trial date was eventually set for April 1984, more than a year hence. Wilder was allowed to return to Florida in 1983 because of what he insisted were pressing business affairs. A full report of his legal situation in Australia was sent to authorities in Palm Beach.

"That was the point that they should have locked him up and thrown the key away," said a rueful Arthur Newcomb. "Had they done that, the FBI and all those other girls would never have had a problem." As far as the Palm Beach County detective was concerned, "the system dropped the ball."

Newcomb had reasons to be critical. Wilder's probation in the 1980 Palm Beach rape specifically prohibited him from misrepresenting himself or his employment; that meant no posing as a photographer or model-agency scout. Because of the line Wilder had handed to the teenagers at Manly, there seemed good cause for Palm Beach authorities to charge him with violating his probation. They could have jailed him immediately, pending the results of a hearing.

Instead, Wilder was merely asked to post $1,000 bond to ensure his appearance in court, and no other jurisdictions were notified of the Palm Beach bond or of Wilder's arraignment in Australia. Not even Detective Newcomb, the original arresting officer, was aware of the developments in Wilder's case.

No new incidents concerning Wilder were reported to the police in 1983. As the date for his trial in Australia came nearer, Wilder's anxiety grew continually. If he was found guilty, as he feared he would be, his mask of status and respectability would be stripped away. The specter of jail loomed over him. He began to unravel.

The 1984 Miami Grand Prix, two days of sports-car racing, was scheduled for Saturday and Sunday, February 25 and 26. Some of the world's best drivers were competing — and though Wilder's probation specifically restricted him to Palm Beach County, nothing could keep him away. He arrived in Miami Saturday morning and drove a black Porsche 911 in a preliminary event called the Camel GTU, finishing 17th, in the middle of the pack, and winning $400. The next day he returned as a spectator, parking his white Porsche 911 Carrera across two spaces so the car wouldn't be scratched.

Exciting, glamorous, highly media-visible, the Grand Prix offered excellent marketing opportunities for all sorts of companies. Cuban-born Rosario Gonzalez, 20, was one of 11 young women hired for $200 a day to hand out samples of Mejoral, a painkiller sold mainly in the Caribbean. A computer sciences student at Miami-Dade Community College, Rosario was undeniably beautiful: five feet six inches tall, with light brown hair framing large, almond-shaped hazel eyes, and a heart-stopping smile. She was nice, too, as sweet and uncomplicated as she was lovely. "This girl was perfect," said her fiancé, 21-year-old William Londos. "The

At a session held for the media during the 1983 Miss Florida pageant in Fort Lauderdale, a photographer happened to catch Christopher Wilder in one of his frames. Wilder had used phony press credentials from an Australian magazine to finagle his way into the session.

Wilder sits in his rain-spattered black Porsche and, at far right, confers with a member of his crew at the Sun Bank 24 Hours of Daytona race on February 4, 1984. A lackluster competitor as usual, Wilder dropped out of the competition when his car developed brake trouble and bumped a guardrail around midnight.

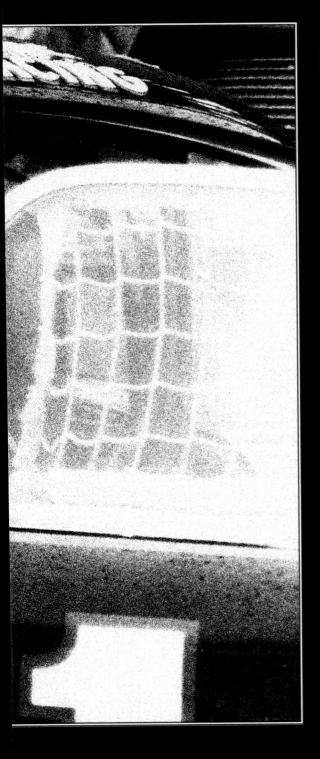

ROSARIO GONZALEZ

first time I ever saw her I said, this is the kind of girl you marry." They planned a June wedding. Meantime, the Grand Prix offered her a chance to make a little money and possibly further the modeling career she thought of pursuing.

On Sunday afternoon at 1:30 Gonzalez, wearing red shorts and a white T-shirt with "Mejoral" on it, went to the company tent to get her purse. It was the last certain sighting of her. One witness later remembered seeing her speaking with a tanned, balding, bearded man at the site of the Grand Prix, and in another possible sighting, a young woman and a man who seemed to match Gonzalez's and Wilder's descriptions were reported in a nearby restaurant. After that, nothing.

By 7 p.m., Rosario Gonzalez's parents began to worry. Their daughter was the sort who came home on time or telephoned to explain why she'd be late. At 9 p.m., they began calling area hospitals, fearing an accident. At 1 a.m., they phoned the police and then went downtown to search the area around the site of the Grand Prix. The race was long over. By 3 a.m., they had found Rosario's gray Oldsmobile Cutlass parked in front of the Dupont Plaza Hotel on the Miami River.

The police started their own unsuccessful search for Gonzalez. Subsequently, investigators learned that another model had introduced her to Christopher Wilder a year or so before, and that he had taken some pictures of her—for the cover of a romance novel, he'd said. Gonzalez told her fiancé about the photo session. "She never saw the pictures and never heard from him again," said Londos.

On Monday, March 5, a week and a day after Rosario's disappearance, Elizabeth Kenyon, 23, a teacher of emotionally disturbed youngsters at Coral Gables High School in suburban Miami, left school after class and simply vanished. When she didn't show up that night, her worried roommate phoned Beth's parents in Pompano Beach, 35 miles up the coast. She had visited them Sunday, they said, but they hadn't seen her since. Because she lived in Dade County, the Kenyons phoned the Metro-Dade police, who took down the description of a slender, lovely young woman with long brown hair and a dazzling smile. In 1982 Beth had been Orange Bowl princess and a Miss Florida finalist.

The police saw no reason to suspect foul play and listed her as a missing person.

The next morning, Tuesday, March 6, William and Dolores Kenyon went to their daughter's apartment and started calling everyone in her address book.

One of the names familiar to the Kenyons was Chris Wilder's. Beth had gone out with him a few times after meeting him at the 1982 Miss Florida Pageant and had introduced him to her parents. She told her mother that he seemed a perfect gentleman; he never made a pass, never even tried to kiss her. As far as she was concerned their relationship wasn't a serious one, and when Wilder asked her to marry him she had tactfully declined. The Kenyons found Wilder polite, but they thought him too old for Beth. The relationship had seemed to taper off. Curiously, though, his name had come up just the day before Beth disappeared. She told her parents that she had missed out on a $4,000 modeling job that Wilder had found for her at the Miami Grand Prix because she'd been out of town. The Kenyons called him at home and left a message on his answering machine.

That same Tuesday, Chris Wilder arrived for work around 6:30 a.m. with cuts and bandages on both hands. When his partner, Zeke Kimbrell, and their secretary, Frances Savage, asked about the injuries, Wilder said that the dogs had been fighting, and when he pulled them apart he got scratched. During the fight, he added, they broke a sliding glass door, and the youngest dog, Turbo, had cut its foot and messed up the place with blood.

Wilder sent some Sawtel workmen to the house to fix the glass, which had a waist-high hole in it. One workman who knew the dogs was surprised to hear they'd been fighting, since they'd always seemed so gentle. He also thought it was odd that the animals didn't appear to have been injured in any way. The crew was a little surprised when Wilder joined them at the house, since it was something he rarely bothered to do. Nor did he simply supervise; he busied himself cleaning up spots of blood by the swimming pool. When a workman tried to go into a bathroom, it was locked. Wilder said bloody rags from the dogfight were in there and curtly told the man to use the other bathroom. No one thought much about any of this, not at the time.

On Wednesday, after getting a call from the Kenyons, Ron Stone, an insurance agent who had dated Beth Kenyon, stopped by a Shell service station near her school where she often bought gas. Questioned by Stone, attendant Richard Norman remembered that she'd come in for $10 worth of gas about 2 o'clock on Monday afternoon. A man in a Cadillac Eldorado—Norman thought the color was light green—pulled in behind Beth and paid cash for the gas. They seemed in a hurry. When Norman tried to wipe Beth's windshield, she told him to skip it; she had to rush to the airport. The attendant overheard Beth ask her companion how she looked and heard him say approvingly that she looked just fine. She also asked who'd take the pictures, and he said he'd be doing it himself. The cars drove away together in the direction of Miami International Airport.

That same day, Beth Kenyon's maroon Chrysler convertible was found backed into a long-term parking slot in Building Five at Miami International. The front license plate had been removed, perhaps because someone wanted to delay identification of the car. Kenyon's books and sunglasses were inside. There was no sign of a struggle.

On Thursday, March 8, Wilder visited his probation officer, dropped off his racing jumpsuit with a seamstress to be monogrammed, and returned the call the Kenyons had made two days before. He told them that he hadn't seen Beth for a month.

Following up on Ron Stone's discovery at the Shell station, William Kenyon and his son, William junior, went there themselves on Saturday. They took along photographs of men friends from Beth's scrapbook to show to station attendant Richard Norman. That's the man, he said, pointing to a snapshot of Christopher Wilder. From that moment on, William Kenyon was completely convinced that it was Wilder who had taken his daughter.

The Kenyons had just hired private investigators Ken Whitaker, Sr., a former FBI agent, and his son Ken junior to look for Beth, and later that Saturday Ken junior went to see Norman himself and confirmed his identification of Wilder.

**A pane in the sliding glass door at left,
between Wilder's living room and pool, was
broken on the day Beth Kenyon disappeared.
He blamed the damage on his dogs.**

The senior Whitaker phoned Wilder, who in quick, clipped tones again denied having seen Beth recently. Whitaker told him that a witness had reported seeing them together on Monday, March 5. Wilder denied it but agreed to meet Ken Whitaker junior and the witness the next day. Wilder called the Kenyons to say he didn't understand why the private detective was bothering him and again insisted that he knew nothing of Beth's disappearance.

On Saturday evening, William Kenyon and his son staked out Wilder's house in Boynton Beach, taking with them a pair of binoculars and a .38-caliber revolver. The place seemed deserted, and they decided to call it quits around 10 p.m. As they were leaving, Beth's father noticed a curtain being drawn back at one of Wilder's windows.

Ken Whitaker junior and Richard Norman arrived at Wilder's house next morning, as arranged. The dogs barked when the doorbell rang, but nobody answered. Taking advantage of Wilder's apparent absence, Whitaker rummaged through a garbage can outside and found a photograph of Wilder at a car race. A phone call to a friend involved in car racing turned up the interesting fact that Chris Wilder had participated in the Miami Grand Prix on Saturday and that on Sunday, the day Rosario Gonzalez vanished, he had drifted around through the crowd of spectators. He had his camera with him.

The detective got in touch with the Palm Beach County police department on the off chance that they might have information about Wilder and discovered he had a criminal record. That night, Whitaker was sorting through notes and photos relating to the Kenyon case when his girlfriend, herself a sometime beauty contestant, looked over his shoulder at one of the pictures and said, "Ken, during the Miss Florida Pageant this guy was all over the place trying to solicit us to take topless photos." The man in the photograph was Christopher Wilder.

They began to put two and two together. Whitaker's girlfriend had met Rosario Gonzalez at another pageant. From the information he'd gotten from the Palm Beach police, Whitaker had some understanding of Wilder's method of approaching young women. The detective now saw a pattern, and he also saw a link in the disappearances of Gonzalez and Kenyon. The link was Wilder. Whitaker phoned the Miami police and related his suspicions.

On Monday morning, another investigator put a call in to the Miami police. Coral Gables police officer Clifford

Fry, who'd met Beth Kenyon when he was on patrol near her school, had gotten in touch with the family when he heard she was missing. The Kenyons mentioned Wilder to Fry, and when he discovered what Wilder's police record was like he concluded that Beth was in big trouble—and he also wondered whether her disappearance was related to Rosario Gonzalez's. Fry phoned the Miami police. The detective who took the call, Harvey Wasserman, had an instantaneous reaction: "All of a sudden all the hairs on the back of your neck stand up on end and you get a cold chill."

The day Fry and Wasserman talked was March 12, and Chris Wilder was purchasing another car. This vehicle was a departure from his usual flashy style; it was an ordinary-looking sedan, a white 1973 Chrysler New Yorker with a blue vinyl top—not the kind of car people would be likely to take note of and remember.

Two Whitaker operatives caught up with Chris Wilder at his Sawtel office on Monday afternoon. He insisted that he hadn't been with Beth Kenyon on the previous Monday, not at the Shell station, or anywhere else; he'd been right here, in the office, from 3:30 p.m. to about 6:30 p.m. He left the detectives for a few minutes and returned with his partner, Zeke Kimbrell. Kimbrell backed up Wilder's story. He said that Chris had been at the office from 3 p.m. until at least 5 p.m., when Kimbrell had left for the day.

But there was a mistake in the alibi, and the Whitaker investigators picked it up. In the course of questioning, Kimbrell nervously blurted out a comment about Beth's car being found at the airport; Wilder had told him, he said. However, nothing about her car or the airport had been published, and no one had told Wilder about it. The investigators were instantly sure that he had to be involved in Beth Kenyon's disappearance.

Tuesday, March 13, marked Wilder's 39th birthday. Sixteen days had now passed since Rosario Gonzalez's disappearance, eight days since Beth Kenyon's, and three days since Richard Norman had identified Wilder as the man he'd seen with her. Wilder visited his sex therapist, Ginger Bush, and afterward got together with several members of his racing team. They thought he seemed preoccupied, and he asked them if they'd noticed an unpleasant odor in the trunk of his Cadillac. He said he'd used a lot of baking soda trying to get rid of it. They smelled nothing, which apparently relieved his mind.

That day, the Metro-Dade police reclassified Beth

$50,000 REWARD

...quest any information on
...zabeth Kenyon, W/F,
...B. 1/11/61,
..., 130 lbs.,
...lder length brown hair.

She was last seen on 3/5/84 at the Shell Gas Station located at Bird and Douglas Road driving a 1982 Chrysler LeBaron convertible, white over brown, New York tag 910 ICS. The vehicle was later recovered at Miami International Airport.

Elizabeth Kenyon — Safe Return

...th can be left with any servant of God at any church.
Negotiations can be worked out with him or her.

No questions asked.

Clinging to the hope that Beth Kenyon was still alive, her family offered a $50,000 reward for her safe return.

Kenyon as a possible homicide. Miami Detective Harvey Wasserman was responsible for the move; he'd called the Metro-Dade police to tell them what he'd gleaned from Ken Whitaker and from Palm Beach County's records on Wilder. The department found itself in the difficult position of investigating a man who already knew he was under suspicion in some quarters. Wary of doing anything that might make Wilder bolt, Metro-Dade detectives started verifying the information they'd gotten from Wasserman and also from Ken Whitaker junior, who turned over his files on the case to them and was ordered to stop his investigation. Meanwhile, Wilder went about his business.

He skipped a scheduled session with his sex therapist on March 15 and failed to show up at his office—he'd left Boynton Beach for a trip to Daytona Beach, 150 miles up the coast, where he rented a room in a Howard Johnson's motel. He was later identified as the man who'd been seen stalking pretty girls on and near the beach. Fifteen-year-old Colleen Orsborn lived on a street where Wilder was seen. She vanished that day and was never seen again.

The next day the *Miami Herald* ran a story

A utility company lineman spotted Terry Ferguson's body floating in this central Florida creek three days after her abduction.

TERRY FERGUSON

saying that an unnamed Boynton Beach photographer and racecar driver with a history of sex crimes was wanted for questioning in the disappearance of the two Miami women. During the afternoon Zeke Kimbrell got a call from Wilder, who said that he was in Tallahassee. At 11 o'clock that night he screeched to a stop in his partner's driveway. Wilder had read the *Herald*'s story, and he knew he was the subject. He was starting to panic. Now telling his partner the cops wanted to frame him for Beth Kenyon's disappearance, he started weeping. Kimbrell had never seen him in such a state. "I'm not going to jail," Wilder wailed. "I'll kill myself."

Wilder had plenty of reason to be frightened, but time hadn't run out for him quite yet, and he now moved quickly to make arrangements for his getaway from Boynton Beach. On Saturday, March 17, he called a Sawtel employee in the morning and told him to come over to his house and take his three dogs to a kennel. Tossing a suitcase into the white Chrysler, Wilder drove to the office to say goodbye to Kimbrell—and to pocket two of his partner's credit cards, one from Visa and the other from Texaco. Since both of the cards were duplicates, Kimbrell wasn't likely to notice the theft soon. Shortly afterward, Wilder was on his way out of town.

Chris Wilder hadn't told Kimbrell where he was going; perhaps he didn't have any idea himself. But when he made his farewell he probably had a pretty good idea of some of the things he was going to do.

On Sunday morning, March 18, Terry Ferguson told her mother that she was going shopping with a couple of friends at the Merritt Square Mall on Merritt Island, midway up the Florida peninsula. A willowy, 21-year-old brown-eyed brunette, Ferguson worked at a T-shirt-printing shop, but she thought she might be happier as a cosmetologist, or even as a fashion model. When her friends turned out to be busy, Terry Ferguson drove to the shopping mall by herself, parking her 1977 Pontiac Sunbird near the J. C. Penney store.

Her father, a police officer, found the car that night when he went looking for his daughter. Inside the locked auto he could see the blouse and jeans she'd worn when she left home. He and Terry's boyfriend, Dan Bednarz, remained with the car until 4:30 a.m. When she failed to show up at work that day, her father called the police and filed a missing persons report.

Terry Ferguson's corpse was found three days later, on Wednesday, March 21. A utilities company lineman working on a power pole spotted the dead woman floating face-down in a creek north of Haines City, 60 miles inland from Melbourne. She was dressed in a pink shirt over a tank top and Calvin Klein jeans; it was the kind of outfit Chris Wilder would have approved of. There was no evidence of rape, but she'd been beaten savagely, probably with a tire iron, before being strangled.

In the ensuing police investigation, a woman reported that she'd seen Ferguson in the mall talking with a tanned, balding, bearded man. Shown photographs of Wilder, she was certain he was the man. The police also talked to a tow-truck operator who said that at 4 p.m. on March 18 he'd been called to haul a white Chrysler from deep sand along a little-used road just off state highway 27 near Canaveral Groves. The driver had paid with a credit card in the name L. K. Kimbrell. "The guy was nice and friendly," said the tow-truck driver. "I'm certain there was no girl in the back seat, but I never did look in the trunk."

On Monday, March 19, Wilder drove across the state to Tampa, where he cashed two checks totaling $4,530 on his account at the North Carolina National Bank. The withdrawals all but emptied his account, but he smilingly told the teller he'd just made a real-estate deal he was very

pleased with. He was playing the rich, successful business-man for an audience of one, and it was pure fantasy. He'd made no such deal.

Linda Grober, a pretty blonde 19-year-old student at Florida State University in Tallahassee in the Florida panhandle, was shopping for greeting cards in Maas Bros. department store in the Governor's Square Mall around noon on Tuesday, March 20, when a well-dressed stranger carrying a camera approached her. Introducing himself as Lynn Bishop, he said he needed a photographic model and began describing the details of the job, including the pay and the hours. Talking steadily, in a businesslike and polite manner, he walked out of the mall with Grober toward his car. When he suggested they drive to his studio, she declined the offer. She was turning away to go to her car when he spun her around by the shoulder, punched her hard in the

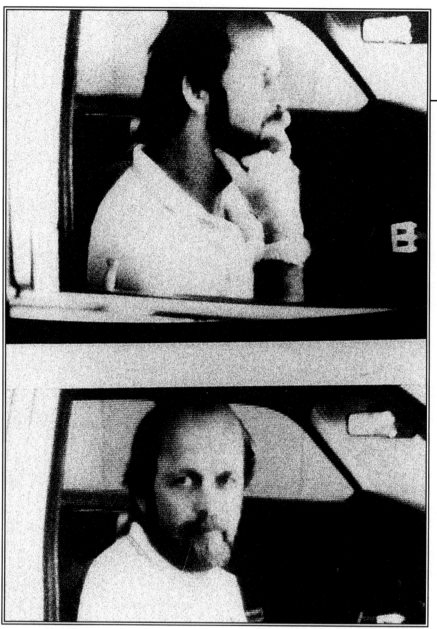

The drive-in window surveillance camera at a Tampa, Florida, branch of North Carolina National Bank filmed Chris Wilder as he was cashing a check for $280 on March 19, 1984.

sometimes trying to make Grober comfortable and calling her "sweet pea" and "good little girl," other times threatening death and pinching her nostrils together so tightly that she thought she would suffocate.

Wilder also stopped to do some shopping at one point; still in the trunk, Grober could hear cars and guessed they were in a large parking lot. She was afraid to scream for help because Wilder said he was leaving a tape recorder on; if he heard her voice on it when he got back, he said, he'd kill her.

After dark, he hauled her out of the trunk and zipped her into a sleeping bag. From then on, she rode in the front seat to Bainbridge, Georgia, 40 miles from Tallahassee. He checked into the Glen Oaks Motel, paying cash, and carried her over his shoulder into the room.

From inside the sleeping bag, it sounded to Grober as if her captor was doing some sort of chore with tools. When he finally let her out of the bag he promised he'd kill her if she tried to escape. "You're here to please me," he said. "You're here to make me feel good."

Wilder turned on the television, stripped Grober, and masturbated while he watched bikini-clad women working out and dancing in a movie called *Getting Physical.* Then he brought out a 15-foot extension cord he'd converted into a torture device. At one end the cord had been split lengthwise and the plastic covering the wires had been stripped. A dimmer knob had been added midway along the cord. At the motel he'd replaced the duct tape over Grober's eyes with a bandanna; it had loosened a little, and she was able to catch a glimpse of the device. Maybe that was what he'd been working on, Grober thought.

Wrapping the bare wires around Grober's little toes, Wilder plugged the other end of the cord into a wall outlet. He raped her and forced her to stimulate him orally. Afterward he gave Grober a sip of soda, almost as if he was apologizing for what he'd done. All the while he jolted her re-

stomach, clubbed her on the head, and shoved her, unconscious, into the car.

Wilder was singing along with the tape playing on the Chrysler's stereo when Grober came to. She was in the backseat, her hands tied behind her to the seat belt. After a while he stopped in a wooded area, where he choked her until she again lost consciousness. The next thing she was aware of was Wilder taping her eyes. Next he stuffed a sock into her mouth, which he then covered with duct tape. He hogtied her, with her hands and feet behind her and nearly touching, and dumped her into the trunk.

They took off again, but from time to time Wilder stopped the car and went to the trunk. He was erratic, peatedly by turning the dimmer knob—just a little or a lot, depending on how big a shock he felt like giving her. Wilder also varied the length of the shocks, and he threatened to make them even longer. "If you make one move, I'll light you up," he said. "I can bring you over the brink of death and back again." He'd fantasized over and over about the pleasure he'd get from terrorizing and torturing a woman, yet what he was doing left him curiously unsatisfied.

Nor did it make him feel good when Grober pretended— or tried to pretend—that she was his willing, passionate partner. He'd instructed her to say, "I want you all night long," and "I am here to please you forever." But when she said these things, it didn't do anything for him. The words only disappointed him.

Maybe the problem was the bandanna over her eyes—it just didn't look natural to him. Wilder was prepared for this eventuality. He took the bandanna off and told Grober to lie down on her back on the bed and close her eyes. He uncapped a white plastic bottle of Super glue and, almost solicitously telling her that her eyes might smart for a few minutes, squeezed beads of glue onto her eyelids. Tidily, he screwed the top back on, then picked up the hair dryer he'd brought along and aimed a stream of hot air at her face to help the adhesive dry quickly.

Grober got his permission to go to the bathroom, where she managed to pry her eyes open slightly. Not noticing what she'd done, Wilder, who was back to watching the movie, told her to dance along with the performers on the screen and remarked that in a while he'd shave off her pubic hair.

The thought of Wilder with a razor in his hand was unbearable to Grober, and she resolved to escape. Following orders, she began dancing. Wilder hardly glanced at her, concentrating instead on the movie. This was her chance: She yanked the electrical cord from the wall

and scrambled for the door. He came after her, grabbing at her, swinging the hair dryer and splitting her scalp. He gouged her eye. They grappled and fought, biting, punching, and kicking. She grabbed his genitals and yanked them hard. He hammered her over the head with a shoe, dropped it, and seized her neck and started throttling her. Grober pretended to lose consciousness, and Wilder relaxed his grip. Taking him by surprise, she jabbed her fingers into his eyes, squirmed out of his grasp, and dashed to the bathroom. Locking the door behind her, she started screaming and pounding on the walls.

Linda Grober was tortured and raped in Room 30 of the Glen Oaks Motel in Bainbridge, Georgia.

Wilder panicked. He grabbed his suitcase, the sleeping bag, and Linda Grober's clothing and ran naked out the door, almost colliding with a truckdriver who'd been eavesdropping on what sounded to him like a couple enjoying themselves immensely. "Sorry, man," Wilder said as he streaked toward his Chrysler.

Linda Grober waited until she was sure her assailant had really gone. She sat on the bathroom floor for perhaps 30 minutes, blood pouring from her gashed head. Then she wrapped a bedsheet around her bloody, bruised body and ran for the motel manager's office. She yelled through the locked door that she had been raped, to phone the police, she needed help.

The night manager refused to let her in and yelled for her to use the pay phone outside. She shrieked that she didn't have a goddamn quarter, then boiled over, just erupted in hurt and outrage and started swearing a blue streak. That impressed the manager, and he called the police. When they arrived, Grober was sitting alone by the swimming pool.

Meanwhile, Wilder was racing back to Governor's Square Mall in Tallahassee. He drove Linda Grober's car across the street and parked it at a bar, to confuse investigators. In the bar, he nursed a vodka and tonic while he thought things over. He tried to pick up a woman patron, telling her that it was her lucky day, that he was a professional photographer and would make her famous. She wasn't impressed. He let it go.

When the cops got to the Glen Oaks Motel in Bainbridge, they found some clothes Grober's attacker had left behind in the motel room, including socks printed with kangaroos. Grober thought she'd seen an Australian document, a passport perhaps, among her torturer's belongings. Because she'd been kidnapped and taken across a state line, the FBI entered the investigation. Agents were already aware that Miami-area police suspected Chris Wilder was involved in the disappearances of Beth Kenyon and Rosario Gonzalez. That seemed even more likely after Linda Grober, who'd been remarkably observant throughout her ordeal, picked him out from a group of photographs. The FBI got a warrant to search Wilder's house on March 22, but they found nothing of real interest except a piece of paper with the word *Kenyon* written on it.

By then, Wilder was in Beaumont, Texas, approaching young women. One of them was Terry Walden, a 23-year-old wife, mother, and nursing student at Lamar University. She came home for lunch and told her husband, John, that as she walked to the parking lot after classes, a man had offered her a modeling job. She had declined, she said. The offer was not surprising. A slender, hazel-eyed blonde of five feet four inches and 105 pounds, Terry Walden "was an eye-catcher," as a fellow student put it, adding, "but she never looked back at anybody."

The next day, Friday, March 23, Walden dropped off her four-year-old daughter, Mindy, at the Baby Red Bird Nursery School, kissed her, and said she'd pick her up later that day. When she failed to collect Mindy, John Walden reported his wife missing.

That afternoon, a schoolgirl saw a white Chrysler speeding down a dusty country road between two rice fields outside Beaumont. The driver was tanned, balding, and bearded, and his female passenger's head was resting against the window, as if she were asleep. An hour later, the girl saw the car come back, only now the driver was alone.

Terry Walden's body was found three days later, on March 26, floating in a canal along that same dirt road—ironically, it was named Walden Road. She was fully clothed, except for her brassiere, which was found nearby in the canal. She had been bound with nylon cord and gagged with duct tape, then beaten and strangled. There were three stab wounds in her chest, two of which went clear through to her back. She had bled to death.

By chance, a self-defense seminar sponsored by the Beaumont police department had been scheduled for March 27. The discovery of Terry Walden's body produced a huge turnout of 1,400 alarmed women. It was more than the hall could handle, and a second seminar had to be held to accommodate them all. By then, Chris Wilder was long gone from Beaumont. Abandoning the white Chrysler immediately after killing Terry Walden on the 23d, he'd taken off in her rust-colored 1981 Mercury Cougar.

Wilder was spotted in Dallas on Saturday, March 24, when he tried but failed to make any headway with Tiffany Conley, a model working at an exhibit promoting the upcoming Dallas Grand Prix; Conley knew as much as he did about a racing car on display. That, she later told authorities, made him huffy, and he walked away.

From Dallas, Wilder gunned on another 210 miles to Oklahoma City, where he took a room at a Holiday Inn, paying for it with Kimbrell's Visa card. Sunday morning he went stalking at the Crossroads Mall. Seventeen-year-old

Lisa Henson was mildly interested in the proposal he made about modeling. As she was talking with him, she noticed a severe scratch on the white of one eyeball—it was made by one of Linda Grober's fingernails. After Henson refused to leave with him, Wilder gave up on Crossroads Mall.

That afternoon, Suzanne Logan, British-born and recently married, went to Oklahoma City's Penn Square Mall to see about a wrist watch she was buying on layaway; on the way she had dropped off her husband, Brian, at the Sav-A-Stop convenience store where he worked. Logan held down a secretarial job, but her real interest was in a more glamorous career in fashion design and modeling. She had already assembled a photo portfolio. Clerks at the mall remembered seeing her chatting with a tanned, balding, bearded man. She failed to pick up Brian after work, and he went to the police.

Wilder took Logan 180 miles north to Newton, Kansas, and checked into Room 30 of the I-35 Inn. In the morning he ate breakfast alone at a pancake house next door to the motel. He seemed nervous and ate quickly, according to his waitress. After breakfast he drove to Milford Reservoir, 90 miles northeast of Newton near Junction City. Taking Logan out of the car, he stabbed her below the left shoulder blade with such force that the tip of the knife exited above the left breast. He dumped her under a cedar tree.

A fisherman found Suzanne Logan, bound with nylon cord and duct tape, less than an hour later. By then she had bled to death. Her brown hair had been cut off and her pubic hair shaved. Her chest was bruised, and her right eye was blackened from the beating she'd gotten. There were bite marks on both her breasts, and the flesh along her backbone had been pricked a half-dozen times with the point of a knife just deeply enough to bring agonizing pain.

Driving fast, by nightfall on Monday Wilder was in Denver, 500 miles from Junction City. The next day, March 27, Wilder saw an interesting ad in the paper and drove over to suburban Aurora, where he paid $245 cash for the .357 magnum Colt Trooper revolver a service station employee was selling. Wilder spent that night in Wheat Ridge, another Denver suburb, once again paying for his room with his partner's Visa card.

By midmorning, Wednesday March 28, the fugitive was in a lodge at the Loveland ski area in the Colorado Rockies. Thirteen-year-old Jessica Ballard* didn't quite know what to make of the balding man with the brush-cut beard who handed her a card from Casa Blanca Modeling in Denver. He was doing action shots of skiers, he said, and she had just the look he needed. He asked if she'd like to meet some of the other photographers with him, but Jessica wisely said that she was waiting for a friend.

Striking out in Loveland, Wilder drove on to the little town of Rifle, and, after spending the night there at the Red River Inn, he arrived at Grand Junction, Colorado, the next morning, Thursday the 29th. He was still driving Terry Walden's Cougar. He bought gas, had breakfast, and went to a barbershop for a haircut. Following the directions the barber had given him, Wilder got to the Mesa Mall by noon, nicely dressed in jeans, a sweater, and cowboy boots.

Wilder spotted blonde, blue-eyed Karen Spurlock as she was on her way into a department store. Spurlock gave him the cold shoulder when he asked her if she was interested in modeling. He followed her anyway, and in the lingerie department he tried to get her attention a second time, handing her a business card. "Look, I'm legit," he said. "This is just to show you I'm legit." She didn't like the look of his eyes. "They were very intense eyes, beady eyes, sort of what I'd call mouse eyes," she said later. "Very round, like a rat."

Unlike Spurlock, Sheryl Bonaventura, 18, wasn't at all put off when Wilder came up to her. A popular student at Grand Junction High, she had stopped at the mall to buy face cream before a ski trip to Aspen. Wilder would naturally notice her. She was five-seven, 110 pounds, blonde, blue-eyed—and an aspiring model. Driving up in her Mazda RX-7, she wore faded jeans, a white sweatshirt with the word *Cherokee* on the front, and rust-colored cowboy boots with silver toecaps. She shared a pizza with a pal, then headed to a drugstore for her face cream. Shortly before 2 p.m., two other friends bicycling around the mall saw her sitting in her Mazda and called out "Hi, Sheryl." She returned their greeting. There was a man squatting by the car's open window talking with Sheryl. The friends later picked the man out of a photo lineup. He was Chris Wilder.

When Sheryl failed to meet yet another pal at 2 p.m. that afternoon, the friend called the Bonaventuras. That evening they found Sheryl's Mazda parked at the mall, its sunroof halfway open and the doors unlocked. Sheryl's sunglasses, which she depended on because her eyes were very light-sensitive, were still inside. Her parents checked with Sheryl's boyfriend, Terry Shanahan, who hadn't seen her.

Wilder and Bonaventura had lunch that afternoon at a

Terry Walden's body was found in this canal several miles west of Beaumont, Texas, on March 26, 1984, three days after she was abducted by Wilder.

TERRY WALDEN

drive-in restaurant in Silverton, a mining hamlet 100 miles south of Grand Junction. The owner, Kathryn Litchliter, had been making chili when the two came in. She found herself talking with the young woman, who introduced herself as Sheryl Bonaventura and said that her grandfather had once been a baker in Silverton. She told Litchliter that her companion was a photographer and that they were going to Las Vegas to take some pictures, with a stop in Durango on the way. The young woman spoke nervously, breathlessly; Litchliter thought she was volunteering an aw-

ful lot of information for such a casual conversation. Litchliter invited Bonaventura to sign the guest register. "The man gave her a look like, 'don't sign it,' and she didn't," recalled Litchliter.

That night, Wilder and Bonaventura checked into a Durango motel. They were seen the next day at Four Corners Monument, a scenic spot 70 miles farther southwest where the states of New Mexico, Utah, Colorado, and Arizona share borders. At 3 p.m. the same day, March 30, Wilder checked into the Page Boy Motel, in Page, Arizona, 150

Surrounded by police markers, Suzanne Logan's body lies beneath a cedar tree at Kansas's Milford Reservoir on March 26, 1984.

SUZANNE LOGAN

miles west of Four Corners. The next morning, a maid saw him hustle a young blonde woman into a car and speed away. That was the last time anyone saw Sheryl Bonaventura until her nude body was found on May 3, lying in the open near the Kanab River across the Utah line from Page. Her left breast had been mutilated, and she'd been stabbed through the heart. A bullet fired by the .357 magnum had gone through one arm and into her back. It appeared that her arms had been tied behind her.

Chris Wilder had a drink at the bar of Caesar's Palace in Las Vegas late on the night of March 31. *Seventeen* magazine was holding a cover-model competition at the Meadows Mall the next day. It was Michelle Korfman's first beauty contest. The second of three daughters born to a Las Vegas casino executive, 17-year-old Michelle was tall and slender, with dark hair and striking blue eyes. The Korfman family lived in Boulder City, 25 miles south of Las Vegas, because it seemed safer than the gambling mecca. For Michelle, the beauty contest actually was something of a lark. A bright, ambitious young woman, she was interested

Christopher Wilder used this hunting knife, shown actual size, to intimidate, torture, and kill many of his victims.

in politics and was planning to attend the University of Nevada in the fall. Although she had a good deal of confidence, she was self-conscious enough about the *Seventeen* contest that she had asked her family and friends not to come to the mall. She drove there alone in her brown 1982 Camaro—a reward from her father for good grades—and joined the other contestants.

The mother of one of the other young women was there taking photographs, and after Christopher Wilder's picture had been shown in news reports, she realized that he was one of the onlookers she'd caught with her camera. In the photo she took he is half-sitting, half-leaning against something about the height of a tall stool, his left knee cocked up, the foot hooked behind his right leg. His hands are clasped together. He is wearing white trousers, a plaid shirt, a brown jacket, and a neatly trimmed beard. He is staring hard in the direction of the contestants.

Police learned later that the man had talked to several contestants about using them for a photo layout. All of them had turned him down—except, apparently, Michelle Korfman. Two teenage girls who were at the mall, neither of them a contestant, had agreed to meet him in front of Caesar's Palace, but he didn't show up. Wilder registered that evening at the Gold Key motel in Las Vegas; amazingly, he used his own name.

Anthony Korfman, Michelle's father, offered a $10,000 reward, but it never was picked up. Her body was identified via dental x-rays in mid-June, after being found in a southern California forest and lying unclaimed for a month in a Los Angeles morgue as Jane Doe #39.

SHERYL BONAVENTURA

On April 2, Zeke Kimbrell opened the Visa bill he'd just received. It contained charge upon charge he hadn't made—but he knew instantly who had. He telephoned the FBI. The paper trail of chits was a great break for the investigators. They furnished solid evidence that Wilder had passed through towns and cities where women had been abducted, and Kimbrell was instructed to let the charges keep rolling in. It ordinarily took several days for charges to get through the processing system, so they wouldn't help Wilder's pursuers catch up with him unless he took a break from his marathon long-distance driving and stayed put for a while.

It wasn't Kimbrell's first contact with the FBI. Since he was Wilder's partner and friend, he'd been interviewed soon after Wilder left Boynton Beach. He had admitted in the interview that he'd been lying when he backed up the alibi Wilder had given when one of the investigators hired by the Kenyons asked him to account for his whereabouts on the afternoon Beth disappeared. "The investigator was just some kid," explained Kimbrell. "If it had been the cops who asked, I would have told the truth."

Chris Wilder arrived in Lomita, California, some 15 miles south of Los Angeles, the day after Zeke Kimbrell phoned the FBI about the Visa bill. He got a $39 room at the seedy Proud Parrot motel. A desk clerk noticed him during the evening, a crazed look on his face, banging furiously on the soft-drink machine; everybody gets sore at thieving coin machines, but this was different. The next morning Wilder breakfasted at a coffee shop, gassed up with Texaco, and headed for the Del Amo Fashion

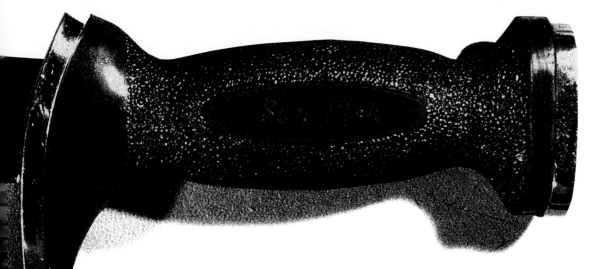

Center, a shopping mall two miles from the Proud Parrot.

On her way to the same mall was 16-year-old Tina Marie Risico. A pretty, slightly chubby, blue-eyed blonde, Tina Marie planned to apply for a summer job selling cheese and sausage at a Hickory Farms store. Life had never been easy for her. Shortly after she was born her father, a petty criminal named Jasper Joe Risico, deserted her and her mother, Carol Sokolowski, who started running around with motorcycle gangs. Home for the girl and her mother was with grandmother Sokolowski in a little tract house that frequently reverberated with loud fights between the two women. But Tina Marie, who was sexually assaulted at the age of 13, had learned to cope. She had dropped out of high school but had returned and was now making good grades. She'd been working part-time at a restaurant, saving her money, and now wanted a better job so she could buy a car.

She felt great when she left the Hickory Farms store. The manager, finding her smart, pleasant, and energetic, had hired her for the summer.

Christopher Wilder had spotted her in the store. He was waiting outside.

To a 16-year-old with her heart set on a car, Wilder's low-key line about modeling sounded pretty good. And when he handed her a $100 bill as a sort of signing bonus, her streetwise radar clicked off. She climbed into the Cougar and they drove first to the beach for some photos, then into the hills for more shots. Look at the mountains, he said, posing her. She did—and when she looked back, he was aiming his .357 magnum at her.

Wilder jammed the barrel into her mouth and cocked the hammer. He took out a wicked-looking knife and ran it under her chin, and down her throat, chest, and stomach. Back in the car, he raped her. He gave her the instructions he'd given Linda Grober: She was to act passionate and submit to whatever he wanted. If she resisted, he'd kill her.

They spent that night of April 4 in a San Diego motel, where Wilder raped her again and shocked her with his modified extension cord, burning her neck, stomach, and breasts. He told Tina Marie that he didn't want to remind her how to act all the time; he wanted her to remember. He got furiously angry when she flinched or cried out in pain at the shocks. By way of further warning, he told her that he and a friend named Pedro sold girls to a Mexican white slavery ring. Tina Marie's alternatives: Be good to him or vanish forever.

Next morning they drove east 120 miles to the Salton Sea, where Wilder parked and chopped off her long hair; it irritated him because it sometimes fell across her face and kept him from seeing her expressions. They stopped at a motel. She endured oral sex, more rape, and electrical shocks because she failed to satisfy him. At one point, he jammed one of the wires deep into her ear.

Late in the afternoon the television was playing as usual. A news show came on, and Tina Marie saw her abductor's photograph appear on the screen and found out just what kind of man was holding her captive—a suspected serial killer. At a press conference earlier in the day, Christopher Wilder had been named to the FBI's 10 most wanted list. He was named as the prime suspect in the deaths of Terry Ferguson and Terry Walden, whose bodies had already been found, and was linked with the disappearances of four women still missing as of that day: Rosario Gonzalez, Beth Kenyon, Sheryl Bonaventura, and Suzanne Logan. Wilder's abandoned white Chrysler had been found near Beaumont early that same morning, and the FBI said the killer might be driving Terry Walden's Cougar.

Wilder was in a sweat. Afraid he'd be recognized, he shaved off his beard and announced that they were going to New York. He checked out, shoved Tina Marie into the car, and raced on another 400 miles to a motel in Pres-

cott, Arizona. At the motel, Wilder raped and tortured Tina Marie again.

On April 7, local police in Florida and in Nevada thought for a little while that they'd found the killer. The madam at the Mustang Ranch, a legal brothel near Reno, called police to report that Wilder was there. When sheriff's deputies from two counties rushed in, they saw a tanned, balding, bearded man who was a dead ringer for Wilder sipping a beer. However, he turned out to be an innocent carpenter from California. The other Wilder look-alike, a medical technician, was picked up as he was looking at a pornographic magazine in the Top Banana, a Coral Gables store. It wasn't the first time he'd had trouble because of his appearance. Six days earlier he'd been nabbed by FBI agents at a nude beach on Florida's Sugarloaf Key.

On the day the erroneous arrests were made, Wilder and Tina Marie were on the way to Missouri, where they spent a night near Joplin. The incessant rape and electrical shocks began to blur in Tina Marie's mind. But she was apparently becoming so submissive that he was confident she would do whatever he said; he no longer worried that she'd try to bolt, as Linda Grober had. He stopped tying her up, and he had her do most of the driving.

Her menstrual period arrived, and that annoyed Wilder. When he demanded anal sex, she was so repelled by the idea that she protested. He punished her with electrical shocks and went ahead.

All along, Wilder had been switching license plates to disguise Terry Walden's Cougar. The original Texas plates had long since given way to Louisiana, New Mexico, and now a set of Arkansas tags that he'd stolen from a silver Cadillac. April 8 and 9 saw Wilder cruising around the Chicago area with his prisoner. By then, Christopher Wilder had in all likelihood seen himself in a videotape that the FBI had obtained from a dating service in Florida and released for broadcast. During a taped interview made for viewing by female clients of the service, a dating counselor had asked Wilder to talk about what sort of man he was and what he expected from life. "I want to meet and enjoy the company of a number of women," he said, gazing levelly into the camcorder.

From Chicago Wilder pushed on east. He informed Tina Marie that he'd decided to replace her with a different girl. He promised Tina Marie that he'd let her go if she'd be the bait; if she refused, he'd kill her. There was no way she

Christopher Wilder takes a closeup look at the contestants in a *Seventeen* magazine cover-model competition at the Meadows Mall in Las Vegas on April 1, 1984. One of the entrants, Michelle Korfman, left the mall with Wilder. Her body was discovered near a southern California roadside rest stop on May 11.

MICHELLE KORFMAN

On the chance that Wilder might shave off some or all of his facial hair, the FBI included two retouched photographs in this wanted poster.

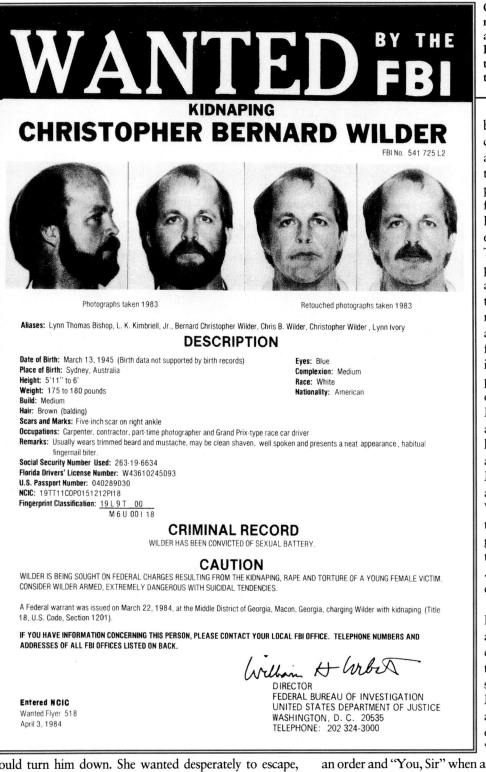

WANTED BY THE FBI

KIDNAPING
CHRISTOPHER BERNARD WILDER

FBI No. 541 725 L2

Photographs taken 1983   Retouched photographs taken 1983

Aliases: Lynn Thomas Bishop, L. K. Kimbriell, Jr., Bernard Christopher Wilder, Chris B. Wilder, Christopher Wilder, Lynn Ivory

DESCRIPTION

Date of Birth: March 13, 1945 (Birth data not supported by birth records)
Place of Birth: Sydney, Australia
Height: 5'11" to 6'
Weight: 175 to 180 pounds
Build: Medium
Hair: Brown (balding)
Scars and Marks: Five-inch scar on right ankle
Occupations: Carpenter, contractor, part-time photographer and Grand Prix-type race car driver
Remarks: Usually wears trimmed beard and mustache, may be clean shaven, well spoken and presents a neat appearance , habitual fingernail biter.
Social Security Number Used: 263-19-6634
Florida Drivers' License Number: W43610245093
U.S. Passport Number: 040289030
NCIC: 19TT11COP0151212PI18
Fingerprint Classification: 19 L 9 T   00
 M 6 U 00 I 18

Eyes: Blue
Complexion: Medium
Race: White
Nationality: American

CRIMINAL RECORD
WILDER HAS BEEN CONVICTED OF SEXUAL BATTERY.

CAUTION
WILDER IS BEING SOUGHT ON FEDERAL CHARGES RESULTING FROM THE KIDNAPING, RAPE AND TORTURE OF A YOUNG FEMALE VICTIM. CONSIDER WILDER ARMED, EXTREMELY DANGEROUS WITH SUICIDAL TENDENCIES.

A Federal warrant was issued on March 22, 1984, at the Middle District of Georgia, Macon, Georgia, charging Wilder with kidnaping (Title 18, U.S. Code, Section 1201).

IF YOU HAVE INFORMATION CONCERNING THIS PERSON, PLEASE CONTACT YOUR LOCAL FBI OFFICE. TELEPHONE NUMBERS AND ADDRESSES OF ALL FBI OFFICES LISTED ON BACK.

William H. Webster
DIRECTOR
FEDERAL BUREAU OF INVESTIGATION
UNITED STATES DEPARTMENT OF JUSTICE
WASHINGTON, D. C. 20535
TELEPHONE: 202 324-3000

Entered NCIC
Wanted Flyer 518
April 3, 1984

broadcasts all over the country, but Wilder was about to use it again. First, though, he had some shopping to do. A favorite perfume of his was "Diane Von Furstenberg," and he wanted to get a bottle to use on Tina Marie's successor. His purchase made, he walked around the mall until he saw the right girl, a pretty brunette about Tina Marie's age. Wilder and Tina Marie followed the girl, who went into several shops; it appeared that she was filling out job applications. Tina Marie made her approach, asking the girl whether she had applied for a job. The answer was yes, and Tina Marie told her that the manager wanted to talk to her. Wilder had no trouble getting Dawnette Sue Wilt to go out to his car. Once there, he showed her the .357 magnum. And he didn't let Tina Marie go.

They were off again. Dawnette was bound hand and foot, and Wilder frequently jammed the gun into her mouth while he instructed her as he had Tina Marie. She would be his for as long as he wanted, and he demanded that she respond, "Yes, Sir" when he gave her an order and "You, Sir" when asked to whom she belonged. He made her spell the word *kill* repeatedly and for emphasis forced her to lick the blade of his 12-inch knife.

On her first night with Wilder, in a motel near Toledo, Dawnette was raped over and over, often with the gun in

could turn him down. She wanted desperately to escape, and she seized the chance.

On April 10, Wilder and Tina Marie stopped at the Southlake Mall near Gary, Indiana. By now his method of stalking young women in malls had been described on

The toughness and savvy that Tina Marie Risico developed during a troubled childhood enabled the 16-year-old to survive nine days as Wilder's captive.

her mouth. Wilder also tied a thin plastic cord around Wilt's breasts so tightly and for so long that they turned blue. After a while he bound her body and allowed her to go to sleep. She woke in the middle of the night to hear him raping Tina Marie on the other bed. In the morning, Wilder raped Dawnette again and gave her excruciatingly long electrical shocks.

Driving east on route I-90, Wilder decided to take a short detour to Niagara Falls. Dawnette stayed in the car, heavily drugged with sleeping pills, while Wilder and Tina Marie mingled with the honeymooners admiring the sight. That night in a motel in Victor, New York, near Rochester, he forced the two young women to perform sexual acts with each other.

Next day, Wilder switched on "Good Morning America," and Tina Marie saw her mother, Carol Sokolowski, pleading with Christopher Wilder not to hurt her daughter. Wilder panicked and told Dawnette and Tina Marie to grab their things and get into the car. They drove south on a small road for about 45 miles until Wilder found the kind of place he was looking for, an isolated, wooded area near Penn Yan, New York. He removed the car keys to make certain that Tina Marie couldn't take off, then he marched Dawnette a few hundred yards into the woods. Following his orders, she knelt down, and he tied her hands and feet behind her. He told her to hold her breath and nod when she couldn't hold it any longer. At her nod, he pinched her nose shut, but Dawnette managed to jerk her head away. He tried several more times to suffocate her in this way but finally gave up.

She knew he meant to kill her, and she pleaded with him simply to shoot her. But Wilder was in charge. He pulled out his knife and stabbed her once in the chest, then twice more in the back. She gasped, "I hate you. I hope you die."

"Shut up, bitch," he said.

Wilder and Tina Marie drove away. She was at the wheel, but after a while Wilder, who'd seemed to her distracted and preoccupied, said he wanted to drive. Turning the car around, he drove back to the woods near Penn Yan, got out, and retraced his footsteps to the place where he'd left Dawnette.

She was gone.

Rushing back to the road, he told Tina Marie they had to get a different car; if Dawnette was still alive, the police might get a description of the Cougar. He sped back toward Victor.

Left for dead, Dawnette had lain on the ground, bleeding profusely but conscious; Wilder's knife had missed her vital organs. Blood soon covered her arms and her hands, and they became so slippery that she was able to free them from the cords. She untied her feet and started walking toward the road. A while later, a motorist slammed on his brakes at the sight of a blood-drenched young woman staggering along. She was rushed to Soldiers and Sailors Hospital in nearby Penn Yan. She would survive.

About an hour after Wilder had stabbed Dawnette Wilt, 33-year-old Beth Dodge arrived at the Eastview Mall near Victor, New York, in her gold 1982 Pontiac Firebird to have lunch. Christopher Wilder pulled in next to Dodge. When she opened her door to get out, he stuck his .357 magnum in her face and climbed in, pushing her over into the passenger seat. He told Tina Marie to follow him in the Cougar. It seemed the perfect chance for her to escape, with him in one car and her in another. But she was too afraid to try; she knew he was a racecar driver and would probably catch up with her and kill her. They left the mall and soon came to a turnout, where Wilder stopped and parked, with Tina Marie still behind him. He pulled Beth Dodge from the car, forced her behind a high mound of gravel, and made her kneel down. He shot her once between the shoulder blades. The bullet pierced her heart, killing her instantly.

Ditching the Cougar, Wilder and Tina Marie headed for Massachusetts on the New York State Thruway in Beth Dodge's Firebird. Some of the air seemed to have gone out of Wilder, and for the first time he opened up a little to Tina Marie, as if he now saw her as a companion and friend. Almost plaintively, he told her that he was rich and had virtually everything anyone could want; he didn't know how he'd got the way he was now. He asked her not to reveal that he'd shaved his beard off and to lie about what kind of car he was driving. He said he was about to set her free, explaining that he didn't want her around when the end came. But Tina Marie didn't believe him. She thought

A videotape that Christopher Wilder made for a Florida dating service in 1981 was distributed by the FBI in an attempt to familiarize television viewers across the country with the fugitive's appearance, voice, and mannerisms.

he was lying about letting her go; she'd been expecting all along to be killed, and she still was, in spite of what he was saying now.

They kept driving, and by evening they were at Logan International Airport in Boston. Wilder walked Tina Marie to the Delta Airlines counter, laid down three $100 bills for a one-way ticket to Los Angeles in the name of Tina Kimbrell, got change for another $100, and handed it to the girl. He made her kiss him on the cheek and said, "All you gotta do, kid, is write a book." He walked away.

Tina Marie Risico bought some French fries. She sat down and looked around for Wilder, but it seemed as if he was really gone. She started to laugh and cry. She sat there laughing and crying and eating her French fries. But not until 2:10 a.m. when Flight 933 began taxiing down the runway for takeoff did Tina Marie believe that she was free.

She'd hardly changed clothes in the nine days she'd been with Wilder, and the first thing she did when she arrived in Los Angeles, on April 13, was to take a cab to a store in Hermosa Beach. While the driver waited, she bought new underwear with the money Wilder had given her. From there she had the driver take her to her boyfriend's house in Torrance. After she'd showered and changed, he took her to Torrance police headquarters.

On the morning of April 13 Wilder was near Boston on Route 128 when he spotted a young woman standing beside her disabled car near Wenham. Wilder pulled over and offered to give her a lift. Thanking him, she hopped into the Firebird, asked him to drive her to her boyfriend's house, and gave him directions. The man's complexion was ashy gray, she noticed, and he seemed exhausted, as if he hadn't rested for days.

Stabbed by Wilder and left to die in a New York woods, 16-year-old Dawnette Wilt saved herself by slipping free of her bonds and flagging down a passing motorist.

They'd gone a very short distance when Wilder suddenly turned off the highway. On the exit ramp, he pulled out his revolver. The car had slowed down for the turn-off, and she started to open the door. Wilder threatened to kill her if she got out, but she leaped from the car. Kicking off her high heels, she started running as fast as she could. Wilder hit the accelerator and roared away.

Wilder headed the Firebird north into New Hampshire on Route 16, a small road that winds through the foothills of the White Mountains. He pulled over twice to throw incriminating articles from the car. Among the things that were later found were Beth Dodge's identification card from the company where she worked and the modified white extension cord.

By 1:30 in the afternoon, he was 12 miles from the Canadian border and chatting with the clerk of a roadside market outside Colebrook, a small New Hampshire town, as he stocked up on sandwiches and sodas. Low on fuel, Wilder stopped in Colebrook at Vic's Getty Station on the corner of Main and Bridge streets. He bought $6.60 worth of super unleaded and asked the attendant, Wayne Delong, what kind of documents he'd need to get into Canada.

Down the street at the Speedy Chef restaurant, three New Hampshire state troopers and the Colebrook police chief were finishing lunch. Trooper Leo Jellison and his partner, Wayne Fortier, both in plain clothes, drove the other trooper and the chief back to Colebrook police headquarters. Then Jellison wheeled his unmarked station wagon back onto Bridge Street and headed toward Main.

As they passed Vic's gas station, Fortier noticed the gold Firebird and snapped alert, since they'd received an all-points teletype about Beth Dodge's murder and her stolen car the day before. Jellison had the bulletin tucked under his sun visor. This vehicle had Massachusetts plates and not New York plates but was otherwise identical to the one described in the teletype. They pulled into the station to take a closer look.

Out of his car and talking to Wayne Delong, the driver turned and looked hard at the two cops as they halted beside the Firebird. He walked in front of their station wagon toward the car.

Faint alarms began to go off in the troopers' minds. They hadn't been notified to be on the lookout for Christopher Wilder in their area, but they'd seen his photograph and had his physical description. Although the driver of the Firebird was clean-shaven, Jellison could see that the skin along his chin and jaw were pale against his tan—"baby white," Jellison thought. An idea was forming in his head—two images merging. "That's the son-of-a-bitch we're looking for," he thought. Or perhaps he said it out loud; afterward he wasn't sure whether he'd actually gotten the words out of his mouth, nor was Wayne Fortier. But he knew who the son-of-a-bitch was: Christopher Wilder.

Jellison leaned out his window. "Sir," he told the man, "I want to talk to you."

Wilder dashed to the Firebird and frantically yanked at the door on the passenger side. It was locked. He scrambled around to the other side of the car, opened the door, and lunged across the seat; it looked to the cops as if he was going for a weapon.

Jellison and Fortier leaped from their station wagon. Jellison ran around the rear of the Firebird and hurled himself in, onto Wilder's back. A big man at six-foot-four and 250 pounds, Jellison grabbed him in a bear hug and pinned his arms to his sides.

The two men wrestled like that for a second or two. Then Jellison heard a boom and felt a sharp pain in his chest. Wilder went limp as Jellison let go and lurched backward. The trooper saw a small red dot in the center of Wilder's back. Jellison looked down at himself and saw a bullet wound in his chest.

Everything had happened very quickly. Just after the first shot, as Fortier reached the Firebird, Wilder's gun fired a second time. The impact of the bullet lifted his torso an inch or two off the seat.

While Jellison, bleeding but not critically wounded, got on his police radio in the wagon, Fortier checked to make sure that Wilder was dead. It was 1:43 p.m., Friday the 13th of April, 1984.

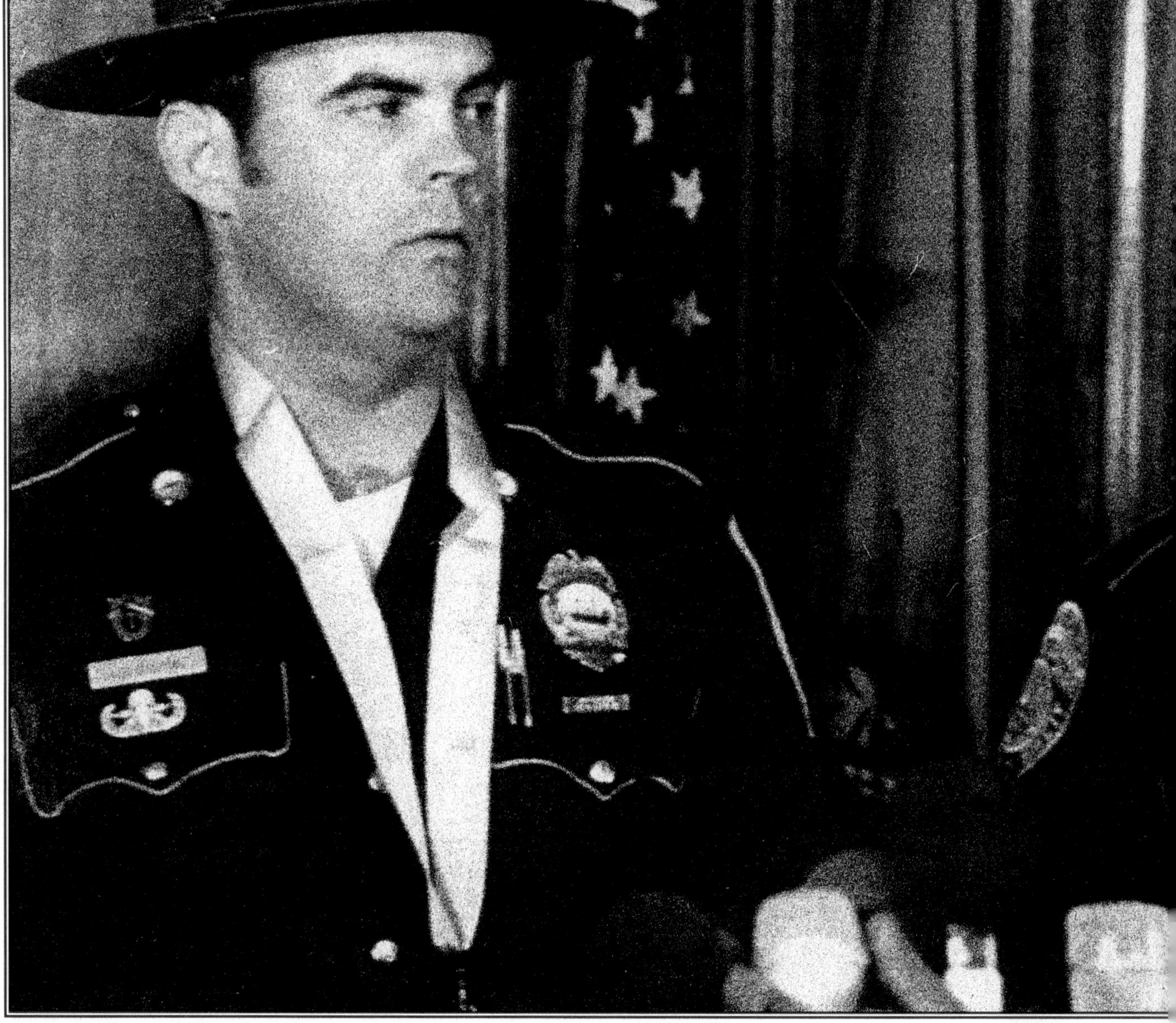

At a ceremony held on June 22, 1984, troopers Leo Jellison *(left)* and Wayne Fortier were awarded the New Hampshire State Police Medal of Valor for putting an end to Christopher Wilder's cross-country rampage.

In the struggle, Wilder had shot himself in the chest. The heavy, jacketed bullet had destroyed his heart entirely before exiting through his back and hitting Jellison with largely spent force. An involuntary muscle spasm shook Wilder after the first bullet hit him and caused the second shot.

The first press reports called Wilder's death a suicide, but the New Hampshire state police angrily countered that it was not. Trooper Howard Weber, who'd had lunch at the Speedy Chef with Jellison and Fortier and arrived at Vic's Getty Station minutes after the shooting, said, "This idea that he committed suicide is a bunch of bull – –. The guy's gun went off during a fight in which he was trying to shoot the trooper."

No one will ever know with certainty how many women Christopher Wilder killed during his murderous seven-week, 8,000-mile rampage; authorities put the number at a minimum of six. Rosario Gonzalez, Beth Kenyon, and Colleen Orsborn are counted among his probable victims, but their bodies have never been found, leaving their families to suffer a painful uncertainty about their fates. As to what became of their bodies—for few doubt they are dead—there is speculation that Wilder may have disposed of them in or near water, as he did with Terry Ferguson, Terry Walden, and Suzanne Logan. Especially in an area like Florida, which abounds with alligators and other predators, a body in water can disappear quickly. It has also been suggested that Gonzalez's and Kenyon's bodies lie hidden beneath the concrete foundation of a building that Wilder's company was working on at the time.

Christopher Wilder's body arrived at Palm Beach International Airport on Tuesday, April 17, in a white cardboard box wrapped in cellophane. Castings of his jaw and teeth were taken to match up with bite marks on suspected victims. His brain was removed, slipped into a jar of formaldehyde, and sent to experts at Beth Israel Hospital in Boston for analysis. They found no abnormalities—no lesions, no growths. It was something invisible in Christopher Wilder that had driven him to torture and murder.

Eleven people attended his funeral on April 18. His brother Stephen had flown in from Australia, and his partner, Zeke Kimbrell, was there. A Roman Catholic priest presided over the brief service. Afterward the body was cremated, and Stephen Wilder carried his brother's ashes back to Australia in a plastic urn. ◆

Christopher Wilder lies dead on the front seat of the Pontiac Firebird he stole from his last victim, Beth Dodge. Because he was known to have a scar on his right ankle, police officers removed his boot to confirm his identity.

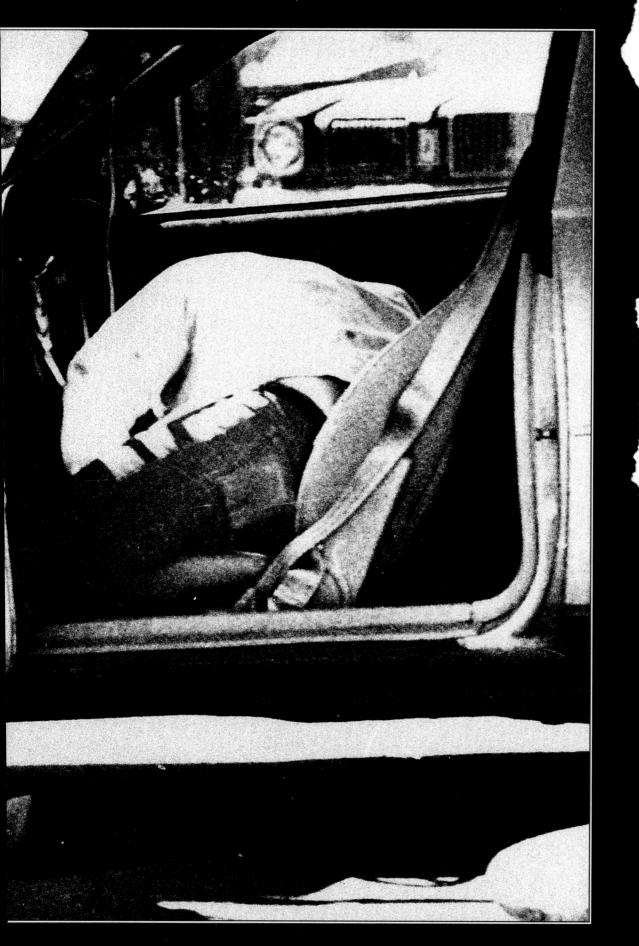

I did a sloppy job, but they deserved it. They had it coming.
CLAUDE DALLAS

2

Mountain Man

It's hard to make out what a quiet man is really like inside, and that's the way it was with Claude Dallas. People in his part of the world, where Oregon and Idaho and Nevada come together and herds of cattle range where the desert isn't too harsh, had contrary opinions about him. Everyone could agree that he was a hard worker, a fellow with the grit to go west alone and turn himself into a cowboy and trapper. But beyond that, the people who had dealings with him split into two camps, and when they talked about what kind of man Claude Dallas was they might as well have been talking about two different men.

One Claude Dallas—the good one—was a polite, soft-spoken man who didn't talk much, not about himself or about anything else much, unless the conversation turned to guns or horses or trapping. Most of the time he preferred to let others do the talking while he did the listening—people liked him for being a good listener. He didn't seem to need steady companionship, and he'd often spend days or weeks alone in the desert, setting up camp and running traplines and enjoying the solitude. This Claude Dallas had a quirk or two—everybody does—and one of his was a distrust of lawmen. He was also a little touchy about his turf, and when he was out on a trapping trip he didn't care to see any strangers, although he welcomed visits from his friends. All in all, they thought, Claude Dallas was a sensible, level-headed person, peaceable and slow to anger, but no weakling. He wasn't the kind to shoot a man without good reason, but he'd do it if he had to, to defend himself.

The other Claude Dallas people talked about was also a man of few words—not because he was thoughtful or shy but because he basically wasn't at all interested in other people, really didn't care much for anybody. He hated it when someone tried to stop him from doing what he wanted to do, and he regarded the law and anybody who represented it with contempt. People called this Claude Dallas a paranoid, a gun nut, a creep, a rattlesnake, a cold, calculating killer.

On a winter day in 1981 two men died out in the high desert of southern Idaho, and the question people would argue about afterward was which Claude Dallas had been there, which Claude Dallas had done the killing.

Claude Lafayette Dallas, Jr., was born on March 11, 1950, in Winchester, Virginia, the second son of Claude senior and his second wife, Jennie. The elder Claude Dallas was a homespun, salty man from hardscrabble Appalachian stock. "My daddy was raised on a farm and he raised me on a farm," Claude senior would tell inquiring journalists. "It gets in your blood." And it stayed in his, even when he had to take on other kinds of work to support his large family—in time there would be nine children, six boys and three girls. He pounded his own work ethic and love for the land into his sons, getting them up to milk the cows before they caught the school bus. He taught them about trapping and hunting, and how to handle guns and horses—not for sport, but as necessities of life, just as they had been on the American frontier. When Claude junior was still a young boy, he discovered from experience how essential such skills were. His father had moved the family from Virginia to a farm in northern Michigan, and the game he and his boys bagged was often the only meat on the dinner table simply because money was short.

Of all the Dallas children, Claude junior was the one who took most readily to his father's earthy view of life. He was, according to his mother, a strongheaded boy. "He knew what he wanted to do and he did it," she said. "Like his daddy." The boy had a stoic toughness, too. On one occasion, a cow he was milking kicked him in the mouth. He kept right on milking, finishing the job even though his lip was "hanging half off," as Claude senior put it.

Claude was still a little boy when his father gave him a horse that had been trained to herd cattle, and the child was soon dreaming of being a cowboy. Claude senior was pleased with the way his son had taken to the horse, which they called Blue Roan. In *Give a Boy a Gun,* the biography he wrote about Claude junior, author Jack Olsen quotes

---

Claude senior bragging about his son's horsemanship: "He could ride anything with four feet." As proud as his father was of Claude junior's ability, however, the boy couldn't always control Blue Roan. Once, when he was about nine, the horse took off with him at a run through some woods. Branches whipped and scratched Claude as he clung to the galloping horse. After a ways he couldn't hold on any longer and fell off, while Blue Roan headed for home. When his father found him his nose was broken and his face was cut. But he wasn't crying. He got back on the horse and rode it into the barn. That was *grit,* Claude senior told Jack Olsen; that was true grit.

Claude junior was no more than eight when he started laying traplines for raccoons and muskrats and whatever else he could snag. Once he trapped a mink and brought it home to his mother so that she could make it into a scarf for herself. She persuaded him to sell it and keep the cash because he'd worked so hard for it.

By the time he was ten Claude had a shotgun of his own, and from then on he was never without a gun of some kind. He went hunting with his father and brothers for deer and game birds—with no regard for legal restrictions as to numbers or season. In a single year they might put up 30 to 50 deer for meat, on top of what they sold to less successful hunters who didn't want to go home empty-handed. When great flocks of migrating Canada geese passed through Michigan, the Dallases were ready. They nailed birds at rest on pond or shore, even though both law and the traditional code of hunters restricted shooting to birds on the wing. "Everyone poached where I grew up," Claude junior would remark years later. "The warden knew it, too." Whether "everyone" did or not, poaching was a way of life for the Dallas clan.

When Claude turned sixteen his father gave him a 30-.06 rifle as a reward for not smoking. Claude senior did that for all his boys, but it seemed to mean something extra to his namesake. "That boy never let loose of a gun," the father said. By this time the Dallases had moved from Michigan to Mount Gilead, Ohio, where Claude senior worked on bridge construction and young Claude put in time at a school that, like the others he'd attended, had little to offer him. According to Claude senior, his son's teachers thought he had the intelligence of a genius, but he was no scholar. What he wanted to know, he learned from his father or found out for himself. He steeped himself in stories of the Old West and the wilderness—Andy Adams's *The Log of a Cowboy,* Owen Wister's *The Virginian,* the fictional works of Jack London, Zane Grey, and Louis L'Amour. He promised his mother he would finish high school, and he did, graduating an undistinguished 65th out of a class of 80.

That was in 1967. His classmates at Mount Gilead High School were going on to college or were on their way to Vietnam, where the United States was embroiled in war. Claude Dallas wasn't doing either of those things. He saw his future elsewhere; he was going west. A classmate, David Hartpence, recalled: "He had that dream from the start. He wanted to get established as a mountain man. I can't remember Claude ever talking about Vietnam. Claude was going to the Rockies, that was it."

His dad gave Claude his 1941 International pickup truck, and before he was 18 he was off to see not just the Rocky Mountains but "the world," as he described his vision to friends and family. The ancient truck gave out before long, so Dallas hitchhiked his way west. He made it to California, where he visited a half sister and worked at various outdoor jobs. But Dallas wasn't ready to settle in there, and when someone happened to tell him about a huge ranch located in the mountains of southeastern Oregon—the most beautiful place in the world, his acquaintance said—Dallas was instantly interested. Called the Alvord Ranch, it was owned by some people named Wilson. They had plenty of jobs for cowboys—real ones who rode horses instead of driving trucks.

Claude Dallas shouldered a 50-pound backpack and set off northward in the spring of 1968. He hitchhiked and walked, sometimes covering 40 miles a day on foot by running part of the distance, or so he said. It was as if he'd started training in earnest to be a mountain man.

The young man who showed up at the Alvord Ranch looked green but sturdy. Hoyt Wilson needed a temporary hand to tear down some old barbed-wire fencing, so he hired Dallas for a week. He finished his assignment in two days. Next, he was sent alone to do some fence-mending high on a mountainside, doing the work of two men in something like half the expected time. Hoyt Wilson was impressed. So were his wife, Mary, and his mother, Coco, both of whom admired the stranger's good manners and clean-cut looks, as well as his remarkable diligence. Wilson hired him on full time.

Hoyt Wilson (*right*) hired greenhorn Claude Dallas as a hand on his 300,000-acre spread near Burns, Oregon. Dallas spent two years acquiring the skills of a cowboy at the Wilson ranch.

Dallas felt comfortable enough with the Wilsons to confide his dream of being a buckaroo, as cowboys are often called in that corner of the world. They obliged him by assigning him a couple of aging nags, one as a saddle horse and the other to haul his gear, and introducing him to cowboy ways of horse handling. But the Alvord's frisky quarter horses, the breed the buckaroos rode when working cattle, threw him repeatedly. Riding Blue Roan around the fields and woods of a dairy farm, Dallas discovered, was a far cry from the serious business at hand. He wasn't quite the horseman his father had made him out to be. But he was determined to learn to handle a quarter horse like the best of them, and when he got thrown he always climbed on again. His father had been right about one thing: Claude Dallas junior had grit.

Some of the other hands doubted that Dallas would ever be a horseman and figured he was only playing at being a cowboy. They laughed when the horses bucked him off and took him even less seriously when he bought the fanciest, most expensive of cowboy rigs, from saddle and bridles to Stetson hat and custom-made boots. He bought himself a Winchester rifle, the storied "gun that won the West," and started packing it wherever he went, then added a pistol to his hip. Dallas's finery and his weapons made him look like something out of a grade-B western movie — but maybe that was the very image the little boy had carried around in his head back East when he dreamed of being a cowboy; he'd never seen the real thing until he landed at the Alvord, and it might have been hard to shake off fantasy.

He worked just as hard at learning how to rope, herd, and brand the Alvord stock. He mastered the techniques of castrating and dehorning calves. And he learned how to stay on a bucking quarter horse.

Other cowhands thought that Dallas never really felt a kinship with horses. He rode them too hard, used them like any other piece of ranch equipment, and sometimes abused them. Once in a while, after he'd been thrown, Dallas would punch a horse in the ribs angrily before climbing back on. It wasn't the right way to treat an animal, even one that was hard to handle.

The way Claude Dallas drove himself to be the best of all cowboy apprentices, to recast himself in the mold of the West, eventually made his colleagues quit laughing and start admiring his dogged effort. The Wilsons appreciated his moderate ways — no smoking, no cussing, no catting around, and only an occasional beer. In time, they came to regard him as more than just an employee. "I got to feeling like he was part of my family," Coco Wilson would say later. Then in the spring of 1970, when Claude Dallas had been at the Alvord for nearly two years and was making his boyhood dream come true, something happened to make him move along.

The problem was his draft board back in Ohio. He had registered as the law required, but once he went west, he didn't bother with forwarding addresses. Apparently the board had mailed a notice directing him to appear for induction into the military. When he failed to respond or show up, it looked as if he was dodging the draft. Dallas learned—how or from whom he didn't reveal to the Wilsons—that the FBI had been called in to track him and was now closing in.

Hoyt Wilson was sympathetic. He didn't see the disciplined Dallas as a common draft dodger, but as an honest, hardworking young man who was carving out his own place in the world. The Wilsons were reluctant to see him go, but they sold Dallas two of their horses, one to ride and one to carry his provisions. From the ranch in Oregon he made a slow, meandering journey that took him southeast and across the state line into northern Nevada. Dallas didn't know for sure where he was heading. He'd know his destination when he got there.

Sporting a high-crowned cowboy hat, an army greatcoat, and silver spurs on his boots, riding one horse and leading another, 20-year-old Claude Dallas cut an unforgettable figure. When he passed close to highways, drivers honked and waved, and he waved back. Once, four carloads of tourists screeched to a halt on Interstate 80 outside Reno. The occupants piled out to take photographs of the horseman from another era making his way across the barren, lonely salt flat.

In the fall of 1970, close to four months after he'd left the Alvord Ranch, Dallas came to Winnemucca, Nevada, a town of about 4,000 that was well supplied with brothels and gambling joints. It wasn't the place for him, and he continued north along U.S. Highway 95 into the Paradise Valley, a forty-by-twelve-mile stretch of parched sagebrush country. Dallas stopped at a little cluster of houses and trailers called Paradise Hill. This was more like his kind of town: just a few people surrounded by wide-open spaces, a really nothing kind of place. He dismounted at a roadside bar and went inside. As always, he was wearing a gun.

George Nielsen's bar didn't even have a name. It was a dark, seedy joint frequented by men as rough edged as the proprietor himself, a beefy 60-year-old who habitually nursed a glass of Early Times whiskey and Seven-up while he dispensed drinks and a barkeep's traditional wisdom and advice. Nielsen took to Dallas instantly. He saw in him a tough young range rider who could hunt and shoot and ride as he himself no longer could. The attraction was mutual. Dallas saw in Nielsen someone who was not unlike his father, a talkative tale spinner who shared his interest in guns and horses and the Old West. They had something else in common, too—a dislike, even loathing, for authority. Law officers were high on Nielsen's list of sons of bitches who deserved to be shot.

Dallas hung around Paradise Hill, making a good impression among its residents. Nielsen's wife, Liz, the head nurse at the little hospital in Winnemucca, was taken by the newcomer's nice manners, and she eventually would feel as close to him as if she had been his mother. Most of the other women in Paradise Hill, at least the older ones, had a soft, maternal spot for Dallas. The men liked his independence; not many young men these days struck out on their own the way this one had. Everything seemed to click, and Claude Dallas was on his way to becoming a hero at the little bar on Highway 95. Or at least a favorite son.

Dallas found work as a buckaroo with the Quarter Circle A Ranch in Paradise Valley. In the beginning some of the other cowboys thought he was a bit of a dude, but they soon got to like him. He was a hard worker who didn't mind getting manure under his fingernails. Besides, there seemed to be something special about him. He had a nice smile and was a good listener, but he didn't talk much, especially about himself. Some hands said he seemed lonesome, like an orphan. Others thought he was so deep and so smart that he was bound to be famous someday. For what, they couldn't say.

Nevertheless, there was one thing that made a lot of the Quarter Circle A cowboys uncomfortable about Dallas—his poaching. He would bring illegal venison into camp and dump it at the chuck wagon, even though the cook didn't need it or want it. Often the meat went to waste, quickly spoiling without refrigeration. Dallas bragged that he had no use for laws against poaching. A man had a right to live off the land. Game wardens meant nothing to

A dirt road winds through the sagebrush of Nevada's sparsely populated Paradise Valley, where Claude Dallas picked up jobs at various cattle ranches. Dallas is shown below with his older friend George Nielsen, a tavern owner in the tiny valley community of Paradise Hill.

him. Dallas wasn't the only person around who thumbed his nose at hunting regulations. George Nielsen, for one, shared his views.

Dallas's rough ways with animals were as obvious as ever. He once knocked a large dog unconscious because it got in his way. Another time he lost his temper at a cow that had fallen down in a chute; he struck the creature with a two-by-four. He was also said to have gone after an unruly stallion with a shoeing hammer. None of this meant much to anyone at the time. It was easy to shrug off because he was good at his work and, besides, all cowpokes got mad once in a while.

Although it wasn't as homey as the Wilsons' Alvord Ranch had been, Dallas liked the Quarter Circle A. On his days off, he often went to Paradise Hill to hang out with Nielsen and his customers. He also spent a lot of free time honing his marksmanship, using ground squirrels and tin cans as his targets. Eventually he'd become a crack shot and could hit a bottle at fifty yards.

Life fell into a pleasant routine, and worries about the draft and the FBI dimmed as the months passed without any further notices.

But trouble struck again. On October 25, 1973, Dallas was taking a nap in his bunkhouse when several FBI agents walked in with a warrant for his arrest on charges of failing to report for induction. Later Dallas would complain bitterly that the agents had roughed him up and knocked the heels off his cowboy boots in the process of handcuffing him and dragging him away. Cuffed and belly-shackled, he had to endure the stares of curious onlookers when he and his captors flew to Ohio. It humiliated Dallas to be treated like a common criminal. And it made him sore that the lawmen had got the drop on him.

Exactly how the agency had found him wasn't clear, but Dallas blamed his bad luck on some pictures taken by a photographer named William Albert Allard. The photographer had shot Dallas and some of his fellow buckaroos at work, and the pictures were published in the National Geographic Society's 1972 book, *The American Cowboy in Life and Legend*. Even though he wasn't readily recognizable and his name wasn't mentioned, Dallas thought someone from the FBI, or maybe from his draft board, had happened to see the book.

In Ohio, Dallas was booked and jailed for 11 days, then released to his father's custody to await his trial in Colum-

At a camp out on the range Claude Dallas *(far right)* takes a break
with five other buckaroos from Nevada's Quarter Circle A Ranch.

bus. With a loan from Coco Wilson for his legal expenses, Dallas hired Andrew Wentworth to defend him. The lawyer liked his client very much, partly because young Dallas was motivated by a belief that he had the right to dictate his own life. "He was probably born 200 years too late," Wentworth remarked. "His problem was that he didn't want anybody telling him what to do."

Dallas's independence, however much his lawyer might value it, was not a defense. But Wentworth found something that was: The Mount Gilead draft board couldn't prove that Dallas had in fact received the second notice the board had sent instructing him to appear for induction. The U.S. attorney dropped the charges the day before the trial date, and Dallas left Ohio early in 1974 — with ugly memories of his encounter with the law and his time in jail.

Out West again, Dallas showed up at the Wilsons' ranch determined to work off the loan from Coco Wilson. The family wasn't surprised. That was the man they knew. But in other ways, Dallas was different. "He came back more savvy, more wary," Hoyt Wilson recalled. "He had felt the heat of authority, and he didn't enjoy it." Hoyt understated Dallas's feelings about his experience. He had hated everything about it, especially the handcuffs.

Ranch hands who'd known him when he first came to the Wilsons' place as a youngster noticed that he was more interested in weapons than ever. He studied books about guns and self-defense and practiced quick-draw techniques, and he peppered his conversation with knowing references to firearms; it sounded as if he'd really done his homework. Whatever he did, wherever he was, he packed a revolver. There was nothing strange about a cowboy carrying a gun, but Dallas took it to extremes. "He's the only man I know who wears his gun just to pick up his mail," observed an old acquaintance.

When Dallas had paid off his debt to Coco Wilson he decided to go back to the Paradise Hill neighborhood. He worked at one ranch and another, but it seemed as if the cowboy life was losing its savor. For some of his jobs, Dallas rode herd on cattle with a truck — certainly more efficient, but not the way of the real buckaroo. After a couple of years, he began to think his days as a buckaroo were about over. "The old-style outfits were going to hell," he said afterwards. "I moved on to other things."

Dallas had been doing some trapping on the side all along, and as he became unhappier with ranch work he began spending more and more time out in rough, wild country alone, setting out his traps. He took bobcats, coyotes, the occasional mountain lion, and whatever else he could get. The life of the trapper offered what Dallas wanted — freedom, independence, a chance to call all the shots himself. And he saw no reason why he couldn't turn a profit with his trapping.

Dallas's friends in Paradise Hill regarded him as an accomplished outdoorsman and hunter; there was no one like him for camping by himself for weeks and months at a time, they agreed. As well as anyone and better than most, he knew the wilderness of northern Nevada. Even so, Dallas knew he had a lot to learn, and he methodically read books about trapping and the habits of coyotes and bobcats. He picked the brains of experienced trappers like Santy Mendieta, a Nevada old-timer who'd trapped something like a hundred thousand animals in some 40 seasons. Dallas tried meticulously to apply what they'd told him about their techniques when he set about laying his own traplines.

Dallas got a Nevada trapping license, then proceeded to ignore the state's rules when it suited him. There wasn't a trapper who didn't ignore some of them some of the time. The game laws were "pinheaded," according to Mendieta, and there were far too many of them. A man could hardly set a trap without breaking some niggling regulation about the exact placement of bait or the kind of device permitted for a particular animal in a particular season.

Although Dallas bent and broke the law, he figured he didn't trap any more than he needed, so he had a right to what he took. The Nevada Fish and Game Department disagreed. In 1976, warden Dale Elliot came across some of Dallas's traps illegally baited with bones, wild-mustang hide, and jack-rabbit fur. He confiscated some of the traps and gave Dallas a citation — standard procedure for game-law violations. The episode ended cordially enough before a justice of the peace, with Dallas paying $100 and getting his traps back. The next time Dale Elliot checked on him, Dallas was clean. He invited Elliot into his camp and gave him a cup of tea.

Dallas lost this round to the Nevada Fish and Game Department. On another occasion he came out the winner — but showed how oddly he could react to authority. In December 1978 game warden Gene Weller came across some illegal traps in a canyon in the Bloody Run Hills, not far from Paradise Hill. None of them had the required tag bearing the trapper's name, and nobody was in sight. Dark was approaching, so Weller returned the next day. A jeep was parked at the mouth of the canyon. It belonged to Claude Dallas, and Weller settled down to wait for him. But by midafternoon the trapper hadn't returned, even though there'd been plenty of time for him to check the traps Weller had seen the day before.

Weller felt uneasy—perhaps Dallas had had an accident, he thought—and decided to radio the county sheriff for help. Two deputies arrived not long before dark, and in checking Dallas's jeep they discovered two loaded weapons, a .300 Savage model 99 rifle and a .44 Ruger revolver. It was against Nevada law to keep a loaded rifle in a vehicle, and the deputies confiscated it and for good measure took the revolver as well, even though it wasn't in violation of the law. Dallas—if he was within earshot—didn't return the signal when one of the men fired his gun into the air. Weller walked to the end of the canyon and back, but the trapper was nowhere to be seen; he'd apparently left the canyon by another route.

It didn't seem normal to Weller for a man to give a game warden such a wide berth, since he wasn't likely to dish out anything stronger than a citation and maybe a lecture. An unnerving thought crossed the warden's mind—maybe Dallas had been somewhere close by all day, watching him.

Three days later Dallas showed up at the county courthouse in Winnemucca demanding the return of his guns. Somebody got hold of Weller, and he and Dallas had a face-to-face talk about the illegal traps. Unfortunately, Weller couldn't prove that Dallas had set them, and the trapper stoutly denied they were his. As to the guns, the deputy sheriff who'd said the rifle was loaded wasn't so sure now that he could swear to it in court. Without his testimony, there wasn't a case against Dallas. The guns were handed over to Dallas, and as he was about to leave he said to Weller: "You are welcome in my camp anytime." Then he added: "Just leave your badge outside." Weller said: "Claude, I can't leave my badge outside." Dallas thought about that for a moment, and said, "Well, then, stay out of my camp."

Dallas seemed to be saying that game wardens didn't need to worry about him as long as they left him alone. But it might be another story if they tried to tell him what to do.

Dallas spent a lot of time camping in the desert, but he wasn't always a nomad. He had permanent quarters of sorts consisting of a trailer and an old school bus in back of George Nielsen's bar. Besides providing his young sidekick with a place to land, Nielsen had a hand in the trapping operation. The bar owner grubstaked Dallas to food, pack animals, camp gear, and mail services, and he also found buyers for the pelts the trapper brought in, legal or not. Nielsen got 40 percent of the take in return for his services, as well as a chance to feel like part of the macho life Dallas was leading.

But Dallas's success as a trapper was only so-so, and adding southern Idaho to the territory he worked didn't help him very much. According to top-notch trapper Santy Mendieta, "He worked hard, but he didn't make good catches. He needed somebody to show him how." Mendieta didn't think much of the take Dallas brought to a fur sale in Winnemucca in 1979. "He'd been out all winter," Mendieta recalled, "and he had fourteen cats. He knew he didn't do good."

Although he had much more freedom as a trapper than he'd had when he was a buckaroo with a boss, Dallas apparently wanted still more. By 1980 he was telling friends that it was time for him to move on, maybe to some lonely, wide-open space in Canada or Alaska. But he wanted to make one last trapping trip to a wild stretch of public land on the south fork of the Owyhee River in Idaho's southwest corner. Dallas had promised himself a solitary winter of trapping, and he had promised George Nielsen bobcat pelts for a fur coat for Liz.

The spot Dallas had picked for his campsite was Bull Basin, some three miles north of the Nevada border, about the same distance east of the Oregon line and, according to a trapper who knew it well, "ten miles from hell and a thousand from anyplace else." Set in the well-watered canyon cut by the Owyhee, Bull Basin was rich in bobcat, deer, and other wildlife. Around this oasis, high desert plateaus stretched in every direction. Bull Basin's isolation didn't bother Dallas at all; he liked being alone.

Escorted by a caravan of off-road vehicles carrying two mules and several hundred pounds of gear and supplies, Dallas arrived at Bull Basin on December 3, 1980. He had grown a beard for warmth in the coming winter, and with his once close-cropped brown hair grown long and pulled back in a ponytail, he looked like nothing so much as an old-time mountain man let loose in the late twentieth cen-

On his way to becoming a full-time trapper, Claude Dallas shows off the coyote and deer pelts he'd taken around his camp near Tonopak, Nevada, in this 1975 snapshot *(above)*. Preparing for a winter of trapping in the wilderness of southern Idaho, Dallas made an advance trip to find a good campsite in November 1980 *(right)*. He decided on a place on the Owyhee River called Bull Basin and returned in December to pitch his tent, which is visible in this aerial view.

tury. George Nielsen was with him, as was Jim Stevens, a potato farmer with a scholarly interest in Indian artifacts and none at all in hunting, trapping, and other pursuits that involved killing animals.

After everything had been unloaded at the rim of the canyon, which was impassable even to off-road vehicles, Dallas's friends bade him good-bye. Stevens promised to return in a month or so with more food and Dallas's mail. The trapper loaded up the mules and led them down to the canyon bottom, where he pitched his big tent and set up its wood stove. Although the deer season was over, Dallas wanted a supply of venison, and he soon bagged two bucks and a doe. He didn't stop with flouting a single regulation and went on to trap a couple of bobcats a few days before the season opened.

Dallas's arrival was noted, but not welcomed, by ranchers Don Carlin and his son Eddy J. Carlin. They operated the 45 Ranch, a spread in Owyhee County—known simply as the Owyhee to the locals—about 12 miles from Bull Basin. They used the basin as a sheltered winter range for their cattle, even though it wasn't actually part of their ranch. The Carlins also trapped coyotes and cats in and around Bull Basin for extra cash, and they didn't like it that Dallas was working an area they'd considered practically their own. Nor was he the only interloper. The Carlins had just discovered that two Oregonians had moved right in on the 45 Ranch itself, laying numerous illegally baited bobcat traps in the heart of Carlin territory.

Eddy Carlin went to Bull Basin for a talk with Dallas about trapping territory. The two men worked out an arrangement that satisfied both of them, but Dallas made it clear that he wasn't going to follow the official trapping calendar. The two revolvers he wore and the illegal meat and skins already in his camp made Carlin uneasy.

The Carlins thought they could put up with Dallas, but something had to be done about the Oregonians; the ranchers didn't want to be blamed for someone else's illegal traplines any more than they wanted to be ripped off. They drove to the nearest telephone, two hours away, and called Conservation Officer William H. Pogue of the Idaho Fish and Game Department. That was at 10 p.m. on Sunday, January 4, 1981.

Pogue was a happily married man and the father of four grown children. There was no real need for him to rush out of the house in the middle of the night in response to the Carlins' call. It could have waited until morning; possibly then someone else could have gone. But he loved his job and he loved the Owyhee. Its desolate beauty held an undying fascination for him, as did the creatures he was charged with protecting. At 50, he was almost as lean and trim as the Marine he had been when he'd married Dee 29 years before. By that night in January 1981 he had been an Idaho game officer for 15 years, as knowledgeable and dedicated an outdoorsman and conservationist as had ever been known in the Owyhee.

Some people said Pogue was hard-nosed and stiff-necked and was not above bullying and threatening in the line of duty. His defenders countered that he had to be tough when he confronted hard-core poachers. Pogue's family and friends knew a softer side. He liked to spend time out in the desert enjoying bird calls and sunsets. An amateur artist, he drew painstakingly detailed, sometimes sentimental pictures of buckaroos and mountain men: a trapper pensively touching a barbed-wire fence, a grizzled cowboy with a bird perched on his finger, a cowhand-barber trimming his buddy's nearly bald head. It took Bill Pogue considerable time to complete his drawings. He had lost the sight of one eye in a long-ago camping accident, which strained his good eye when he worked and confined his sketch periods to about 15 minutes at a stretch.

Although he routinely carried a gun when he was on duty, he hated to use it. Now and again, though, he would shoot a sick or wounded animal to put it out of its misery. Because of the problem he had with his vision, he wasn't much of a marksman. This never seemed to bother him, since he wasn't a hunter and didn't want to be.

It was standard procedure for a warden checking game violations in a remote region such as the Owyhee to take along a partner for backup. Pogue enlisted Wilson Conley Elms, Jr., a soft-spoken, bearded man in his middle thirties who was well over six feet tall and weighed a solid 270 pounds. After four years on the job he still jumped at the chance to go out on a special call. Elms had come up through the academic route, with degrees in geology and game management, but fieldwork as a conservation officer was his life's dream. He would have done it for nothing, his schoolteacher wife suspected.

The two men, dressed in their green Fish and Game uniforms and carrying guns, left for the Carlin ranch around 10:30 that night in a Fish and Game Department Dodge

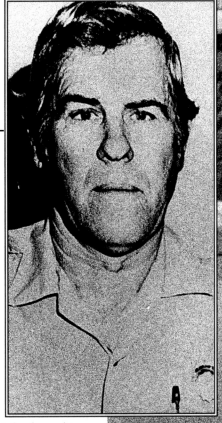

William H. Pogue (*right*) of the Idaho Department of Fish and Game went to Dallas's Bull Basin camp to determine whether he was trapping illegally. Game warden Conley Elms, shown here with Old Blue, his Labrador retriever, accompanied Pogue.

pickup. Early in the morning, after a nap in the truck, Pogue and Elms had breakfast with Don and Eddy Carlin and Eddy's wife, Joann. Don Carlin filled them in about the Oregonians, but nobody brought up the camp in Bull Basin until Joann prodded Eddy into describing Dallas and his setup. After breakfast the two wardens confronted the Oregon trappers working near the ranch house and ticketed them for trapping out of season and using illegally obtained game birds for bait.

Then they asked Eddy Carlin what kind of a man Dallas seemed to be and what they could expect of him. Carlin said he didn't really know, but the man was armed and in his view shouldn't be trusted. He advised the wardens not to turn their backs on him. Pogue nodded. "Right, we'll keep each other covered," he said, and started the truck.

The officers had been invited to have dinner at the 45 Ranch and spend the night. At about 10 p.m. the Carlins gave up waiting for them.

Jim Stevens parked his 1977 Chevrolet Blazer on the canyon rim overlooking Bull Basin at midmorning on January 5, 1981. When Stevens had stopped at the bar in Paradise Hill to pick up supplies and mail for Dallas, George Nielsen had handed him a pistol to use to signal his arrival, in case Dallas was not in his camp.

Stevens fired the gun, waited awhile, then started the descent to the camp carrying a Styrofoam cooler full of Dallas's favorite foods. The trapper met him when he was partway down the trail and seemed glad to see him. Stevens said there was fresh fruit in the cooler as well as brownies and a plastic Cool Whip container full of pistachio pudding his wife had made. Dallas loved Sandra Stevens's pistachio pudding. He grinned with pleasure. "We're going to have a good time!" he said.

Dallas went on up to the Blazer to get the rest of the supplies. Alone in the camp, Stevens glanced into the tent and noted idly the neat stacks of firewood and deer quarters hanging inside. There were two or three pelts stretching, too. Stevens strolled off along the river, eyes scanning the ground for arrowheads or other traces of Old West history.

59

He was concentrating on his search when he heard a shout from the campsite and turned around to see Dallas standing with two men in uniform. Stevens joined them, and Bill Pogue and Conley Elms introduced themselves. Stevens was wearing the pistol Nielsen had pressed on him, and Pogue asked him to hand it over. The warden removed the cartridges, dropped them into Stevens's pocket, then handed the gun back to him. Stevens saw that the shoulder holster in which Dallas had been carrying a .22 pistol was empty; he supposed the wardens had asked him for it. They'd probably missed the .357 Ruger Dallas always wore on his hip, concealed as it was beneath his long coat.

The game wardens turned their attention again to Dallas. They were talking about the illegal deer meat and cats that the Carlins claimed he had and asking for his trapping licenses. To Stevens's relief, Pogue and Elms seemed to have no further interest in him. He wandered back toward the river, tuning in and out of the three voices behind him. It didn't sound to him as if the talk was getting angry, but it wasn't friendly either.

Stevens heard Dallas say that he was a hundred miles from civilization and needed to hang up venison if he wasn't to starve. Pogue said that didn't make any difference to the law. He asked to see the bobcat pelts he understood to be inside the tent. Dallas retorted that his tent was private—did the wardens have a search warrant? Pogue said that they didn't need one, and he told Elms to search the tent. Stevens caught something about a citation, then a word that sounded like "arrest." That puzzled him, since violating a game law wasn't all that serious a crime. Trappers got tickets; they didn't get arrested. Then he heard Elms saying from inside the tent, "There's a raccoon hide in here, too." The warden came out with the bobcat hides. "You know I'm going to tell the judge I got those cats in Nevada," Dallas said coolly. Pogue responded, "We'll still cite you for possession."

Stevens was relieved. It sounded as if the wardens weren't going to arrest Claude after all; they'd only ticket him. He was off the hook.

A moment later, though, Stevens heard his friend ask,

"Are you going to take me in?"

Stevens still had his back turned when he heard a shot, then a voice crying out, "Oh, no!" He swung around to see a flash of gunfire and Dallas with his knees bent, crouching like a trained policeman and holding the .357 with both hands. Pogue reeled, lurched, and fell backward as smoke curled from his chest. Dallas fired twice more. Conley Elms fell and lay still, facedown on the ground.

Jim Stevens was stunned. His ears rang from the noise of the shots. He couldn't grasp what had happened, or why it had happened. As far as he could tell, the game wardens hadn't reached for their guns or shown any intention of harming Dallas. And Dallas hadn't sounded frightened. Why had he shot them?

Suddenly, Stevens was overcome with terror. He saw Dallas going into the tent and coming out with his .22 Marlin rifle. Stevens quickly backed off along the riverbank. Dallas put the muzzle of the rifle just behind Conley Elms's left ear and fired one shot. He moved over to Pogue and did the same thing. The bullets left lethal but very small, neat holes, and in a place that would be scarcely noticeable on a pelt. Any trapper wanting to make sure an animal in a snare was dead would have fired in exactly the same way.

It occurred to Stevens that Dallas now had more reason to kill him than he'd had to kill the wardens. Except for talking, they hadn't done much of anything. But Stevens was an eyewitness to two murders. The farmer walked over to where Dallas was standing, a little way from the bodies. Pogue's handgun lay inches from his fingertips; maybe he'd tried to draw it while reeling back from Dallas's first hit.

The bewildered Stevens choked out a question:

"Why, Claude? *Why?*"

"I swore I'd never get arrested again. And they had handcuffs on them. I'm sorry I got you involved in this."

Dallas didn't seem very concerned about what he'd done; he just seemed worried about what he had to do next. "I've got to get rid of the bodies," he said, "and you've got to help me." Stevens wasn't about to argue with somebody who'd just killed two people, especially since the gun that Nielsen had given him was now unloaded, the cartridges still in his pocket where Pogue had put them.

60

A plan seemed to be taking shape in Dallas's head. He told Stevens to cover the bodies with brush, in case a low-flying plane happened to pass overhead before they could get them out of there. Then Dallas waded to the other side of the river, where he kept the mules. Stevens quickly reloaded his pistol while Dallas was looking in the other direction. Maybe he'd have to shoot Claude to get out of this alive, Stevens thought—but he knew he probably wouldn't be able to pull the trigger.

Across the river, Dallas was having a hard time. The mules had been spooked by the gunfire, and Dallas couldn't catch the larger and stronger of the two animals. With the help of a pan of grain Dallas finally managed to catch the smaller one, a female.

Her first load was Pogue's body. Stevens couldn't believe that he was actually helping to tie a shot-up corpse to a mule. He and Dallas and the mule plodded up the trail to the Blazer. Leaving Pogue's body beside the vehicle, they went down for the second load. Dallas delegated Stevens to wrestle Elms's bloody corpse onto the mule's back while he himself set fire to the two piles of brush to get rid of the pools of blood. The burning was the easy part. Loading the body was hard, and Stevens couldn't do it by himself. He and Dallas together finally managed to manhandle Elms's body onto the mule. Less than halfway up the trail, however, the body shifted off balance, and the mule collapsed.

For Stevens, the next couple of hours were the worst part of what had become a bizarre and mind-numbing nightmare. The two men couldn't wrestle the body back onto the mule. They dragged and heaved; the animal balked, reared, fell down, rolled over. The dead warden's shirt and pants tore. It was hopeless. Dallas said at last: "The only way to get him up is to quarter him."

Stevens felt sick. He didn't have the stomach for anything so ghastly, and he said so. Dallas couldn't go through with butchering Elms's body, either. It seemed there was only one thing to do—he'd have to dump the corpse into the river. Dallas lashed a rope around Elms's ankles and tied the other end of it to the mule's packsaddle. As Dallas began leading the mule down the trail, the boots slipped off the body. He removed the rope from the boots and retied it around the dead man's chest. This time the rope held. Brush and rocks clawed at the warden's body, and by the time Dallas threw it into the river, only a few shreds of clothing clung to the lacerated flesh. To Stevens, it was a vile and callous way to treat a human being, dead or alive. He shivered at the desecration.

Obeying Dallas's instructions, Stevens poured kerosene on the bloody drag marks on the trail and set the fuel on fire. Then the two men carried all the wardens' effects up to the canyon rim, along with the hides and Dallas's rifles and shotgun. On the way up Dallas said to his friend, "This is murder one for me. I didn't weight the body. They're bound to find it in the morning."

Nevertheless, he was determined to get Pogue's body out of there and hide it. That didn't make much sense to Stevens. But at this point, nothing did. He went through the motions of helping Dallas pack the gear into the Blazer. The corpse came last. There was so little room left that its feet stuck out through the open tailgate.

From Bull Basin there was only one place for Claude Dallas to go—Paradise Hill. During the five-hour trip he said to Stevens, "I don't know how you feel about it, but to me it was justifiable homicide. They had no business in my camp." Stevens wondered what Dallas meant by justifiable homicide. The farmer didn't understand why a man was justified in killing two law officers because they'd set foot in his camp. And what Claude was telling him now sounded very different from what he'd said moments after the shooting: "I swore I'd never get arrested again. And they had handcuffs on them." To Stevens, that had sounded like a man resisting arrest.

It was around 10:30 that night when Dallas and Stevens pulled in at the Nielsens' bar in Paradise Hill and rousted out George and Liz. "We're in trouble," Dallas told them. "I dusted two Fish and Game." Not "killed," not "shot dead." The word Dallas used seemed offhand and heartless. He borrowed a pickup truck and a shovel from the shaken Nielsens and drove off alone to bury Pogue's body in a secret grave. Meanwhile, Liz Nielsen steered the distraught and exhausted Stevens into the shower and burned his bloody clothing before he went home to his potato farm eight miles away.

Dallas came back to Paradise Hill with an empty truck and another favor to ask of George Nielsen: He needed a ride to Sand Pass Road, about thirteen miles from town, near the Bloody Run Mountains. Dallas showered, ate, and packed his gear. Nielsen gave him $100.

On the way to the drop-off point, Dallas said to Nielsen,

"I did a sloppy job, but they deserved it. They had it coming." He didn't say why.

At Sand Pass Road Dallas told his friend good-bye and vanished into the night.

On January 6, the day after the shooting, Jim Stevens and the Nielsens went to the Humboldt County sheriff's office in Winnemucca. Conscience, and their certain knowledge that there was no way to conceal the fact that a crime had been committed, prompted them to tell everything they knew. The authorities concluded that they had acted under duress, and none of them was charged as an accessory—even though any of them could possibly have thwarted Dallas's escape, notifying the law while he was out hiding Pogue's body.

A two-pronged search was launched immediately, for the victims and for their alleged killer. Tim Nettleton, the sheriff of Owyhee County, Idaho, where the game wardens had been shot, coordinated the effort. Nettleton had been a good friend of Bill Pogue's, and the search for Claude Dallas became his personal quest. But he didn't expect an early success, since Dallas had gotten a good head start in country that he knew well.

Conley Elms's body was spotted by a news crew aboard a helicopter two days after the killings, floating facedown and naked in the icy river. At the same time, nearly 80 law

Owyhee County Sheriff Tim Nettleton *(right)* coordinated the search for William Pogue's body. As
part of a search party, 27-year-old Steve Pogue, in
the foreground below, looks for his father's body
in a stretch of northern Nevada desert.

officers were scouring the desert around Paradise Hill. Helicopters and small planes equipped with infrared sensors
made repeated passes in the course of a week. Two four-
man SWAT teams from the FBI were on the scene; the
federal agency had come into the case because Dallas
had crossed the Idaho state line into Nevada after
shooting the wardens.

Besides looking for Dallas, the manhunt was also
on the alert for Bill Pogue's body. It appeared that
Dallas probably hadn't driven more than 25 or 30
miles when he left Paradise Hill carrying the corpse in
Nielsen's truck, so the searchers stayed within a 30-mile
radius of the town. But there were too many places to dig

a grave, too many old mine shafts where Pogue's body might have been hidden, and not a trace of it turned up.

Pogue's family and friends wondered why the fugitive couldn't at least have left a note about where he'd hidden the body so it could be retrieved and laid to rest properly. They also wondered why Dallas had gone to the trouble of transporting it all the way from Bull Basin to Paradise Hill before hiding it. But Gene Weller, the Nevada game officer who'd had a run-in with Dallas about traps and guns three years earlier, thought he knew why: "He brought it back to show George Nielsen," he said, "the same way he used to bring back poached deer and lions."

A search of Dallas' makeshift trailer-school bus dwelling behind George Nielsen's bar turned up some interesting surprises. The man who was supposedly fixated on the Old West had a quite modern arsenal. There were 10 handguns and seven rifles, thousands of rounds of ammunition, speed loaders for the handguns, a bulletproof vest, a gas mask, a tanker's helmet, half-a-dozen well-honed knives with extra blades, and a package of human-shaped targets. In addition to the weaponry, Dallas had a little library devoted to guns and combat. Among the magazines were *Shotgun News* and *The American Rifleman*, combat-training manuals, and books with titles such as *The Machine Gun, Kill or Get Killed, Firearm Silencers,* and *No Second Place Winner.* This last book emphasized the need to draw fast in a gunfight and warned the reader, "Be first or be dead—there is no second-place winner in a gun fight."

"Wanted" posters were distributed across the nation and in Canada offering a reward of up to $20,000 for information leading to Dallas's arrest and conviction. FBI agents questioned Dallas's acquaintances, friends, and family to get some hint of who might have helped him or where he might have gone. In March, Idaho Governor John Evans asked the FBI to place Dallas on its 10 most wanted list. There wasn't a vacant slot, the governor was told, but perhaps one would come free. Reports of Dallas sightings from all of the western states, as well as many eastern and southern states and several Canadian provinces, poured into Tim Nettleton's office, eventually mounting into the hundreds. He kept them filed in a large cardboard box in his tiny office. There were more tips than the various law-enforcement departments working on the case could check out, but even the most solid-seeming ones led nowhere.

Spring turned into summer without the authorities discovering a single solid clue about where Dallas was or where he'd been since the killings. The long wait was beginning to wear on Sheriff Nettleton, and he admitted to a reporter, "I want Claude Dallas. I want him bad."

Nearly six months after the shootings, the FBI got a call from a man named Randall Curry, who worked at a steel mill in Sioux Falls, South Dakota. He'd read a story in *Outdoor Life* magazine about Claude Dallas that included the fugitive's photograph and a reproduction of the wanted poster. Curry was certain that the person pictured was a man who called himself Jack Chappel and had worked at the mill during the winter. He wasn't disposed to be friendly, Curry said. Chappel had quit his job at the mill at the end of March, but the fingerprints the FBI found there proved that he was indeed Claude Dallas.

Tim Nettleton began to wonder if the search might go on for a year or even more. "He could be in Alaska, he could be out East, he could be anyplace. It's even possible he might still be in the county," Nettleton said. "There are lots of places for a man to lose himself out here, and Dallas knows most of them. To him, this is home."

The fugitive's friends agreed. Said one: "Claude knows every damn gopher hole and cave in the Northwest." And the press fed the notion that Dallas the mountain man was as comfortable in the desert as an ordinary person in his or her own house. A lot of people began to regard him as a romantic figure, even a hero. He was reported to have the skills to live off the land, picking nutritious plants and setting simple snares for game or cornering high-protein mice and pack rats in caves and abandoned mine shafts. As Dallas was played up, the reputations of William Pogue and Conley Elms declined. It was hinted that they'd done something to trigger the incident. One Dallas loyalist accused Pogue, the more assertive of the two wardens, of "showing too much badge."

Sheriff Nettleton was confident that sooner or later Dallas would make a bad mistake, and the sheriff was pretty sure what it would be: The fugitive would slip into Paradise Hill for a little company and some civilized comforts, and one of the FBI undercover agents assigned to the place would nab him. Nettleton didn't buy the notion that Dallas was making it totally on his own in the wilderness. On the contrary, he was convinced that some of the town's residents were shielding Dallas, keeping him supplied with food, and thumbing their noses at the law. The sheriff had gotten wind

This wanted poster, distributed nationally by Sheriff Tim Nettleton, alerted the public to possible variations in Claude Dallas's appearance, including his hair style.

REWARD UP TO $20,000

For information leading to the Arrest and Conviction of
CLAUDE LAFAYETTE DALLAS, JR.
for the Murder of two Idaho Fish and Game Officers on January 5, 1981.

- Date of Birth: 3-11-50
- Height: 5' 10"
- Weight: 180 lbs.
- Brown Hair (may be shoulder length)

- Brown Eyes
- May have full beard
- Wears glasses
- Social Security No. 270-49-0296

Subject is an accomplished trapper and shooter.

SUBJECT IS ARMED AND EXTREMELY DANGEROUS.

CONTACT —
Sheriff Tim Nettleton, Owyhee County, Idaho - Murphy, Idaho 83650 — (208) 495-2441

of rumors that the fugitive's friends had occasionally left their pickup trucks at prearranged spots in the Nevada desert, gas tanks full and keys in the ignition, so Dallas could stay on the move.

Nettleton's instincts were only a little off the mark. On April 15, 1982, an anonymous caller hoping to collect the reward that was being offered for Dallas informed the FBI office in Reno that he could be found hiding out in a ramshackle trailer in a place called Poverty Flats, a couple of miles outside Paradise Hill off Highway 8A. The trailer belonged to ex-Marine Craig Carver, who'd been a close friend of Dallas's for several years.

FBI agents kept watch on Carver's trailer through binoculars until they were sure their quarry was there. Then they moved.

The light was fading on Sunday, April 18, 1982, when a large party of lawmen converged on Craig Carver's trailer. Other officers on foot and in pickup trucks blocked escape routes. Shortly before dark a Huey helicopter dropped an FBI SWAT team near the trailer. Other SWAT ground units moved in almost simultaneously. An amplified voice from the hovering Huey shouted: "This is the FBI! Claude Dallas, come out with your hands up!"

Dallas burst through a window, hit the ground running, and leaped into an old Ford pickup truck. Seeing his way to the road blocked by a SWAT team, he swung the truck around and smashed through a barbed-wire fence. He bounced across the open desert at a speed that made the old truck shake violently, at the same time firing at the Huey and an observation plane overhead. The truck had gone about a mile when it jolted to a sudden halt, immobilized by a loosened electrical connection. Dallas jumped out with a rifle and flung himself down. Fire came from all sides. He was hit in the left foot, but he managed to crawl into a clump of sagebrush to hide.

By now it was nearly dark, and searchers came close to Dallas's hiding place but passed by without seeing him.

Then a curious thing happened: He called out to the lawmen, "Don't shoot! I'm over here." They turned around and saw him with his hands above his head. "Don't move!" said SWAT team leader David Guilland. "I'm not going to do anything," said Dallas. He surrendered quietly. The whole episode, from his leap through the trailer window to his capture, had lasted only 22 minutes.

Like many other local policemen and federal agents who'd been after Dallas for 15 frustrating months, Nettle-

An anonymous tipster informed authorities that
Claude Dallas was hiding out in this ramshackle
trailer, which belonged to a friend in Poverty
Flats, near Paradise Hill.

ton was a little surprised by Dallas's behavior. "I figured he'd be tougher than that," the sheriff remarked. "But he didn't walk on water or anything. He's just a man." For the people who couldn't understand why Dallas had risked sneaking back to Paradise Hill, Nettleton had a ready explanation: "It's just like a dog that you kick in the side. He runs in a big circle and then comes back home."

Dallas waived extradition from Nevada to Idaho and, wearing bright orange prison clothes and shackles, was driven in a heavily guarded Winnebago to the four-cell jail in Murphy, the Owyhee County seat. He was quiet and

cooperative, except on one point. He told the police that he'd buried Pogue's body, but he doggedly refused to say where. Not even appeals to the family's feelings could soften his unyielding silence.

An Owyhee County grand jury charged Dallas with two counts of first-degree murder. Under ordinary circumstances he would have been tried in the county, but his defense attorneys, Michael Donnelly and William Mauk of Boise, did a survey of 100 county residents of Murphy and found that 60 of them thought that Dallas was guilty as charged and deserved the death penalty. As a cowhand put it, most of the locals had already "done the judge, jury and trial on him." The defense requested a change of venue, and the trial

was moved to the town of Caldwell in neighboring Canyon County and scheduled to begin September 15, 1982.

Even in Canyon County, finding 12 people who could be objective about the case wasn't easy, since there'd been so much pretrial publicity. It took three days of careful sifting before 10 women and two men were seated in the jury box.

From the first day on, the courtroom was jammed with spectators, and the lines were clearly drawn between the pro- and anti-Dallas camps. At the center of the charged atmosphere was Claude

Dallas. He seemed quiet and composed, and he listened attentively to the proceedings, his manner almost scholarly and at times a little puzzled. He was neatly dressed, and his hair was now cut short and his beard was closely trimmed. He neither acted nor looked like the formidable mountain man portrayed in the press.

In their opening statement prosecuting attorneys Michael Kennedy and Clayton Andersen hammered away at the bullets Dallas had fired into the heads of the already wounded game wardens, the gro-tesque manner in which their bodies had been manhandled, the systematic way in which the accused had destroyed evidence. Some 50 witnesses for the prosecution were then called to the stand. Dee Pogue and Sheri Elms, the widows of the victims, told how their husbands had gone out on the night of January 4, 1981, in response to rancher Eddy Carlin's complaint about Dallas's illegal hunting and trapping. Eddy and his father, Don, testified about their meeting with Claude Dallas in Bull Basin, and various experts showed gruesome photographs and videotapes of Elms's body and described its pitiable condition.

Although George Nielsen was probably Dallas's best friend, he took the stand as a prosecution witness. Nielsen repeated what Dallas had said when he showed up in Paradise Hill after the shootings: "I dusted two Fish and Game." The bar owner also recalled the comment Dallas made just before being dropped off near the Bloody Run Mountains: "I did a sloppy job, but they deserved it. They had it coming." Dallas hadn't said anything to Nielsen about shooting the wardens in self-defense or being afraid they'd arrest him.

The prosecutors were counting on Jim Stevens's testimony to seal Dallas's conviction. Unfortunately, though, there were critical gaps and uncertainties in his story. The potato farmer explained that everything happened so fast when the wardens were shot that he couldn't swear to the exact sequence of events. As to whether Bill Pogue had drawn his gun first, or whether he'd even drawn it at all, Stevens couldn't say; all he knew for sure was that when Pogue lay sprawled on the ground the gun was near his hand. Stevens also admitted that he hadn't been looking at Conley Elms at the moment Dallas fired at him and couldn't say whether the game officer had gone for his gun.

As to what might have motivated the killings, Stevens repeated what Dallas had blurted out after he'd shot the wardens: "I swore I would never be arrested again." Stevens wasn't allowed to say anything more, nor were the attorneys on either side allowed to ask questions or reveal anything about Dallas's previous record; the rules of evidence didn't permit it.

The defense opened with a parade of character witnesses for Dallas. The composite picture they created was that of a peaceable, trustworthy person — not a trigger-happy man looking for trouble. As for Bill Pogue, he was labeled "a hard-nosed-so-and-so," "quarrelsome," "aggressive,"

"someone who pushed his weight around." That wasn't the way his friends and family and fellow wardens knew him, but the damage had been done; the prosecution couldn't erase the implication that Pogue might have threatened Dallas or even gone so far as to pull a gun on the trapper. One game warden who was attending the trial remarked sourly to another, "I didn't know an officer had to go on trial for being killed."

When Dallas came to the stand, he was regarded with rapt attention by the 15 or so women, mainly local housewives, who'd been attending the trial religiously and were the defendant's ardent admirers. Calling themselves the Dallas Cheerleaders, they sent Dallas mash notes and murmured and nodded happily when a point was made in his favor. As far as the cheerleaders were concerned, Dallas was on trial because he'd stood up for what he believed in — a man's right to live by his own code. Besides that, they liked his gentlemanly manners.

Prompted by his lawyers, Dallas engagingly related the story of his life as a buckaroo and trapper. He spoke simply and directly, once in a while showing a flash of humor or catching a juror's eye.

Claude Dallas's account of what had taken place in Bull Basin cast the two game wardens as the aggressors. "They acted as if I had just robbed a bank," he claimed. It was William Pogue, according to Dallas, who came on strongest, repeatedly moving his hand toward his gun. But Conley Elms had also made Dallas apprehensive when it looked to him as if Elms was about to reach under his jacket for a gun. When Dallas protested a search of his tent without a warrant, Pogue supposedly replied, "Dallas, you can go easy or you can go hard. It doesn't make any difference to me." When he was asked to explain what he thought going hard meant, Dallas answered, "Well, hard — that's only one way. That's dead." The trapper testified that he'd called Pogue "crazy" for talking as if he'd shoot a man over a game violation.

Then came Dallas's version of the shooting. Pogue, he testified, said, "I'll carry you out," and drew his gun. "I went for mine. He fired one round. I fired. And I fired again," Dallas told the court. He claimed that he fired a round at Conley Elms because the warden was going for his gun, then got off two more shots at Pogue and a second at Elms. Dallas flatly contradicted Jim Stevens's testimony that the trapper had held his .357 Ruger in two hands and as-

sumed a professional-looking crouch when he took aim at the wardens.

Dallas continued: "And I just ran back and into my tent and grabbed my .22 and shot both men in the head." Asked why he had shot each of the officers one last time with the .22 Marlin rifle, Dallas explained, "Well, I was a little bit out of my head at that stage. I was afraid. I was wound up." The killings, he said, had been justifiable homicide because "those men were going to kill me. All I wanted to do was keep those men from killing me."

Dallas wrung himself an advantage when he answered a question he'd been refusing to answer ever since his capture. When prosecutor Anderson asked him if he could point out the site of Bill Pogue's grave on a map, Dallas responded agreeably, "I would be happy to," as if he was pleased to be able to bestow a favor, and indicated a desolate area of sagebrush and blowing sand southwest of Paradise Hill, not far from Sand Pass Road and the Bloody Run Mountains. None of the attorneys asked Dallas why he'd gone to the trouble of transporting the body all the way from Bull Basin to Paradise Hill before burying it, and he didn't volunteer an explanation. A search party was immediately organized and, using Dallas's directions, found Pogue's body that same day. Animals, probably coyotes, had discovered the shallow grave and scattered the bones.

However helpful he'd been about William Pogue's body, Dallas drew an apparent blank on the subject of the warden's gun, insisting politely that he couldn't remember what had become of it. Without the gun, it wasn't possible to prove that Pogue had in fact fired it, as Dallas had sworn. By the same token, however, the fact that the gun was missing meant that the prosecution couldn't prove their contention that Pogue *hadn't* fired at Dallas. Asked what had become of the .357 Ruger and the .22 Marlin rifle, Dallas said he buried them within four or five miles of Pogue's grave but couldn't be any more precise than that.

At the conclusion of the trial, the defense's summation rested entirely on Claude Dallas's version of events and Bill Pogue's supposed brutality. And it had been a very persuasive version: Dallas had seemed certain about what had passed between him and the two game wardens. Jim Stevens, on the other hand, had admitted that there were things he hadn't seen and details he no longer felt so sure of after the passage of almost two years' time. It had also come out that some of his testimony was inconsistent with what

he'd reported to authorities on the day after the shooting.

The gravest conflict between Dallas and Stevens concerned motive. The defendant insisted that Pogue, and possibly Elms as well, had been on the point of shooting him. If Dallas was telling the truth, he'd had the right to kill them. There was no way to reconcile his story of self-defense with what Stevens recalled him saying at Bull Basin: "I swore I'd never get arrested again. And they had handcuffs on them." Because of the rules of evidence, the prosecution wasn't allowed to get into Dallas's arrest on draft charges. The possibility that the experience had made him profoundly, even dangerously, resentful of lawmen in general went unexplored.

After seven days of quarrelsome deliberation, the jurors returned to the courtroom with a verdict that satisfied no one but themselves. They found Dallas not guilty of first degree murder, guilty of two counts of voluntary manslaughter, guilty of two counts of using a firearm to commit a crime, guilty of concealing evidence, and not guilty of resisting arrest.

Convinced that Dallas had lied on the stand, Prosecutor Clayton Andersen termed the verdict "a tremendous injustice." A statement from the Idaho Department of Fish and Game was even more scathing: The verdict "cheapened and jeopardized the lives of all police officers. We feel that the jury has told us some people can live off the land without social responsibility, that laws should not be enforced—that the last man alive is the one telling the truth." Disappointed with the verdict, Sheriff Tim Nettleton of Owyhee County said flatly, "No two ways about it. It should have been murder." Dallas and his attorneys were also unhappy; the case had seemed to go in their favor, and they'd become hopeful that the jury would find Dallas not guilty on every count. Supporting his son all the way, Claude Dallas senior denounced the results as "shitty."

The trapper knew he was going to jail, but he was confident he wouldn't be sentenced to more than two or three years. He figured he could live with that.

Judge Lodge, who was known as a careful and fair-minded jurist, was thoroughly dismayed by the jury's verdict—and thoroughly hamstrung by it. When Dallas returned to court for sentencing, the judge lashed out at him: "Mr. Dallas, I can consciously tell you, sincerely tell you, that I do not believe the issue of self-defense arose at Bull Camp. Your actions were motivated by a desire to ensure your own freedom as opposed to an actual threat to life or limb." Rejecting Dallas's contention that he'd shot the wardens in self-defense, Judge Lodge said he was satisfied that neither Pogue nor Elms had drawn on Dallas. Labeling the killings unjustified and morally reprehensible, the judge told the defendant, "Your actions were void of any remorse or feeling."

Claude Dallas didn't get the two or three years he'd expected. Instead, Judge Lodge gave him the longest sentence the law allowed—a total of 30 years.

Thirty years behind bars: it was inconceivable to a man who cherished his independence above all. Claude Dallas started serving his term at the Idaho State Penitentiary on January 5, 1983. He behaved himself and worked hard at the jobs assigned to him. And people outside didn't forget him. He got a gratifying amount of mail, from friends and even from admiring strangers who'd read about him or followed his story on television.

One of Dallas's staunchest supporters was Geneva Holman. She and her banker husband, Herb, had first met Dallas at George Nielsen's bar around 1975 during one of their frequent trips to Paradise Valley to hunt chukar, a kind of partridge. The Holmans had helped raise $28,000 for his legal expenses. On Easter Sunday, March 30, 1986, Geneva Holman visited Dallas at the penitentiary. She would be the last of his old friends to meet him within prison walls for quite a while.

At 8:30 that evening a routine head count revealed that one man was missing. Worried guards counted again. By 10 o'clock officials confirmed that Claude Dallas had broken out of the penitentiary, snipping his way through the two chain-link fences that surrounded the building where he'd met with Holman. He left behind the wire cutters he'd used. Holman was questioned and her car was checked for Dallas's fingerprints, but investigators couldn't find any evidence connecting her to the escape.

The hunt was on again. The media rehashed what Claude Dallas fans had said when he'd eluded his pursuers after the Bull Basin shootings: He was a real mountain man who knew how to live off the land, even in the most desolate sagebrush country. Owyhee County's Sheriff Tim Nettleton scoffed at such notions. "He can't survive without help," he said. Sheriff's Captain Tom Taylor, one of the coordinators of the search in ION, the nickname for the area where

Idaho, Oregon, and Nevada meet, was even more emphatic. "He's going to stay where he has support and can get assistance," he said. "He probably just goes from doorstep to doorstep for handouts."

Even though returning to Paradise Hill had been his undoing in 1982, investigators were hopeful Dallas would make the same mistake again. And indeed, bloodhounds sniffing a barstool at Nielsen's place picked up the fugitive's scent and followed it for a ways into the desert before losing it. In spite of the bloodhounds, residents of the area, George Nielsen among them, claimed to know nothing of Dallas's whereabouts. On May 16, forty-seven days after his escape, Dallas was placed on the FBI's 10 most wanted list.

Dallas's second stint on the lam was almost as frustrating for lawmen as his first had been. If all the leads they got were accurate, the fugitive was covering a lot of territory, from his habitual ION stomping grounds to South Dakota, California, and Mexico. Meanwhile, FBI agents were keeping a number of Dallas's friends under surveillance. One of them was Danny Martinez, a Paradise Valley buckaroo and George Nielsen protégé who'd testified on Dallas's behalf at his trial. Six months after his friend's Easter escape Martinez moved to the ranching community of Riverside in southern California, and FBI agents quickly discovered the address of the house he rented there. Martinez was a talkative type, and pretty soon lots of folks around Riverside knew that he was friendly with the celebrated Claude Dallas.

On March 8, 1987, almost a year after his escape, Claude Dallas walked out of a Stop 'N Go convenience store in Riverside with an armload of groceries, including a Dr. Pepper. Acting on a tip, a dozen or so FBI agents were outside waiting for him. They surrounded the startled Dallas and wrestled him to the ground, but he didn't put up a fight.

Dallas, who'd been calling himself Al Shrank, looked quite different. He'd replaced his eyeglasses with contact lenses, shaved his beard, grown a sizable mustache, and had discarded his trademark cowboy hat. But he was afraid that these superficial changes wouldn't disguise him well enough, so he'd gone to Mexico for plastic surgery. Dallas told investigators that, besides the four months he'd spent in Mexico, he'd been in San Francisco, Los Angeles, and Eugene, Oregon.

Extradited to Idaho for a second time, Dallas was charged with one count of escaping from the state penitentiary. If he was found guilty—and it seemed certain that he would

After Claude Dallas's escape from the Idaho State Penitentiary in 1986, a bloodhound *(above, right)* tries in vain to track the fugitive near his old haunt of Paradise Hill, Nevada. Below, a penitentiary guard checks cars following the escape. On March 10, 1987, two days after his capture in Riverside, California, Dallas is escorted from the county jail to a court hearing.

be—he would be sentenced to as many as five additional years in prison.

But there was a catch, and that was Claude Dallas's proven skill as his own best witness. At his trial, which began September 1, 1987, in Ada County, Dallas claimed that officials at the Idaho Penitentiary had been plotting to kill him because in their eyes he was a "cop killer." Several inmates he'd served time with appeared in court to back up his claim. The alleged plan called for secretly fomenting a riot and using it as an excuse for guards to kill Dallas. There hadn't been any riot, supposedly because the inmates got wind of the administration's plan and refused to be pawns. Dallas had supposedly fled without knowing that the inmates had effectively foiled the plot.

The scenario seemed too fantastic to credit, if only because it would have been virtually impossible for prison officials to keep their complicity in a riot secret. Nevertheless, Dallas won the sympathy of the jurors. After deliberating for only five and a half hours, the jury filed into the courtroom with a verdict. Two of the jurors were sobbing, and three others were wiping their eyes; later on the foreman would say all of the 12 members had been teary-eyed in the course of their deliberations. The foreman handed the verdict to the judge to announce. "I won't keep you in suspense, Mr. Dallas," he said. "You've been acquitted."

There were gasps of protest and cries of joy in the courtroom. The verdict flew in the face of reality and even of the defendant's own testimony, for Dallas never denied that he had escaped from the penitentiary. As peculiar as the verdict seemed, it was a fitting sequel to the one reached at Claude Dallas's murder trial three years earlier. In that case, the jury had chosen to believe him when he said he was in fear of his life at the hands of game wardens. Now, a second jury had believed him when he said he was the target of a murderous plot by prison officials. Pointing out how Dallas had claimed self-defense as his motive at both trials, Jerry Conley, the director of the Idaho Fish and Game Department remarked sourly, "He says, 'I'm an innocent little guy who's being picked on by these big fat bullies.'"

Whatever their opinion of the jury's verdict, Dallas watchers gave him high marks for his performance on the stand. Attorney William Mauk, who'd defended him when he was tried for murdering William Pogue and Conley Elms, called him "the best natural witness I've ever seen." Speaking as if he were a director and Dallas an actor,

Mauk ticked off his former client's skills: He was good at making eye contact with individuals, he spoke slowly and convincingly, he understood his own defense thoroughly and articulated it clearly. And there was something powerful about him—even "intimidating," Mauk thought. Edward Lodge, the presiding judge at Dallas's murder trial, recalled his skill in establishing rapport with jurors—but implied that his credibility was open to question. Another observer remarked that the defendant possessed "a certain charisma."

Such comments seemed to sting the foreman, who denied that the jury had been swayed by Dallas's supposedly charismatic personality. Their verdict dismayed Ada County Sheriff Vaughn Killeen. "I suppose most of those people on the jury would take Claude home for dinner and pat him on the back," he said, adding, "Killers aren't necessarily unlikable people, as Claude Dallas has proven very, very well." Sheriff Killeen agreed with the fine review Claude Dallas had gotten from other critics. "He smiles at the right times," the sheriff commented. "He's very sure of himself. A person like that looks like he's very truthful." Lest anyone misunderstand his opinion of Dallas, the sheriff summed it up succinctly: "He's an accomplished liar."

Claude Dallas, at 37, went back to prison. Although he'd been found innocent, he suffered a penalty for escaping: The year of credit he'd earned for good behavior was taken away from him, and he was also out of pocket the $109 it cost the prison to repair the fences he'd cut through.

Dallas still had his coterie of fans who saw him as the personification of all that was great about the pioneer West. In their eyes, his conviction in his 1982 trial had been a travesty of justice. Sheriff Tim Nettleton of Owyhee County, Idaho, in whose territory wardens William Pogue and Conley Elms had died so violently, saw Claude Dallas with eyes unclouded by romanticism and nostalgia. "Dallas lived by his own code," Nettleton once remarked. "Like a lot of people who live out there, he simply felt the law didn't apply to him. Those canyons were his territory, and he believed he could do what he wanted out there."

If the sheriff was right—if that is what Claude Dallas truly believed and if that is why he killed two men—Dallas found out how terribly mistaken he had been. Perhaps it was like waking from a little boy's dream of being a cowboy to discover what dreadful things can happen when dreams come true.◆

On the Lam

The character a person displays in planning and pulling off a crime carries over to the character of his flight. Of the eight people featured in the following pages, ace robber John Dillinger, for instance, became a mythic figure in American crime annals for his bold strikes against banks and the fearless, arrogant cat-and-mouse game he played—by his own rules— with his pursuers. Where Dillinger chose his own course, a low-level mobster accustomed to swimming with the sharks of the Mafia can't stray too far from familiar territory. A cop with good instincts can be pretty certain that such a fish will be caught in home waters. For the same reason, when a true-believing fanatic has fixed on a particular notion such as hatred of the income tax, a smart police officer searches among birds of the same ideological feather. And if the target is the matriarch of a criminal clan, the place to look is at home, in the bosom of the family.

Ma

"Ma" Barker, born Arizona Clark, never forgot the day she saw Jesse James ride through Carthage, Missouri, near her family's Ozark foothills home when she was 10 years old. Soon afterward, little Arizona was weeping bitterly about her hero's death: In 1882 he was gunned down by Bob Ford, a former member of James's gang, so he could collect a $10,000 reward. Her childhood infatuation with the outlaw mystique would never diminish.

In 1892, at the age of 20, Arizona Clark married George Barker, a poor sharecropper. Over the next 10 years she gave birth to four boys: Herman, Lloyd, Arthur, and Fred. Her timid husband yielded all control over the children to his overbearing wife, who instilled in them a fierce loyalty to the family and an equally resolute contempt for the law.

From their earliest years the boys stole whatever trinkets they were tall enough to pluck from shop counters. When they got in trouble with the police, their mother was certain they were being persecuted. Thus when she heard that 18-year-old Herman had been arrested for theft, she stormed into the police station to protest his innocence. Alternating between tearful pleading and angry denunciations, Ma Barker so unnerved the police that they caved in and released Herman.

In 1915 the Barkers moved from little Webb City, Missouri, to Tulsa, Oklahoma. Although it was their first time in a big city, the boys soon made contact with sophisti-

In this photograph dating from the early 1930s, an aging Ma Barker looks like a respectable matriarch.

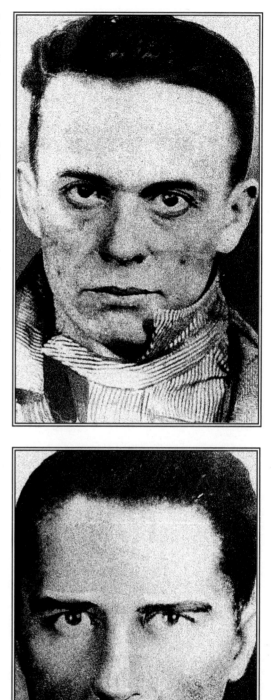

Arthur "Doc" Barker *(top right)* served time in Oklahoma for killing a night watchman during a robbery. A prison buddy of Doc's brother Fred, Alvin Karpis *(below)* joined forces with the Barker clan in 1931, after completing a sentence for car theft and burglary.

cated criminals, and their home became a favorite refuge for big-time thieves such as Al Spencer, Frank Nash, Francis Keating, and a parade of other felons. Under Ma's approving eye, the Barker boys listened attentively to the tales told around the dinner table of past hauls and plans for future heists. Such talk wasn't George Barker's cup of tea. He left the family and moved to Welch, Oklahoma.

Despite the tutelage of veteran criminals, the Barkers had only spotty success. Lloyd landed in Leavenworth, sentenced to 25 years for holding up a post office in 1922. Soon after, Arthur—known as Doc—was found guilty of killing a night watchman during a robbery and was sent to the Oklahoma State Prison. In 1926 Fred was arrested for bank robbery and sentenced to 5 to 10 years. Herman, who was wounded in a shootout with police in 1927, killed himself rather than face capture.

Ma worked tirelessly for her children's release. She hired lawyers and wrote a stream of letters to wardens, parole boards, and governors. By 1932 Fred and Doc were back home with their mother (Lloyd would languish in prison until 1947). Ma also took in Fred's former cellmate, Alvin Karpis, and treated him as one of her own. The Barkers and the adopted Karpis got a new lease on criminal life, and the infamous Barker-Karpis gang was born.

With the help of a revolving cast of associates, the gang traveled the Midwest, robbing everything from big-city banks to small-town groceries, killing policemen without compunction. Contrary to the legend that would envelop the gang, Ma took little or no active role in the planning and execution of its crimes. For someone who'd raised a lawless brood and relished the

criminal life herself, Ma appeared to be a simple sort, enamored of playing bingo, going to movies, and listening to hillbilly music on the radio. She missed the boys when they were on the road and prepared lavish feasts of fried chicken, mashed potatoes, and biscuits to celebrate their return. And she was a useful cover. "When we traveled together," remembered Karpis, "we moved as a mother and three sons. What could look more innocent?"

In 1933 the gang kidnapped St. Paul brewer William A. Hamm, collecting $100,000 in ransom. The following year they nabbed another St. Paul victim, banker Edward George Bremer, and doubled their previous take. There was, however, a downside to the gang's lucrative kidnappings. Such crimes fell within the bailiwick of the FBI, which quickly orchestrated a nationwide manhunt for Ma and the boys. The FBI painted a black picture of her as a predator more vicious than John Dillinger *(pages 79-82)* or his accomplice Baby Face Nelson; Ma Barker was, according to Director J. Edgar Hoover, a "Gila monster," a "she-wolf," a "beast of prey."

The gang decided it would be smart to split up for a while. Fred, always the most devoted son, took Ma to Florida and rented a house in Oklawaha. Karpis went to Cuba, and Doc headed for Chicago. He was apprehended there without a fight on January 8, 1935. In his apartment FBI agents found a map of Florida. There was a circle drawn around Oklawaha.

Eight days later, 14 FBI agents surrounded Fred and Ma's Florida hideout and demanded their surrender. In answer, machine-gun fire sprayed from the house. The ensuing battle went on for six hours. Then the house fell silent. The Barkers' black handyman was outside with the agents, and at their urging he went into the house to have a look around. He found both of his employers dead.

As to the fate of Ma's remaining boys, Karpis, who was named Public Enemy Number One after the Florida shootout, was captured May 1, 1936, in New Orleans. Imprisoned for the Hamm and Bremer kidnappings from 1936 until 1969, Karpis died of an overdose of sleeping pills in 1979. Doc was sent to Alcatraz for the same crimes and died during an escape attempt in 1939. Lloyd was killed by his wife in 1949, two years after he finally got out of Leavenworth.

George Barker buried his family one by one in a field near his filling station in Welch, Oklahoma. When curious travelers inquired about the graves, George would simply reply, "That's Ma and the boys." ◆

Officials inspect the Oklawaha, Florida, house where Ma and Fred Barker had been killed the day before in a shootout with the FBI.

Public Enemy Number One

No other bandit ever captured the American imagination as thoroughly as John Dillinger. In his brief, frenetic career, the one-time Indiana farm boy swashbuckled across the Depression-torn Midwest robbing banks and becoming a legend even before his criminal exploits were cut short. His notoriety was so great that when FBI chief J. Edgar Hoover created the title 'Public Enemy Number One," the first man he bestowed it on was Dillinger.

To many dirt-poor, down-and-out farmers and factory workers in the early 1930s, however, John Dillinger was not a public enemy, scarcely even a criminal. They viewed his thieving as a fair means of evening out the very uneven Depression-era distribution of wealth. As far as they were concerned, Dillinger robbed only the rich when he stuck up a bank; presumably no one else had enough money to have a bank account.

Dillinger was, in the eyes of his admirers, one of them. The girlfriend of one of his accomplices echoed public sentiment when he remarked, "Johnnie's just an ordinary fellow. Of course, he goes out and holds up banks and things, but he's really just like any other fellow, aside from that." His skill on the baseball diamond gave the big-time bank robber an apple-pie, all-American gloss. His sister's husband, Emmett Hancock, described Dillinger as "a good batter, good fielder, and fast—he could steal anything, so they said."

Although Dillinger went on to become a remarkably successful criminal, he showed little promise of any kind as a youth. After dropping out of high school at 16, he spent a lot of time hanging around pool halls. He joined the navy when he was 20 years old but repeatedly went AWOL. Back home after his short stint of sailoring, he worked off and on as a machinist.

But Dillinger wasn't an ordinary working man at heart. On September 6, 1924, at the age of 21, he got his first taste of armed robbery when he and an ex-con named Edgar Singleton tried to hold up a 65-year-old grocer, Frank Morgan. Morgan put up a fight and managed to knock Dillinger's gun out of his hand. The robbers fled but were quickly arrested.

At his trial, Dillinger pleaded guilty in the hopes of being given a lenient sentence. Instead, Judge Joseph Williams dished out the maximum sentence—up to 20 years in prison.

During the nearly nine years that he served, Dillinger grew bitter and hard. He also became wise in the fine points of crime, thanks to two fellow inmates, convicted bank robbers Harry Pierpont and Homer Van Meter. When Dillinger was released on May 22, 1933, from the Indiana State Prison at Michigan City, he went away clutching a graduation present from Pierpont—a list of Midwestern banks that he considered prime targets.

On July 17 Dillinger and several confederates hit the first of the institutions from the list, the Dalesville, Indiana, Commercial Bank. The haul amounted to $3,500. Still using Pierpont's guide, Dillinger followed up this success with a string of robberies in Indiana, Ohio, and Pennsylvania.

On a visit to his family's farm in 1934, John Dillinger poses holding the wooden gun that he used to escape from an Indiana jail. A real submachine gun is tucked under his other arm.

Ties loosened and sleeves rolled up in the July heat, sensation-seeking
Chicagoans pack the sidewalk in front of the Biograph theater on the night moviegoer
Dillinger was felled by FBI agents waiting for him outside.

He invested his earnings in weapons that he smuggled into the Michigan City prison to help Pierpont and nine other inmates stage a successful breakout on September 26. As it happened, Dillinger was serving time in the Lima, Ohio, jail that day; he'd been arrested six days earlier on charges of holding up a local bank. Returning the favor, Pierpont engineered Dillinger's escape, in the course of which the town's sheriff was shot and killed.

Dillinger and Pierpont now joined forces with several other criminals, including the machine-gun virtuoso Lester Gillis, better known as Baby Face Nelson. They collected an arsenal of Thompson submachine guns, shotguns, and bulletproof vests by robbing small-town police stations, then moved north to hit banks in the Chicago and Milwaukee areas. Dubbed the Terror Gang, they quickly became a national sensation. The Indiana National Guard was mobilized to deploy tanks, airplanes, and poison gas to corner Dillinger, and the state's American Legion offered to form a vigilante force with its 30,000 members.

In late December 1933 the gang took a break from bank robbery and went on vacation to Daytona Beach, Florida, where they welcomed the New Year by firing their Tommy guns over the ocean. From Florida the robbers traveled to Tucson, Arizona. There they had a piece of bad luck. A fire broke out in their hotel, and two gang members paid firemen several hundred dollars to carry their luggage to safety. Surprised by the generous tip, one fireman wondered why the suitcase he was carrying was so heavy. Taking a peek inside, he discovered a submachine gun and several pistols. The holiday was over.

Extradited to Indiana to face a bank

robbery charge, Dillinger was placed in a supposedly escape-proof jail at Crown Point, where he passed the time whittling and chatting with other inmates. On March 3, 1934, Dillinger grabbed a guard and jabbed a gun in his ribs. At Dillinger's direction, the guard hailed a coworker, who was armed with a .45-caliber automatic. Taking the pistol from him, Dillinger rounded up all the guards on duty and the warden as well. He locked them up in a cell and then ostentatiously displayed the gun he'd used at the outset: It had been whittled from the top of a washboard and blackened with shoe polish. Leaving his captives to their embarrassment, he headed for the prison garage, where he commandeered a car, took a guard and a mechanic hostage, and forced them to drive him to Illinois.

Indiana officials were livid. J. Edgar Hoover, however, was delighted. Dillinger had violated a new law that made transporting a stolen vehicle across state lines a federal crime, and it was the FBI's responsibility to apprehend such felons. Dubbing Dillinger Public Enemy Number One, Hoover appointed FBI agent Melvin Purvis to head up a special detail charged with catching the enemy. With Hoover's blessing, Purvis adopted a strategy of shooting first and asking questions later.

On the loose again, Dillinger hit banks in South Dakota and Iowa. Between jobs, Dillinger and girlfriend Billie Frechette took a brief trip back home to Indiana. On April 6 they attended a family get-together at the Dillinger farm in Mooresville, and friends and neighbors stopped by to chat with the homegrown hero. Two FBI men who had the farmhouse under surveillance saw the cars coming and going, but they didn't

catch on to the fact that it was Dillinger everyone had come to see. He left Mooresville that evening. The FBI agents were the last people around to know he'd been in town.

Just two weeks later, the FBI got another chance to land Dillinger and several girlfriends and confederates, including Baby Face Nelson. Picking up his trail, Purvis's detail tracked him to the Little Bohemia Lodge, a resort in northern Wisconsin. On the night of April 22, Dillinger was inside the lodge when agents began converging on it. Then three men came out of the lodge and got into a car. Jumping to the conclusion that it was Dillinger and two other gang members, trigger-happy agents loosed a hail of gunfire in the direction of the car. One man was killed and the other two were wounded; all three proved to be innocent guests, not gangsters. While the FBI guns were blazing away, Dillinger and several others climbed out a back window of the lodge without being detected. Meanwhile, Baby Face Nelson, who'd been staying in a cottage on the grounds, stepped out and began firing, killing one agent and wounding two others. Nelson also managed to slip away, and Purvis mounted an all-night siege of the lodge, unaware that his quarry had fled.

For three months after the Little Bohemia raid, it seemed to the frustrated FBI as though Dillinger had disappeared from the face of the earth. In fact, the elusive gangster was in Chicago, undergoing plastic surgery and having his fingerprints treated with acid to alter their patterns. He hid in plain sight, attending baseball games, movies, and nightclubs with a new girlfriend Polly Hamilton.

He had been introduced to Hamilton by

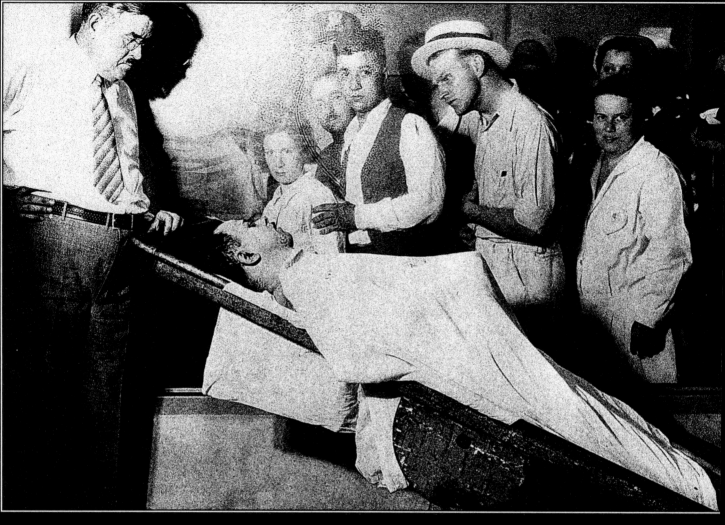

At the viewing held at the Cook County morgue in July of 1934, members of the public get a closeup look at the corpse of famous criminal John Dillinger after a long wait in line.

Anna Sage, an old acquaintance and a one-time madam in East Chicago. She was being threatened with deportation to her native Romania, and it occurred to her that helping the FBI capture Dillinger might make the federal government look on her more kindly. In addition, there was the lure of the $25,000 reward on Dillinger's head. Fixing up Dillinger with Hamilton—who knew nothing about her friend's scheme—would make it easier for Sage to keep track of him. Once the match was made, she got in touch with Melvin Purvis. Together, the two laid a trap.

At 10:40 p.m. on July 22, 1934, Dillinger, Hamilton, and Sage left the Biograph theater on Chicago's North Lincoln Avenue, where they had just seen Clark Gable, Myrna Loy, and William Powell in *Manhattan Melodrama*, a gangster movie.

As the three strolled along, Dillinger glanced idly at a man standing in a doorway, attempting to light a cigar. The man was Melvin Purvis, and the cigar was the signal to other agents to close in.

At Purvis's signal Sage stepped back, pulling Polly Hamilton with her. Before Dillinger could react, an FBI agent ran up behind him and fired point-blank into the back of his head. Three more shots smashed into Dillinger, but he was already dead. He was 31 years old.

Drawn by radio broadcasts, thousands rushed to the Biograph. The pool of Dillinger's blood on the pavement outside had not yet dried, and people dipped handkerchiefs or the hems of their skirts into it for

a gruesome souvenir. Seeing a car with license plates from Dillinger's home state of Indiana parked nearby, fans began to dismantle it. (It turned out to belong not to Dillinger but to some unlucky Hoosier.) At the morgue, attendants propped the gangster's body up so that the people filing past could get a better look at it. At times, the line of people waiting to get in was a quarter-mile long.

The spectacle moved from Chicago to Mooresville, which was jammed with 5,000 mourners and spectactors on the day of Dillinger's funeral. After the burial there were so many attempts to dig up the body that the family was forced to cap the grave with three feet of concrete.

As to the woman who set Dillinger up for death, Anna Sage collected $5,000 as her reward, but she was deported to Romania anyway. She died there in 1947. ◆

A Day at the Races

As Charles S. Ross and his former secretary Florence Freihage were on their way home after dining together at a hotel outside Chicago on a September evening in 1937, he watched the headlights of another car hanging steadily in his rearview mirror. "I don't like the looks of this," he said to Freihage. "I'll cut over to the side and let him pass." Instead, the other car drew level, swerved in front of Ross's sedan, and forced him to stop on the quiet suburban road. A young man waving a revolver sprang out of the other car and shouted, "This is a kidnapping." He ordered Ross into his car, where an accomplice was waiting at the wheel. They sped off, leaving Freihage unharmed — and with a clear image of the kidnapper's curly brown hair and sharp features.

The man who had abducted the 72-year-old retired greeting-card manufacturer was John Henry Seadlund. A small-time thief and bank robber, he'd also carried out an earlier kidnapping but had released the victim when her husband refused to pay the ransom Seadlund demanded. For Ross's release, Seadlund set the ransom at $50,000 and mailed detailed instructions for the payoff, which Ross's wife and friends carried out to the letter.

Thus at 6 p.m. on October 8, thirteen days after the abduction, George Kukovac, a veteran motorcyclist hired for the occasion, started out from the Chicago suburb of Oak Park in the direction of Rockford, Illinois. Dressed in white coveralls and a white helmet and riding a red-and-black Harley-Davidson, he had with him a package containing the ransom in 5-, 10-, and 20-dollar bills. When he was five miles from Rockford, a car pulled up to within 10 feet of the motorcycle's back wheel and

Kidnapper and murderer John Henry Seadlund snaps his fingers in reaction to the news that he has been condemned to the electric chair.

A party of civilians returns home by bobsled after helping law enforcement officials retrieve the bodies of Charles Ross and John Gray from a crypt at Seadlund's Wisconsin hideout. At right, a member of the party inspects the interior of the crypt.

flashed its lights—the signal to proceed with the drop-off. Kukovac threw the package to the side of the road and drove on for another 300 feet. Then, as he had been instructed, he ran the motorcycle off the road and continued on toward Rockford on foot. Behind him, Seadlund seized the money and took off.

Ross was being guarded by Seadlund's accomplice, John Gray, at a hideout in Minnesota. When Seadlund returned with the ransom, they packed up and moved their victim to another hideout, in a remote woodland near Spooner, Wisconsin. Seadlund had promised to return Ross unharmed, but he didn't fulfill his side of the bargain. On October 10 he shot Gray in the face from point-blank range, then struck Ross a blow that shattered his skull.

After burying the bodies, Seadlund went

on a spending spree that took him to racetracks all over the country. He went west to Seattle, then back to Chicago and on to New York, Philadelphia, Washington, Miami, New Orleans, and Los Angeles. Where he'd been was no secret, for the FBI had broadcast the serial numbers of the ransom money to banks and other businesses handling large amounts of cash, and agents soon learned that many of the bills were being used for betting.

Almost four months passed before Seadlund finally hung around one track long enough for FBI agents to catch up with him. On January 4, 1938, he placed his first bet at the Santa Anita Race Track near Los Angeles and returned the next day and the next. Officials at the track, on the look-

out for a curly-haired, sharp-featured 26-year-old man, alerted the FBI. Agents armed with lists of serial numbers posed as assistants to the betting-window clerks, and on January 14 Seadlund was apprehended when he stepped up to put some money down on a favorite horse.

Seadlund confessed to murdering Ross and Gray and led FBI investigators to the site in Wisconsin where he'd buried his two victims. Then, even though he was in chains, he tried to run off into the woods. He didn't get far. On July 14, 1938, Seadlund died in the electric chair. ◆

84

KARLETON ARMSTRONG

Blowup

From their vantage point on a knoll overlooking the University of Wisconsin campus in Madison, four young men stared at the fireball rising hundreds of feet into the dark summer sky. "God," one of them whispered, "it's like an atom bomb."

Not quite. But the bomb they'd concocted—1,700 pounds of fertilizer soaked with fuel oil and stuffed into a stolen van—had torn apart Sterling Hall, a six-story building of reinforced concrete, and shattered windows 10 blocks away. The bombers—Karleton Armstrong, a 22-year-old chemistry student; his brother Dwight, an 18-year-old high-school dropout; Leo F. Burt, a 22-year-old competitive rower and a reporter for the *Daily Cardinal* campus paper; and David S. Fine, 18, a *Daily Cardinal* editor—hadn't dreamed that their crude device packed so much destructive power.

The bombers' target on the night of August 24, 1970, was the U.S. Army's Mathematical Research Center, which occupied three floors in Sterling Hall. The explosion was yet another protest against the nation's involvement in the Vietnam War, which was being hotly, sometimes violently opposed by student activists. Ringleader Karl Armstrong's antiwar sentiments developed after he entered the University of Wisconsin in 1964. As a freshman, he enrolled in the campus Air Force ROTC training program, but within a year

he turned against the military and became a war resister.

At first committed to peaceful protest, Karl eventually decided that violent action was necessary—but only against property, for he didn't want to hurt anyone if he could help it. In December 1969 he single-handedly firebombed the Quonset hut occupied by the university's Air Force ROTC. On New Year's Eve, Karl and Dwight, a student pilot, stole a small plane and flew

As he leaves a court hearing in 1973, Karl Armstrong clenches his fist in the salute widely used at the time by opponents of the Vietnam War.

some 30 miles north of Madison to an army ordnance plant. Passing overhead, they tossed out two 10-pound jars, each filled with a homemade explosive, but they didn't go off. The week after New Year's Karl firebombed a university gymnasium, but he had less success with his next target, a power station. He'd scaled the plant's security fence and was preparing to set off a bundle of dynamite when he saw an employee watching him from a distance. Armstrong dropped what he was doing and ran away.

Such events were dress rehearsals for the assault on Sterling Hall. The conspirators determined to set off their explosion at 3:45 a.m., when the building would presumably be deserted. On the 24th, Karl, accompanied by Leo Burt, slowly and carefully drove the van to Sterling Hall. Dwight sat nearby in the getaway car while David Fine took up his position in a phone booth within sight of the building.

Surprised to see lights burning in Sterling Hall, Karl nevertheless lit the bomb's 10-foot fuse. After quickly checking several ground-floor windows without seeing anyone inside, he and Burt took off running toward Dwight's car. Fine was watching, and when he saw Karl waving, he picked up the phone and dialed the Madison police department. "Okay, pig, there's a bomb in the Math Research Center," Fine said. Warning the policeman at the

other end of the line to clear the building and call the hospital, he signed off saying, "This is no bullshit, man!" Two minutes later the bomb exploded.

After watching the stunning results of their handiwork from the knoll, the four drove around listening to the radio for news about the explosion. The sheer size of the blast had made them nervous, and their nervousness turned to horror when they tuned in to a shocking report: Five people had been found in Sterling Hall. Four were injured, and one was dead. Robert Fass-

nacht, a 33-year-old physics graduate student who'd been working on an experiment in a basement laboratory.

Leo Burt began to moan and cry, and Fine worried that his paper-route customers would get suspicious when he didn't make his rounds in the morning. It was too dangerous to stay in Madison, so the bombers decided to go to Ann Arbor, Michigan. Through the radical grapevine they'd heard about a group there called the White Panthers; perhaps they'd be able to help the bombers get to Canada, a haven at

the time for antiwar Americans who'd run afoul of the law.

Because of Fassnacht's death, however, the Ann Arbor radicals refused to get involved. Burt and Fine suggested splitting up and meeting again in a week in New York City. The two of them had contacts there who could furnish false identification documents that would make it much easier to get into Canada undetected. The plan sounded good to the Armstrongs. They dropped Burt and Fine off at a Greyhound bus station, then headed east.

The van bomb detonated at the University of Wisconsin's Sterling Hall propelled one of the van's wheels through two concrete walls. The blast damaged 31 other campus buildings.

Burt and Fine got their fake IDs in New York—then immediately took off for Canada. After a down-and-out week of waiting, during which Dwight resorted to panhandling in Times Square to buy food and cigarettes, the brothers admitted they'd been stood up. They'd have to risk the border crossing into Canada without false IDs.

The trip from New York to the border was also going to be a risky business: On September 2, the FBI charged the four bombers with conspiracy, sabotage, and the destruction of U.S. government prop-

erty. Afraid the car they'd been driving might be traced, the Armstrongs stole a nearly new, expensive Pontiac and left New York on September 4—the same day that they, Fine, and Burt were added to the FBI's most wanted list. Ordinarily it contains no more than 10 names at a time, but the agency considered the bombing so serious an offense that the list was expanded to 14 to accommodate the Madison four.

Later that day Karl and Dwight wheeled into the quiet town of Little Falls, New York. When the police chief spotted two dirty, long-haired young men driving such a nice car, he couldn't help wondering how they'd acquired it. The Armstrongs were taken into custody on suspicion of auto theft and brought to the station house, where Dwight saw on the chief's desk a newspaper headlined "Suspects Named in Bombing." "All right if I read the paper?" Dwight asked. Getting the okay, he slipped it into his pocket. Twenty minutes later, the chief let them go; the car had checked out. It was a lucky break for the Armstrongs: The theft of the Pontiac had been reported, but the car's license number had been entered incorrectly into the police computer.

After their close call the brothers drove on toward Canada. Over the radio came their father's voice begging them to turn themselves in. Karl was already filled with remorse about Fassnacht's death and miserable about the damage the fatal bombing had done to the antiwar movement, and now, when he heard his father, tears pooled in his eyes.

In Montreal, Canadian sympathizers shuttled the Armstrongs from one safe house to another. The brothers were broke, so one night they hid in a movie theater until the other patrons had left, hoping to surprise a manager and make off with the day's receipts. But the only person they found was a janitor, so they left empty-

handed. When the Armstrongs' benefactors heard about the attempted robbery, they decided the two had been in Montreal long enough. In December 1970 they were put on a train to Toronto with phony baptismal certificates for identification.

Naomi Wall, an American living in Toronto who'd sheltered a number of her draft-dodging countrymen, took Karl and Dwight under her wing. She gave them a $25-a-week allowance and arranged a succession of rooms with trustworthy families. Dwight soon took to selling drugs and bragging about his past, and for his own good Wall shipped him off to British Columbia. Karl, on the other hand, lived quietly, working in menial jobs and moving to a different residence every month or so.

For over a year Karl Armstrong escaped the attention of the police. Then on February 16, 1972, he answered his landlord's knock on the door of his room to find several Royal Canadian Mounted Police officers with drawn guns outside. One of Dwight's drug-dealer friends had turned Karl in, in hopes of getting a lighter sentence on a drug charge.

Karl Armstrong was extradited to Wisconsin, where he pleaded guilty to second-degree murder and arson and was sentenced on November 1, 1973, to 23 years in prison. In 1976 he and Naomi Wall, his Toronto savior, were married, but they divorced after he was paroled in 1980.

After his release from prison, Karl returned to Madison, where he became a fixture just a few blocks from the rebuilt Sterling Hall, selling fruit drinks from his "Loose Juice" vending cart.

David Fine was arrested in San Rafael, California, in 1976, and the following year Dwight Armstrong was captured in Toronto. Both men were tried and sentenced to seven years. As for Leo Burt, his whereabouts were still a mystery in 1993. ◆

Father Knows Best

John List's neighbors in suburban West-field, New Jersey, liked him well enough, even though he was standoffish and a little odd. It was his habit, for instance, to wear a business suit when he mowed the lawn surrounding the huge, shabby mansion where he lived with his wife, Helen, their three children, and his aging mother. The neighbors saw little of Helen List. She was, they knew, suffering so badly from some unnamed chronic illness that by the time Patricia, John junior, and Frederick were teenagers their father bore the burden of raising them and earning a living as well.

On November 9, 1971, the 46-year-old List told his neighbors and his pastor at the Redeemer Lutheran Church that his mother-in-law lay gravely ill in North Carolina; the family was going there to look after her for a few days. But as weeks went by without a word from the Lists, people became alarmed about their prolonged absence. At last the police were notified, and on the night of December 7 they broke down the door of the Lists' darkened home.

Nothing had prepared them for what they found. Funereal organ music was coming from a central sound system, and in the mansion's ballroom the decomposing bodies of 45-year old Helen List, Patricia, 16, John junior, 15, and Frederick, 13, were laid out neatly on the floor. Alma List, John's 85-year-old mother, was discovered upstairs. All five victims had been shot in the head.

A letter addressed to List's minister was taped to a filing cabinet in the house. "I know what has been done is wrong from

In this portrait of the List family, Patricia and John junior stand behind their parents and Frederick, who was the youngest of the three List children.

Separated from the street by a sweep of lawn and surrounded by trees and shrubs, the List family's 19-room Georgian-style mansion burned to the ground 10 months after the murders. The cause of the fire was never determined.

all that I have been taught and that any reasons I give will not make it right," the letter began. "I wasn't earning anywhere near enough to support us. Everything I tried seemed to fall to pieces."

The letter cataloged a series of family disasters. Losing one job after another had left List in debt and unable to pay the mortgage on the mansion his wife had insisted on buying. A syphilis infection passed on to Helen by her first husband had attacked her brain, causing bizarre behavior, spells of fainting, and temporary paralysis. Patricia had turned into a rebellious teenager, fascinated by the occult and intent on a career in theater. Her interests, List wrote, would interfere with her "continuing to be a Christian." He professed to see a positive spiritual benefit in the murders, noting that "at least I'm certain that all have gone to heaven now."

List's 1963 Chevrolet was found abandoned at John F. Kennedy International Airport, but investigators were unable to pick up his trail. Weeks passed, then months, and police began to despair of solving the crime. The tall, thin, colorless accountant seemed to have evaporated.

Although the authorities continued to follow up occasional fruitless leads, 18 years went by without a sign of List. And then, in 1989, he was dragged into the public spotlight by a novel conjunction of forensic science, art, and media hype. The old story of the murders was dusted off and broadcast on a popular television program, "America's Most Wanted," which aims to enlist the assistance of its nationwide audience in finding criminal suspects who have disappeared.

The program's producers hired forensic sculptor Frank Bender to make a bust of List as he might look after nearly two decades on the lam. Working from old photographs and what was known of List's habits, Bender created a balding man with the pasty skin and slack flesh of a person who shunned exercise, and gave him glasses that were thicker than the ones List had worn in 1971.

On May 21, 1989, "America's Most Wanted" unveiled the bust and presented a reenactment of the murders. Three hundred people called in after the show. One of them, an employee at a Richmond, Virginia, accounting firm, reported that a coworker named Robert P. Clark bore a striking resemblance to Bender's sculpture. Eleven days later, FBI agents paid a visit to the firm and came upon Clark in a hallway. He did indeed look like the sculptor's rendition of John List, down to his eyeglasses. A check of his fingerprints proved beyond the shadow of a doubt that Clark was in fact John List.

In the course of his 1990 trial on five counts of murder, investigators revealed that List had spent 16 of his fugitive years in Denver, where he worked as a comptroller and married a woman he met at church. She thought his first wife had died of cancer. List was found guilty and sentenced to five consecutive life terms.

Ironically, List had been unaware of owning a treasure that could have solved his financial problems. In the ceiling of the ballroom where he'd shot his wife and children was a stained-glass skylight made by the renowned turn-of-the-century glass artisan Louis Comfort Tiffany. At the time of the murders the skylight was worth at least $100,000 — twice what List had paid for the house. The skylight was destroyed when fire swept the mansion in 1972.

During the May 21, 1989, broadcast of "America's Most Wanted," host John Walsh displays one of the old photographs of John List that Frank Bender *(right)* analyzed in order to sculpt the bust of the aging List shown here. Remarkably close to reality, the bust led to List's arrest.

A handcuffed List is led away after a hearing in Richmond, Virginia. He had been living in a Richmond suburb under an alias.

Tax Time

Several federal marshals were watching when a meeting of antitax zealots held on the evening of February 13, 1983, in Medina, North Dakota (population 522), broke up. The man the marshals were after was 63-year-old Gordon Kahl, a convicted tax evader wanted for violating his parole. With the marshals following them at a discreet distance, Kahl and five other people drove away in two cars, only to be stopped at a roadblock outside town, where more law enforcement officials were stationed. As several marshals walked up to the cars, Kahl, his son Yori, and Scott Faul jumped out and began shooting. The marshals returned fire, hitting Yori several times and

two of their comrades had already been fatally injured. In the darkness and confusion Gordon Kahl slipped away and disappeared into the prairie.

The marshals had never suspected that serving a warrant on Kahl could end violently. The balding, bespectacled 63-year-old farmer's only run-ins with the law had been over taxes. The income tax, he once told a reporter, was "one of the ten planks of the *Communist Manifesto*." In Kahl's opinion, the planks were also the "ten commandments of Satan." He belonged to an organization of antitax fanatics called Posse Comitatus—Latin for "power of the county"—that didn't recognize any government office higher than that of county sheriff. In spite of their passionate opposition to taxation, Kahl and his fellows seemed harmless enough.

In 1977 Kahl was found guilty of failing to file federal tax returns for 1973 and

1974 and was fined and sentenced to a year in prison. He'd been living in Texas at the time of his offenses, but when he was paroled after seven months, he was granted permission to return to the family farm in his native North Dakota. The terms of his parole banned him from getting involved with the Posse Comitatus or any other like-minded group. Kahl had ignored the restriction, and as a consequence two marshals were dead.

Three days after the shootout, some 75 federal marshals and local police officers stormed Kahl's farmhouse, but the fugitive wasn't there. The hunt expanded across the Dakotas and into Minnesota and Montana, and a $25,000 reward was offered. By the end of May, when Yori Kahl and Scott Faul were convicted of second-degree murder, Gordon Kahl was still at large.

Agents learned that in 1982 Kahl had spent time in Arkansas with fellow tax protesters Leonard and Norma Ginter, outside the hill country hamlet of Smithville. As May turned to June, there was finally a bit of luck: A man answering Kahl's description was reported in Smithville.

On June 3 federal marshals, FBI agents, and state and county police officers surrounded the Ginters' house. Around 6 p.m. Sheriff Gene Matthews, with two federal agents and a state trooper following him, knocked on the door. The Ginters tried to escape but were quickly captured. Inside, Gordon Kahl was lying in wait.

The sheriff stepped through the door and was hit by a bullet that ricocheted from his left arm and ripped into his lung. Matthews managed to fire back before other officers dragged him away. He would die on the operating table that night.

A barrage of gunfire was unleashed on the house, but there wasn't any return fire. To flush Kahl into the open, a smoke bomb was thrown down an air vent. When the bomb went off, a stockpile of ammunition exploded with a deafening noise, and the house caught on fire.

It was close to 10 p.m. when officers wearing gas masks finally ventured into the gutted house. Gordon Kahl was dead on the kitchen floor, slumped over his Ruger Mini-14 semiautomatic rifle. He had been hit only once, by a .41-caliber bullet that had entered his head above the right ear. It appeared that he and Gene Matthews had killed each other, for ballistics tests proved that the bullet had been fired by the sheriff.

Lawmen hunting for fugitive Gordon Kahl, shown above in a 1981 photograph, used a tanklike personnel carrier when they laid siege to his North Dakota farmhouse. It proved to be unoccupied, but a cache of more than 30 weapons was found inside.

ROBERT MATHEWS
Killing the Messenger

Denver talk-show host and disc jockey Alan Berg liked nothing better than making the hackles of his listeners rise—and there were millions and millions of them, since 50,000-watt radio station KOA reached 38 states, Canada, and Mexico. For four hours each weekday morning the outspoken host aired his opinions on everything from papal directives on sex to the need for gun-control laws, taunting and insulting callers who disagreed with him. Berg, who had practiced law for a time, commented to a reporter in 1983, "I stick it to 'em and they love it. Hopefully, my legal training will prevent me from saying the one thing that will kill me."

Berg was Jewish, and he particularly enjoyed sticking it to anti-Semites. None of them hated the disc jockey's caustic cracks more than Robert Mathews, a cement-plant worker and leader of the Order, a neo-Nazi group he founded in 1983. Mathews and his followers—23 at the organization's peak—subscribed to the scurrilous fantasy that the United States is secretly controlled by what they called the Zionist Occupation Government, or ZOG. Mathews drew up a list of people he claimed were ZOG conspirators, including former Secretary of State Henry Kissinger, TV producer Norman Lear, and banker David Rockefeller. With an eye to eventually undermining the U.S. monetary system, Mathews started a counterfeiting operation. In the meantime, the phony money helped keep the group afloat. Ranging through several western states from their headquarters in Metaline Falls, Washington, the Order also funded itself by a string of robberies, including two armored-car heists that netted them a total of $273,345.

Mathews's enemy list continued to

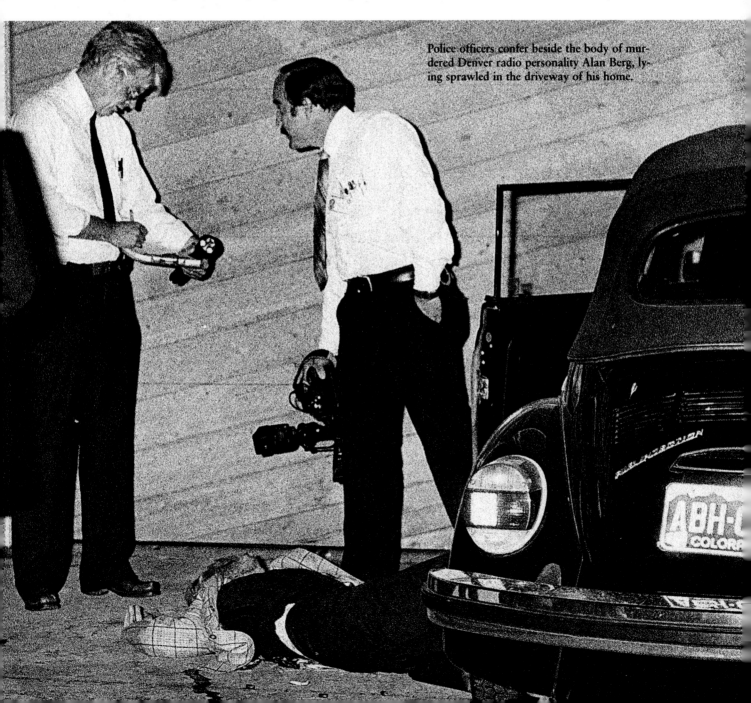

Police officers confer beside the body of murdered Denver radio personality Alan Berg, lying sprawled in the driveway of his home.

grow, and in 1984 Alan Berg's name was added. Berg's offenses included barbed attacks on the *Primrose and Cattlemen's Gazette,* a far-right-wing newspaper aimed at a rural clientele in the Midwest and Plains States. So many advertisers deserted the paper in response to Berg's broadcasts that it was forced to fold. One of the people who lost his job was Order member David Lane, a security guard at the *Gazette.*

On June 18, 1984, the 50-year-old Berg pulled into the driveway of his Denver townhouse at 9:30 p.m. He had just closed the door of his convertible when a car driven by David Lane stopped at the driveway entrance. As Lane, Mathews, and a third Order member watched from the car, Bruce Pierce jumped out and fired 12 rounds from a short-barreled MAC-10 machine pistol into Berg's upper body and face. "Did you see that?" Pierce exclaimed as the hit squad raced away. "It was like we pulled a goddam rug out from under him the way he went down!"

From Berg's house the four men went back to their motel, staying just long enough to see the report of Berg's death on the 10 o'clock news before checking out.

The month after the murder the Order held up a Brink's armored car in Ukiah, California, for a breathtaking $3.6 million. Mathews established a pay scale for his followers of $10,000 every three months plus a $20,000 bonus for each action. He also fantasized about buying laser weapons capable of knocking out the power supplies of Seattle and Los Angeles. The future looked rosy for the Order.

However, Mathews's plans were being seriously threatened. Ten days after Berg was killed, member Tom Martinez had been arrested for passing a number of the

A smiling Robert Mathews holds a trick-or-treat bag stuffed with $25,952 he stole from a Seattle bank.

Order's counterfeit $10 bills. Mathews was confident he could count on his follower's loyalty. For four months Martinez resisted the pressure put on him to reveal what he knew about the Order, but with the specter of a trial looming closer and closer he decided to talk.

With the turncoat's information about Berg's murder and the various robberies, the FBI tracked Mathews to a Portland, Oregon, motel. When agents moved in to arrest him on November 24, Mathews was hit in one hand during the ensuing shootout but managed to escape. He fled to

Whidbey Island in Washington's Puget Sound, where he had already established three safe houses. Over the next two weeks other Order members joined him—and one of them was a traitor. He telephoned the FBI and told them where to find Mathews.

On the morning of December 7 the safe houses were surrounded by more than 200 federal agents. By bullhorn and field telephone they warned the fugitives to surrender, and by 11 p.m. the only holdout left was Mathews.

FBI SWAT teams were moving on the house when from inside a single gunshot rang out, followed by a long wail. Unsure if he had killed himself or was setting a trap for them, the agents temporarily backed off. The next day, after six tear-gas canisters were fired through the windows, an eight-man team emerged from the trees nearby and slipped into the silent house. Suddenly a burst of machine-gun fire cut a Z pattern down from the room overhead through the ceiling. Unhurt, the eight men escaped to the woods.

After dark, agents began firing illumination flares into the house in hopes of forcing Mathews out. But a cache of ammunition exploded when a flare landed on it, and soon the wooden house was afire. As the flames intensified, Mathews ran from window to window shooting into the darkness. The house burned to the ground, and Mathews's charred body was found among the ashes the following day.

With Mathews dead, the Order disintegrated, and by the winter of 1985 all of the members had been arrested on various charges. Bruce Pierce got a total of 250 years for murdering Alan Berg, counterfeiting, and other crimes, while David Lane drew combined sentences of 150 years. ◆

All in the Family

Costabile "Gus" Farace was no big cheese in New York City's underworld—just a murderous little crumb who'd once served time for beating a man to death with a piece of wood and later ran cocaine for Gerard Chilli, a capo in the Mafia's Bonanno crime family. But even little crumbs can become intolerably irritating, and so it would be with Gus Farace.

It was the capo whom undercover agent Everett Hatcher of the U.S. Drug Enforcement Administration was after when he began meeting with Farace in early 1989. Passing himself off as a drug dealer, Hatcher set up a rendezvous with Farace on Staten Island's Bloomingdale Road on the night of February 28, supposedly to make a big cocaine buy. The DEA man wore a radio transmitter, and five backup agents parked out of sight were listening in when Farace arrived and instructed Hatcher to follow him to a diner, where they would talk. Two of the agents tailed Farace's and Hatcher's vehicles for a short distance before losing them in heavy traffic. They didn't know the name of the diner, and to their frustration, Hatcher's

WANTED BY TH

INTERSTATE FLIGHT - MANSLA
PAROLE VIOLATOR

COSTABILE "GUS" FA

DESCRIPTION

Dates of Birth Used, June 20, 1960; January 20, 1959; July 20, 195 January 20, 1960; June 21, 1960; January 21, 1960; Brooklyn, New Height, 6' 2"; Weight, 220 pounds; Build, muscular; Hair, brown; Eyes Complexion, medium; Race, White; Nationality, American; Scars and tattoos of rose with mom and dad on upper left arm; girl on lower calf leg and a butterfly on stomach; Occupation, grocery man; Social Secu Number Used, 087-52-9335.

CAUTION

FARACE SHOULD BE CONSIDERED ARMED AND EXTREMELY DAN OUS IN VIEW OF PRIOR CONVICTION FOR MANSLAUGHTER AND A IN VIEW OF THE NATURE OF THE SUSPECTED CRIME.

FBI

ER;

E

transmitter was broadcasting so badly that they couldn't follow the conversation.

After a fruitless hour spent looking for Hatcher, the agents decided to try the Bloomingdale Road meeting place. Hatcher was there in his car. He was dead, shot four times. There was no sign of Farace— but there was no doubt in the minds of the agents who'd pulled the trigger. Robert M. Stutman, special agent in charge of the DEA's Manhattan office, declared an all-out manhunt. A $280,000 reward was offered, and the 500 lawmen on the case began leaning hard on the Bonanno family, repeatedly raiding the businesses it ran and the social clubs where the mobsters gathered. Toni Farace, Gus's pregnant wife, was brought in on marijuana charges, and in May Gerard Chilli was indicted for loansharking. And, although the Bonanno family was the DEA's primary target, other Mafia families in New York were also feeling the heat.

Despite the pressure, no one came forward to finger Farace. But the fu-

gitive hadn't run far; indeed, he was practically under Stutman's nose, moving from one apartment to another in various parts of New York City and in nearby suburbs.

After eight months and no progress, Stutman decided to make a man-to-man, boss-to-boss appeal in hopes of turning up the heat on Farace and his friends. Early on a November morning, he drove to the Queens residence of John Gotti, the top

EVERETT HATCHER

boss of the Gambino crime family. Stutman's knock on the door was answered by Gotti himself, who was still in his bathrobe. The DEA boss didn't mince words with the mobster. "Our guy got whacked," Stutman said. "I've been bringing pressure. You know how much it costs you in business. John, do what's right, or the pressure isn't going to get easier."

Gotti nodded, his hands in his bathrobe pockets. "There is little I can say, but of

course, I'm sorry." Stutman persisted: "Farace whacked our guy. If you hear where he is, let us know. We want him." Saying nothing, Gotti stepped back and shut the door.

In the end, it wasn't Stutman's visit to Gotti that brought Farace to account but Chilli's decision that he wasn't worth protecting any longer. For one thing, the police raids on his businesses in the wake of Hatcher's murder had cost the capo a lot of money. And then there was the matter of Chilli's daughter, Margaret Scarpa. She had been having an affair with Farace, who had run to her home to hide on the night of the murder. He thereby violated the sacred Mafia rule that prohibited involving the women—wives, lovers, relatives—in crimes. Chilli put out the word: He wanted Gus Farace dead.

On November 18, Farace drove from the apartment where he was staying on Manhattan's upper East Side to Queens to meet Louis Tuzzio, a minor mobster and close friend who'd helped him find hideouts and served as a conduit for messages between Farace and his wife.

But Tuzzio had caved in to mob muscle. Farace arrived at their rendezvous point first, and Tuzzio pulled his van up beside the car where Farace sat waiting. Farace had barely rolled down his window to greet his friend when a gunman in Tuzzio's van opened fire. Gus Farace died on the spot, done in by his own.

Robert Stutman's blunt comment on Farace's violent end could have served as his epitaph: "He died the way he lived, in the gutter." ◆

I've always had this craving for adventure. There is this incredible thrill to being a crook."

RONALD BIGGS

3

Great Train Robber

On the terrace of a stylish apartment in Rio de Janeiro a tanned, handsome, middle-aged man is relaxing with a newspaper. The lead story's headline reads "BIGGS ELUDES YARD AGAIN!" The man lifts a steaming cup of coffee, takes a sip, turns to face the camera, and says, "There's nothing like a good, satisfying cup of coffee when you're on the run."

The star of this 1982 commercial can speak with great authority when the topic is life on the run: Ronald Biggs was in on the storied, stupendous heist known as the Great Train Robbery and, in the aftermath of the crime, led Scotland Yard on a merry chase that would eventually span years and continents. His first-rate performance as a fugitive turned him into a celebrity. To millions of fans who have followed his career in newspapers, books, and movies and on television, Biggs is a hero, a sort of working-class Robin Hood who made off with a small fortune and never hurt a fly; a generous, charming, kindhearted fellow who was outnumbered and outgunned but who outfoxed his enemies anyway.

Cleverness, however, doesn't account completely for Biggs's triumph. Over and over he has gotten out of jams because of incredible luck. It seems to have stalked him as relentlessly as Scotland Yard. What's more, he's had a good time. "I've always had this craving for adventure," Biggs explains. "There is this incredible thrill to being a crook."

Where Ronald Biggs is these days is no secret—indeed, Scotland Yard has known for years where to find him. But as long as he keeps himself in good graces with the Brazilian government and stays put, Biggs is untouchable.

Rio natives are fond of their foreign fugitive. A familiar figure in bars and clubs, along palm-lined boulevards, on beaches strewn with gorgeous women in string bikinis, Biggs is one of the city's major tourist attractions. Several nights a week he holds forth at a local bar entertaining tourists with his exploits (talk isn't cheap; he gets a percentage of the house take). The Great Train Robbery is interesting, but what people really want to hear about is his repeated escapes from the clutches of the law. Ronald Biggs is a criminal dozens of times over, but his marathon battle for freedom can squeeze a drop of sympathy from the sternest of souls.

Ronald Arthur Biggs was born in London on August 8, 1929, thirty-four years to the day before he became a Great Train Robber. His father worked as a bus driver by day and a cook by night, and his mother was a housewife. The family bonds were strong: "I was superprotected," Biggs later remembered. "My mother always made sure that my cap was square on my head and my socks were pulled up. It was a loving family life." There was always enough money to get by. Ronnie, the youngest of the Biggses' brood of four, helped clean the house or performed errands for neighbors to earn a few shillings to buy candy and other treats.

A timid lad, Ronnie was tormented by grammar-school bullies. One day, he raced home with one of them at his heels. But when he knocked frantically at the door, his father refused to let him in, telling Ronnie he had to stand up for himself. Forced to fight, Ronnie managed to punch his enemy in the nose. It was a rout. The bully ran away, and Ronnie earned a shilling from his proud dad and a new respect among the boys at school.

The fight didn't turn Ronnie into a ruffian—he never would acquire a taste for violence—but it won him the opportunity to try out for a gang of shoplifting schoolmates, even though the leader said Ronnie probably couldn't "nick stuff." On the contrary, he came away from his trial run at two neighborhood stores with a record amount of loot. His criminal career had begun.

Ronnie was a good student, the pride of his parents, who had no idea what he and his friends were up to. The more he stole, the more he enjoyed it. "There is no explanation for some of the things that I stole," Biggs said of his youthful thefts. "For instance, a friend and I stole a brush from a public toilet. God knows why, it was just something to take, something to have a laugh about and throw away later."

Besides having fun, Ronnie also had a long lucky streak: He didn't get caught stealing until, at the age of 15, he pocketed some lead refills for a mechanical pencil in a stationery store and was nabbed by the store detective. More such setbacks followed for the once-uncatchable Ronnie. In June of that year he was arrested for stealing radio parts and given a year's probation. In November he was charged with stealing and selling his brother's gold Rolex watch — an impulsive act that landed him in a juvenile institution for several months.

By now out of school, Biggs made a number of stabs at earning a living honestly. Among other bouts of employment, he worked as a parts numberer in an aircraft plant, a drill operator, a sign-painter's assistant, a helper in a radio repair shop. In 1947 Biggs enlisted in the Royal Air Force for an eight-year stint as a regular, with four more years in the reserves to follow. But he soon discovered that the military life wasn't for him and went AWOL. Returning to London, he joined forces with several other thieves. They stole from trucks, stripped valuable lead fittings from rooftops, and broke into shops. Biggs took some of the stolen goods to a fence, but then he made the mistake of romancing the fence's wife. The jealous husband got even by turning Biggs in to the police. He was dishonorably discharged from the RAF and sentenced to six months in a prison known as Wormwood Scrubs.

Although Biggs complained about having to eat too much porridge there, jail nevertheless had its good points. "In prisons you meet interesting people, bigger and better crooks," he recalled much later. "Nobody at all talks about going straight and anyone who does is thought to be a chump. All, or practically all, jobs are put together behind prison walls. You might get a big tough safecracker who would tell you that, 'I've got a beauty and when I get out I want a couple of real game blokes.' Everyone fancies himself as being real game and there are plenty of volunteers."

Shortly after his release from jail in the summer of 1949, Biggs and a friend stole a Studebaker late one night. Speeding around a corner, they spotted a police car in the deserted street. The police gave chase, and the two thieves leaped from the Studebaker and sprinted off. "Boy, I really did run," Biggs remembered, "straight into a cul-de-sac. Anyhow this policeman did the flying-tackle bit and we were taken back to the station. He said to me there, 'Christ,

sonny, you can run, but I can run faster.' He could too."

The punishment for this escapade was a three-month stint in Wormwood Scrubs. It would prove fateful: While he was there he met a smart, smooth-talking convict named Bruce Reynolds, future mastermind of the Great Train Robbery. In addition to their taste for thievery, the two men discovered that they had other things in common. Both were, as Biggs said, "sensual" people who enthusiastically pursued women. Both of them liked modern jazz and enjoyed reading; the American fiction writers Ernest Hemingway and John Steinbeck were particular favorites.

Two months after his release, Biggs was arrested for breaking into a store and sent back to Wormwood Scrubs. A prison psychiatrist assigned to evaluate Biggs informed him that his IQ was far above average and advised, "There is a good future for you if you pull yourself together."

Biggs wasn't interested in pulling himself together. From Wormword Scrubs he was transferred to a work farm in Wales. In that rural setting, freedom called. With an Irish companion named Paddy, Biggs climbed over a gate and struck out across the Welsh countryside. A few days later they reached London, where they broke into the house of a bookmaker who supposedly had £10,000 in cookie tins hidden under his bed. The tins, however, were filled with papers, and all Biggs and Paddy got away with was £200. The police caught Biggs before long, and he received a sentence of three and a half years.

Sent to Lewes prison this time, Biggs was pleased to find that the jazz-loving Bruce Reynolds was doing time there. They became fast friends, endlessly discussing future projects. One especially interesting topic they tossed around was train robbery. From a former post-office mail sorter doing time at Lewes, they learned that huge sums of money were periodically carried by train from various parts of the country to London. These trains, said the ex-postal worker, were not well guarded. Furthermore, determining their schedules wouldn't be hard; a nice bribe was sure to loosen lips in the postal service. Reynolds, in particular, was fascinated. He was, as Biggs put it, always looking for the "big touch."

At Lewes Biggs took a carpentry course. He was a natural at the craft, scoring top marks for his work. Applying his new skills, he made some wood supports for inmates Eric "Birdseye Bertie" Flower and John Smith to use in their attempt to go over the prison walls. The effort failed, but

luckily prison authorities didn't find out that Biggs had helped Flower and Smith.

Carpentry, Biggs realized, could open an avenue into a different sort of life. Should stealing fail to provide a future livelihood, construction work might be quite satisfying. However, he wasn't ready for that yet, and when he was released from prison in 1952, one of his first moves was to look up fellow parolee Bruce Reynolds. They quickly picked up the topic of train robbing. But talk of money-stuffed railroad cars was still just talk, and Biggs joined several other ex-cons in a string of small-time jobs. This spree came to a bruising end when they wrecked a stolen car. Once more, Ronald Biggs was off to jail; he spent most of the three-year sentence at Wandsworth, a dirty, decrepit prison in London that was notorious for its tough guards. His only consolation was that Bruce Reynolds was also in Wandsworth, serving three years for assaulting a bookmaker.

Free again in December of 1955, Biggs got a job as a pipe-layer, but he also moonlighted as a thief. He moved in with a woman named Rose, who'd been Bruce Reynolds's girlfriend until he got interested in someone else and palmed her off on his buddy.

For two years Biggs stuck with Rose and pursued his dual career. One autumn morning in 1957 he got onto the commuter train he rode to work and noticed an attractive young woman. She was reading *Tess of the D'Urbervilles*, a classic English novel that Biggs had also read during a stretch in prison. The book made for a fine opening gambit, and Biggs commented on the plot. It didn't occur to 18-year-old Charmian Powell that a serious reader could also be a crook, and the two started to chat. She was the auburn-haired daughter of suburban schoolteachers—a proper, well-brought-up girl, but a very unhappy one. She didn't get along with her father, who criticized her savagely whenever her grades fell short of the highest level. At the time she met Biggs, Powell had recently been turned down by the university she'd hoped to attend and was still smarting from her father's threat to kick her out of the house as punishment.

Biggs was 28 years old, good-looking, cheeky, and seemed to have an air of the unusual about him—of danger, perhaps. When he and Powell became lovers, she discovered he *was* unusual, at least to a middle-class girl like her, for he told her everything about his past, crimes and all. Though shocked, she'd fallen for him hard, and she focused

Newlyweds Ronald and Charmian Biggs smile happily after a civil ceremony on February 20, 1960. The groom had been released from prison two months earlier, after serving 21 months for robbing a pharmacy.

on his virtues instead of his vices; he was a good man at heart, she felt—kind, considerate, never violent.

Life at home was becoming so unbearable for Powell that she decided to move out. She and Biggs talked about going away together, and he proposed financing their fun with money that she would steal from the precious-metals company she worked for. Powell protested at first; she couldn't imagine doing such a thing, and besides, she might go to prison. But she loved Ronnie Biggs to distraction, and she went through with the theft. To Biggs's disappointment Powell pocketed a mere £200. But she got away with the crime, after a fashion. When Powell's employer discovered the theft, her father made restitution, and no charges were brought against her.

Powell and Biggs left London the next morning for a tour of England's West Country. They weren't alone. Biggs didn't have a car, and Mike Haynes, a crony who'd often chauffeured him and Powell on dates, had agreed to drive them. Powell didn't much like Haynes, but she was stuck with him.

After two weeks of touring, the lovers settled into an apartment in the country town of Swanage, and Haynes returned to London. Soon, however, Biggs asked him to come back. He and Powell were running out of money, and he wanted Haynes's help in a little thieving. Biggs suggested a grandiose scheme—going after the payroll of a nearby RAF camp—but they rejected it for something more modest. They hit a shop that sold cameras, watches, and other articles easy to fence in London.

The job went off without a hitch, and brimming with confidence, the two men decided to steal the weekly receipts of a local movie theater. When the men broke into the theater in the middle of the night, however, they didn't find any money. When they came out they saw a policeman down the street. He started after them, but they shook him off, running up one fire escape to the roof of the theater and down another.

A week later a policeman came to their door. Because of the recent spate of robberies in town, the identity of temporary residents was being checked out. Claiming to be a London physician, Biggs gave the cop a phony name and address. The officer apologized for bothering him. He had hardly left when Biggs, Powell, and Haynes realized what trouble they'd be in if and when the police tried to verify the information. They climbed out the apartment window and

started walking. Two hours later, they came to a hamlet where they found a parked car with the key in the ignition. They climbed in and headed toward London with Haynes at the wheel. The police, however, were by now looking for them and had set up a roadblock on the route they'd taken. Haynes roared through the roadblock. A little farther on, the three fugitives abandoned the car and headed off across the fields, but police dogs soon tracked them down.

For their misadventures, Powell and Haynes were given two years on probation while Biggs spent nearly two years in prison. Powell visited and wrote her lover faithfully, and when he was released in December 1959, the two of them bought a bottle of champagne and headed for a hotel.

They decided to get married, and Biggs swore that he would give up his light-fingered ways. He meant it. After the wedding in February of 1960, he signed on as a carpenter for a construction company. Later that year Charmian Biggs gave birth to a son, Nicholas. The family moved from the apartment they'd been living in to a house, and Biggs soon set up a construction business of his own. He stayed in contact with old friends such as Mike Haynes, but for the time being, marriage, fatherhood, and honest work agreed with him.

But only for the time being. It was money, or not enough of it, that would make him break his promise. The house the family had been renting was up for sale, and to buy it required a fat down payment. Biggs also wanted capital to expand his business, and there was soon another mouth to feed—Christopher, born in March 1963.

Biggs thought he might be able to get a loan from Bruce Reynolds, his jailhouse mate. To his disappointment, Reynolds said that he didn't have any money to spare at the moment, since he was planning a big job. Would Biggs like to help out? Biggs said he definitely wasn't interested, but Reynolds persisted. This job, he said, was special. "It's a big one. I can't give you too many details at the moment, but it's very, very big." When Biggs remained adamant, Reynolds said, "O.K., going straight is fine, but what if I told you that your minimum whack would be £40,000?"

Suddenly Biggs was interested—very, very interested. But there was a catch: Reynolds said that before Biggs could sign on or be let in on the job's specifics he'd have to find someone who could drive a railroad locomotive. Biggs knew instantly what Reynolds had in mind—a fabulous train robbery of the kind they'd talked about during their

prison days. As luck would have it, Biggs happened to know a freight-yard engineer. He'd met Peter—to protect his friend, Biggs never revealed his last name—when he was hired to do some work on Peter's bungalow. Biggs paid a visit to Peter to feel him out about participating in a heist, and when Biggs mentioned a fee of thousands of pounds the engineer leaped at the opportunity. Biggs remembered Peter's saying, "I've been working on the railways for God knows how long and now I'm working past my retirement age. All I will get when I go is a gold watch and fifteen bob a week. So why not?"

With his engineer problem solved, Reynolds filled Biggs in on his train-robbing scheme. It sounded fine to Biggs. "I always had confidence in Bruce Reynolds as a crook," he later wrote. "I thought that anything he put together was bound to be good. Looking back, I do not think that many crooks at that time would have turned the job down."

Reynolds had been quietly recruiting a train crew for a year. In all, some 20 men would have a hand in the heist. Following the advice of the postal worker who'd been his fellow convict at Lewes prison back in 1950, Reynolds bribed several post-office employees, and he also paid off some railroad men to help him pick his target.

The target seemed almost too good to be true. A Royal Mail train leaving Glasgow on August 6 would carry an unusually large shipment of cash from banks in Scotland and northern England for delivery to their London offices. The run would be the first after the annual three-day August bank holiday, when hordes of vacationers customarily head north and spend heavily. Reynolds's informants told him the train might carry as much as £6 million, the equivalent of some $16,800,000. Virtually all of the money would be in the form of used £1 and £5 notes. Except for a small percentage that might be marked, the money would be impossible to trace.

A typical Glasgow-to-London mail train was a dozen cars long, with 70 or so clerks sorting letters in most of the cars during the overnight run. All of the loot would be in the High Value Package coach, a car that was usually the second one from the engine. Except for the locks on the HVP coach doors and the metal cages where the bags of money were stored, security would be nil, since the last mail train robbery had occurred more than a century earlier.

After weeks of exploring the line the train traveled, Reynolds found what looked like a perfect spot for rail piracy,

just outside the little farming town of Leighton Buzzard, about 50 minutes from the end of the run in London. He planned the operation carefully. As the train passed through the town at 3:10 a.m. on August 7, the engineer would see an amber warning signal beside the tracks and begin to slow down. At a railway crossing a few hundred yards farther on, a red signal light on a gantry would command him to bring the train to a full stop. There the locomotive and the first two cars would be uncoupled from the rest of the cars and driven on down the line a mile to an overpass, the site Reynolds had chosen for ransacking the High Value Package coach. The bags of money would be thrown down an embankment to vehicles waiting on the road below.

Reynolds knew that a full-scale hunt for the robbers was sure to be launched as soon as the robbery was reported. With all roads in the area under close watch, the best course of action would be for the gang to hole up in the neighborhood for a while. After a little house hunting, the plotters found a suitably deserted place about 20 miles from Leighton Buzzard. Called Leatherslade Farm, the house was invisible from the road, and the nearest building was half a mile away. To eliminate fingerprints and other clues that were bound to accumulate in the house, an accomplice was hired to burn the place down after the robbers decamped.

Painstaking preparations went on throughout the summer. Four gang members were assigned to learn how to uncouple railway cars, and two others were to be responsible for manipulating the signal lights. Of the equipment needed for the operation, some was bought and much was stolen. For transportation the gang acquired two Land Rovers, a small van, two Jaguars, and a five-ton truck they painted to look like an army vehicle. The robbers bought military uniforms to wear during the drive to the train and railroad workers' blue overalls to put on over the uniforms just before boarding. In addition there were masks, walkie-talkies, radios to listen in on police frequencies, handcuffs, electrical equipment for rigging the signal lights, axes for breaking into the money coach, and gloves—plus food, sleeping bags, and other supplies for the stay at Leatherslade Farm. The only weapons stockpiled were ax handles wrapped in adhesive tape; the leaders didn't want to hurt anyone if they could help it.

On August 6 Biggs, Peter, and four other members of the gang rode out to Leatherslade Farm in one of the Land Rovers. When Peter learned that the vehicle had been stolen,

he exclaimed, "Christ, you can get bloody pinched for a thing like that."

By evening the entire team was assembled and ready for action. But word soon came from an informant that the mail train was carrying much less cash than they'd expected. A far larger shipment would be on board the following night. For the next 24 hours the robbers lay low and passed the time as best they could; Biggs and another gang member played several rounds of Monopoly. When night came at last, everyone donned his military uniform and gave the gear a last check. At 12:10 a.m. Bruce Reynolds gave the go-ahead order, and the men took their assigned seats in

the Land Rovers and the truck and set out into the night.

The operation was carried out with dazzling efficiency. With a veteran of the run, 57-year-old engineer Jack Mills, at the controls, the mail train reached Leighton Buzzard right on time. When Mills saw the amber signal light ahead, he applied the brakes gently. Next, the rigged red signal came into view, and Mills brought the train to a stop. His assistant climbed out of the cab to call the next station from a trackside telephone. But the phone was dead—the gang had cut its wires. Now wearing their overalls and masks, several robbers grabbed the assistant engineer and threw him down the steep embankment. Several others went after

the engineer. But Jack Mills didn't give up easily; he fought his assailants until one of them hit him on the head with a tape-wrapped ax handle. Meanwhile, the locomotive and the front two cars were being uncoupled from the rest of the train. Peter took over at the controls.

The train couldn't move ahead immediately. Uncoupling had released the vacuum in the brake system, and the brakes would remain locked until the vacuum was reestablished. It was only a matter of a few moments, but one impatient robber couldn't wait. He wrenched Peter away from the controls and forced the dazed and bleeding Jack Mills into his place. "Move this train," the gang member commanded, "or you'll get some more stick." By now, the vacuum had built up again, and the train began to move forward.

After that, it was easy. At the overpass Biggs carried out his assigned task of escorting Peter to one of the Land Rovers and waiting there with him until the job was finished. The raiders broke into the HVP coach and ordered the astonished workers to lie on the floor and stay there for a half-hour. Forming a human chain, the gang passed 125 bags of money from the coach down the embankment and loaded them into the waiting truck. It wasn't big enough to hold all the bags, so the robbers had to leave a few behind.

On the way back to Leatherslade Farm the men listened to police radio frequencies. But not until they were turning into the farm driveway, about a half-hour later, was an alarm about the robbery broadcast. They stayed tuned in and soon heard a stunned policeman say, "You won't believe this, but they've stolen a train."

The robbers couldn't restrain themselves as they counted

Three men film the site where bags of money were tossed from the mail coach, then passed from hand to hand down the embankment to a waiting truck. At right, a British Rail engineer and a policeman chat beside the coach after it was driven on down the line to the next station.

their booty. The count took an entire day because there were thousands upon thousands of bills in the money bags. As the sorting into piles went on, one man started dancing the twist, and another burst out singing the current pop hit "I Like It, I Like It." The take wasn't the £6 million they had hoped for, but they weren't complaining: the bags they'd made off with contained £2,631,000, equivalent to about $7.3 million. Biggs's share should have been some £140,000, and he took it on faith that the haystack of bills

he got was close to that figure. Later, he heard that another gang member had managed to grab some of his bills, but he wasn't sure whether to believe the tale.

While the gang members divided the money they stayed tuned to police broadcasts—and began to worry that the farm wasn't such a safe haven after all. Just as Reynolds had expected, the police immediately put up roadblocks and scoured the countryside around Leighton Buzzard. He had assumed they would soon shift their focus to other areas, but that didn't appear to be happening. The hunt continued to fix on the neighborhood, as if the police thought the robbers hadn't fled. These tactics were based on a bit of information provided by one of the mail sorters on the HVP coach: The robbers had told them to lie down on the coach floor and stay there for a half-hour. To the police, the time period hinted that the robbers might be lying low somewhere within 30 minutes or so of Leighton Buzzard. The gang had good reason to worry.

Clutching money-stuffed bags and suitcases, the men soon began slipping away from the farm. Biggs caught a ride home with Reynolds, and when Charmian greeted him at the door, he said, "Have you got a kiss for your clever little husband?" Then he opened the suitcase he was lugging to show her the bundles of bills inside. As a precaution against a possible police search of his house, Biggs split up most of his haul and entrusted it to several friends for safekeeping. But he wasn't really worried about being found out: He got the word from the arsonist's contact man that the farmhouse had been torched as planned.

But the arsonist lied when he reported he'd carried out his job. Unbeknown to anybody in the gang, he'd taken the big advance he'd gotten and run away, leaving a houseful of clues for the police.

On August 12 a nosy herdsman went poking around the deserted farm. His suspicions were aroused by the phony army truck he saw in a shed, and he tipped off the police. Scotland Yard agents sifting through the house lifted Ronnie Biggs's fingerprints from a plate, a ketchup bottle, and the Monopoly set he'd used.

On August 24 a dozen Scotland Yard officers showed up at the Biggses' house. Charmian met them at the door and explained that her husband was at work. When she offered to telephone him, the officer in charge said, "Oh no you don't. Sit down. We'll all sit down until Ronnie comes home, shall we?" Biggs pulled up in front of the house at 7 o'clock. When the police took him away they wouldn't even let him say good-bye to his children, and Charmian was kept at arm's length.

Her loyalty unshaken, she visited her jailed husband as often as she could. Knowing he might be in prison as many as 30 years if he was found guilty, Biggs told Charmian, "You're only 24—you've got your whole life ahead of you. If I go down for a long spell in the boob, I want you to know you are free to live your life as a single person. So if you meet a fellow, go out and have some fun." Charmian didn't want to have fun with another fellow. "You know there'll never be anyone else but you," she replied.

Besides Biggs, 11 other gang members were caught in the initial sweep, and they all went on trial in February 1964. (Peter, the engineer, was one of the lucky robbers who were never caught.) Biggs was found guilty, and the judge gave him the maximum possible sentence of 30 years. In his closing remarks, he called Biggs "a specious and facile liar" and noted that he had perjured himself time and again. The train robber appeared to take his stiff punishment and the judge's hard words in stride. Wrote one reporter, "Biggs, a slight smile on his face, winked at his wife as he left the dock."

Biggs found himself back in Wandsworth prison, the one he hated more than any other. One of the convicted gang members escaped after only four months in prison, and officials feared he might engineer an escape for Biggs. As a consequence Biggs was classified a "special watch" prisoner. He was kept under close surveillance and regularly moved from one cell to another to foil any escape plan.

After two months of such treatment he was so fed up that he wrote to his Member of Parliament to complain about the restraints he had to endure as a special watch prisoner:

"In an interview with the governor I told him I was anxious to settle down, keep out of trouble and hope to earn maximum remission. And that is what I want to do, but the overall effect of the extra aggravation I am being subjected to is making it very hard for me. I have much patience and equanimity but I am rapidly losing both and, quite frankly, rather than finding it more difficult to escape I am finding it difficult not to!

"I would greatly appreciate any help you can give me in these matters.

"Yours faithfully,

"R. A. Biggs

"PS: Good luck in the forthcoming election!"

Just convicted of robbery and sentenced to 30 years in prison, a dejected Ronald Biggs is escorted from court by a policeman.

The letter did no good, and Biggs was increasingly depressed by the constraints he was living under. It didn't help his mood to hear one guard's repeated jibe: "How long to go now, Ronnie? Twenty-nine years? Or is it thirty?"

Biggs spent the days sewing mailbags — a task whose irony he didn't find amusing. He found some comfort, though, in talking with a tough con named Paul Seabourne, who was also assigned to the mailbag detail. Seabourne was nearing the end of a four-year sentence, and he offered to help Biggs escape once he was on the outside himself. Month after month they turned over various schemes for springing Biggs from prison. The most radical was a helicopter pickup from the prison yard, but they decided it was unworkable. Seabourne suggested a commando raid against the Wandsworth gatehouse, but Biggs didn't like the idea of violence. They finally settled on a plan that took advantage of the fact that a street ran alongside one of the 20-foot walls surrounding Wandsworth's exercise yard. They envisioned a tall van beside the wall; on the van's roof would be a platform high enough to reach the top of the wall. The two plotters left the plan at that; Seabourne would work out the engineering details when he got out of prison. And Biggs and Seabourne agreed that two could escape just as easily as one. Eric Flower, Biggs's old prison chum of some 15 years' standing, had arrived at Wandsworth to serve 12 years for armed robbery. He would go over the wall with Ronnie.

Seabourne was released in May 1965. Drawing on some of the train-robbery money held by Biggs's friends, he enlisted two accomplices and got hold of a van. The escape team painted the van to look like a mail truck, cut a trapdoor in its roof, and built a platform with a hinged base mounted inside. Thus equipped, the platform could be raised to the wall's top. The men also bought a long rope ladder. The time for breakout was set for July 8 at 3:10 p.m., when Biggs and Flower would be exercising.

At 3:09 the van and a getaway car parked outside the exercise yard wall. The trapdoor opened and the platform rose through it, bearing Seabourne and one of his accomplices. The two men lowered the rope ladder, and Biggs and Flower sprinted toward it, closely followed by a pair of guards. By prearrangement, two prisoners knocked down the guards with a flying block, and several other prisoners stepped in to detain them for five minutes. Realizing this was their big chance when they saw what Biggs and Flower were up to, two other inmates scrambled up the ladder behind them. Nobody objected, and the four escapees, along with Seabourne and his helper, piled into the getaway car. The driver roared away toward a nearby railway station, where Biggs and Flower switched to a second car. The two interlopers took their leave there, shouting "Thanks, Biggsie, and good luck."

Indeed, Biggs had far better luck than Seabourne did. The plan had called for setting the van on fire at the last minute, but getting two extra prisoners over the wall had eaten up precious time. Fearing that the cops might be on their trail any moment, the men had abandoned the van and fled, leaving behind enough evidence for the police to arrest Seabourne and his helper; they both went to prison for aiding the escape.

The press had a heyday with the flight, portraying the escape team as bold, resourceful swashbucklers, perhaps dangerous ones. Scotland Yard issued a warning: "As there is a possibility that these men may be armed, members of the public who may encounter them are advised to contact the police at once, without approaching them."

Ronald Biggs hated guns and anything else that smacked of violence, and encountering the public was the last thing he had in mind. He and Flower hid out in London, then slipped out of the city to the seaside town of Bognor Regis, where they stayed for a month.

The newspapers kept their front pages plastered with headlines about the daring escape and the ghostlike disappearance of the prisoners, and embarrassed authorities kept a large task force of hunters on the trail. Biggs and Flower realized that England wouldn't be safe for them for a long time—in fact, it might never again be safe for them. They would have to go abroad.

Flower had underworld friends experienced in spiriting fugitives out of the country and on to a new life—for a suitable fee. Biggs had already spent £20,000 on lawyers' fees and about £10,000 on the prison escape; in addition, he had given many thousands of pounds to friends. Now he agreed on a £40,000 package deal to get himself and Flower to a safe haven—exactly where that might be they hadn't yet decided. In addition to items such as false passports and transportation, the money Biggs paid covered plastic surgery to be performed by a doctor in Paris. "We were offered the complete range of surgery available," Biggs remembered, "including £1,000 per finger to have our fingerprints removed; there was a price list for everything—eyelids, lips, ears, etc." Flower opted for a new nose only, while Biggs decided to have a face-lift as well as a nose job.

In October 1965 Biggs and Flower, wearing seaman's clothes, were escorted to a hiding place in the hold of a freighter bound for Belgium. When they landed, a chauffeured car was waiting for them. After restoring themselves with a delicious meal of snails and chicken in red wine, they were driven to Paris. They were taken to a pleasant apartment, and their escorts urged them to stay put; if they went out, they risked being recognized. But Biggs and Flower couldn't resist the temptations of Paris. One night they went drinking; another night, Biggs remembered, "I went out and found myself a prostitute. It was something of a relief after being holed up with Eric Flower."

Between nights on the town the men concluded that their final destination must be an English-speaking country where they'd blend in inconspicuously, and a newspaper story they read one dank, cold Paris morning made up their minds for them. A reporter who'd recently been to Australia raved about the heat and the beaches full of bathing beauties. "That's the place for us," Flower said. "Yes, Ron, let's make it Aussie." It sounded perfect to Biggs, too.

Biggs hadn't expected plastic surgery to be so painful. Lying in his hospital bed after the operation, he almost went out of his mind: "For the first and only time in my life I contemplated suicide. I wanted to get up and throw myself out of the window. I didn't care how high or low it was." Fortunately the pain soon subsided, and when the 140 stitches were at last removed, Biggs was pleased with his new look. "It was a very different face from the one with which I had gone into the clinic," he reported later. "I decided to grow a moustache which, with the new face, a

In a lane between Wandsworth prison and the fenced gardens of residences occupied by prison guards, investigators cluster near the furniture van that Biggs, his friend Eric Flower, and two other prisoners had used the day before in their escape over the wall behind. The two friends who engineered the operation were arrested after police found their fingerprints in the abandoned van.

One of Biggs's aliases, Terence Cook, is misspelled on this income statement from the Melbourne construction company he worked for in 1968 and 1969.

short haircut and some dark glasses, gave me an altogether changed appearance." His new passport was in the name of Terence Furminger—a real Englishman who was paid £1,000 for cooperating.

The £40,000 fee paid for Charmian, Nicky, and Chris to spend five days in Paris with Biggs at Christmastime. Then, on December 29, he was off to Australia—alone.

On New Year's Eve Ronald Biggs—or Terry Furminger—landed in Sydney, checked into a hotel, and went out to celebrate his successful trip. Eric Flower had arrived in the city a week earlier and had promptly gotten a job pumping gas. Biggs, however, had left France with £700, so he could afford to spend his time at the beach developing his tan and meeting women. Charmian wrote regularly, sending her letters in care of a taxi driver Biggs had made friends with.

Biggs's new life was off to a good start, but he didn't forget that he was the object of an international manhunt. He had his first brush with danger in February after Charmian sent a magazine with £200 tucked between the pages. Post office inspectors discovered the bills and went to the taxi driver's house looking for Terry Furminger. As soon as Biggs learned of their visit, he and Flower got out of Sydney and headed for the city of Adelaide, 800 miles away. Once there, Biggs took the precaution of changing his name to Terry King. He landed a job in a furniture factory, and Flower, who was now known as Bob Burley, went to work at a garage.

Although he found plenty of women to keep him company, Biggs missed his wife and children sorely. Charmian was eager to join him, and with the aid of the same experts who had gotten Biggs out of England, she acquired a passport in the name of Margaret Furminger, the real wife of the real Terence Furminger. In June 1966 she, Nicky, and Chris arrived in Australia. In her luggage Charmian was carrying £7,000. About £40,000 of the money Biggs had parceled out to friends immediately after the train robbery remained in England, but he knew that some of them might not let go of it now. Practically speaking, the £7,000 was probably the last of the train robbery loot the Biggses would see.

It was delightful for the family to be together again, but in the back of Biggs's mind there was the constant lurking fear of Scotland Yard. In fact, the agency had no idea where he was, though it had received reports alleging his presence in various far-flung locations, including Singapore, Canada, Cyprus, Indonesia, Mexico, and New Guinea.

In April 1967 the third Biggs son, Farley, was born. But a week later his parents' happiness was overshadowed by a worrisome unsigned letter delivered from England: "Things moving in an unpleasant direction. Photo found. Suggest change of scenery and name." Biggs didn't know what photo the writer was talking about, but he didn't take any chances and quickly arranged to move the family from Adelaide to Melbourne. Once there, Biggs and Charmian began calling themselves Terry and Charm Cook; they hadn't seen fit to change the boys' names before, and they didn't now. Biggs went to work for a construction firm, and Charmian found a job at a cookie factory.

In the wake of the letter Biggs couldn't shake the sense of being hunted, and he became positively alarmed when one of the Great Train Robbers turned himself in and two others were captured in 1968. The media gave especially big play to the arrest of robbery mastermind Bruce Reynolds, who'd spent several of his four years on the lam in Mexico. Biggs grew even more alarmed when he saw his own photograph in several newspaper stories about the robbery. In early 1969 a women's magazine serialized the memoirs Reynolds's wife wrote to make some money, and the accompanying photograph of Biggs was a particularly good one—good enough to make him fear that plastic surgery hadn't changed his face enough to deceive people after all. For the moment, however, nobody challenged his identity as Terry Cook.

During this tense period a welcome figure from Biggs's past resurfaced. Biggs was at a construction site when he noticed a new worker carrying a sheet of glass. It was Mike Haynes—the same Mike Haynes who'd accompanied Biggs and Charmian when they were on the lam with the £200 she had pilfered from her employer in 1957. Unlike Biggs, Haynes had immigrated to Australia legally to start a new life. He was glad to see his mate from the old days and would soon show how true a friend he was.

Things were about to heat up for Ronnie Biggs. In March 1969 a man from Adelaide who'd known him as Terry King saw one of the newspaper photographs and made the connection between King and Biggs. He told the police and added that King had been good friends with one Bob Burley. Burley—that is, Eric Flower—hid when the police came knocking at his door. He immediately called Biggs, then fled

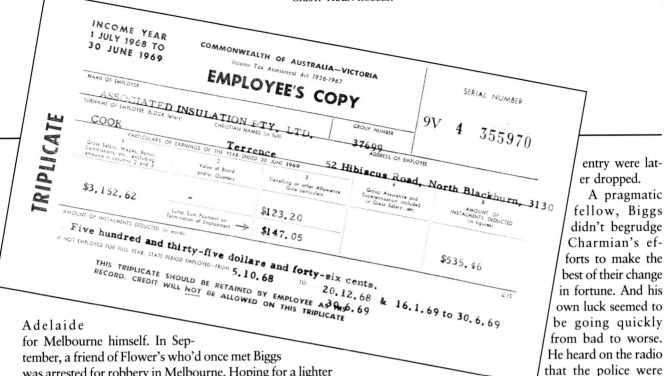

Adelaide
for Melbourne himself. In September, a friend of Flower's who'd once met Biggs was arrested for robbery in Melbourne. Hoping for a lighter sentence, he told the police that Biggs was living somewhere in Australia. The police launched an investigation, and on October 16 Biggs was watching when his photograph appeared on a television news report.

The report also mentioned his children's names. Biggs knew that the jig was up; the chances of another family having a Nicholas, a Christopher, and a Farley seemed slight. That was it. Early the next morning Charmian drove him to a hotel on the outskirts of Melbourne, where he registered under a false name. He and Charmian were to meet that evening, but she didn't keep the date. Biggs guessed that the police, having discovered where they were living, came looking for him and arrested Charmian.

His guess was correct. She was charged with illegal immigration and grilled about her husband's whereabouts. "Do yourself a favor, lady," one interrogator advised her. "You've had a good run for your money. Tell us where he is and make it easy on yourself." But she wouldn't tell the police what they wanted to know.

When Charmian didn't show up, Biggs left the hotel and took refuge with a friend, who found a hideout for him in the Dandenong Hills near Melbourne. Radio broadcasts and the newspapers his friend brought kept Biggs abreast of his own story. Thus he learned that two days after her arrest Charmian had sold her life story to a newspaper magnate for a tidy $65,000. Moreover, she declared at a hearing after her arrest that she had come to Australia only because her husband had pressured her. Charmian said that her children were very happy in their new home, and she requested permission to remain in Australia. The sympathetic judge ordered her released on bail, and the charges of illegal

entry were later dropped.

A pragmatic fellow, Biggs didn't begrudge Charmian's efforts to make the best of their change in fortune. And his own luck seemed to be going quickly from bad to worse. He heard on the radio that the police were going to search the Dandenongs, which had a reputation as a convenient hiding place for criminals. Biggs immediately asked his friend to carry an SOS message to Mike Haynes. Haynes arrived that evening and whisked the fugitive away to another hideout.

Soon there was more bad news. The police had found Eric Flower, who now faced being sent back to prison in England. Happily, though, the *Sunday Mirror* had something entertaining and encouraging for Biggs to read on October 26—it was the first installment of Charmian's memoirs. In an interview with the two reporters who put her story on paper Charmian said she dreaded hearing some day that the hunt for her husband was over; it would be "cruel and wicked" were he to wind up in jail again for his part in the Great Train Robbery. She claimed she had no regrets about her life and declared that "meeting Ronald Biggs was the greatest thing that ever happened to me."

If the thought of Biggs behind bars was dreadful to Charmian, it was completely unbearable to him. Biggs, who by now was living with Mike Haynes and his wife, wondered if he could drop out of sight in the rough, frontierlike western reaches of Australia. But one day Haynes, all on his own, made his friend a magnanimous offer—his passport. Instantly Biggs's chances of remaining free seemed far brighter: With Haynes's passport (properly doctored, of course) he could leave Australia for a safe haven elsewhere in the world—a European country perhaps, or maybe Japan or South Africa.

These places were rejected, however, after Biggs looked through some travel brochures about South America that Haynes's wife, Jesse, brought him. Biggs's eye was drawn to a photograph in one of the brochures showing Sugarloaf Mountain thrusting skyward above the harbor of Rio de Janeiro. Somehow, the picture struck a sympathetic chord in the music-loving Biggs, bringing to his mind the steps and rhythms of Brazil's sensuous samba. "This is the place for me," he declared. Mike Haynes was just as enthusiastic. "South America!" he exclaimed. "That's where all the Nazi war criminals are hiding out. It's a natural for you to wind up in."

A luxury liner with a stop scheduled in Panama in Central America was set to sail from Melbourne on February 5, and Jesse Haynes booked passage for Biggs, using money Charmian had earned from her memoirs. To reduce the risk of being recognized when he went to board the ship, Biggs ate huge amounts of spaghetti to gain weight and cut his hair very short. As his day of departure neared, the now chubby Biggs put on sunglasses and left the safety of the Haynes home for a shopping center to get a photograph of himself made in an automatic booth. He added what he hoped would pass for the official government seal stamped on passport images.

Charmian came to see him to say good-bye just before he left Australia. They drank champagne and talked for hours. Their hope was that she and the boys could join him in South America in a year or so. "I've coped before and I can cope again," Charmian said. She mightn't have been so optimistic if she'd known that she and Biggs wouldn't see each other again for four years.

On February 5 Mike and Jesse Haynes accompanied Biggs to the ship. There they worked a simple ruse: Mike went through passport control as himself, then boarded the ship by way of the gangplank reserved for passengers. Jesse and Biggs, who was wearing his dark glasses, boarded the ship by the visitors' gangplank. In a cabin toilet, Biggs replaced Haynes's passport photo with his own. The real Mike Haynes and his wife left the ship, and the phony Mike Haynes was off for Panama.

The voyage was blissful. Biggs spent his days sunbathing and swimming and his nights partying. "My philosophy was to enjoy the trip to the maximum, to treat it like a last fling," he said later. His fling included women—he found plenty of companions on board to help him while away the hours. Biggs's shipboard fun was expensive, and when he reached Panama on February 25 he had only $300 of the $2,000 Charmian had given him for the trip. Fortunately,

he'd made a friend during the trip who invited Biggs to stay at his home in Caracas, Venezuela. It wasn't squarely on the road to Rio, but Biggs was in no hurry. The understanding Charmian cabled him more money, and after two weeks in the Venezuelan capital, he flew to Brazil on March 11.

Biggs was anxious about getting through passport control at the Rio de Janeiro airport. "My imagination was working overtime as I visualized all kinds of Interpol wanted posters exhibiting my photograph, convinced that the officials at the check need only compare the passport with the wanted poster and that would be my lot, the door would burst open and the police grab me." Luckily for Biggs, nothing of the kind happened, and he got out of the airport with no trouble at all.

By another stroke of luck, on the flight from Caracas Biggs had met an American with several friends in Rio. The man helped smooth Biggs's way into his new life with an introduction to an English-speaking ex-show girl named Nadine Mitchell. She was a Christian Scientist, and although Biggs wasn't a religious man, he accepted her invitation to a church service. Once again Biggsian luck prevailed. Among the churchgoers was a Swiss stockbroker who now and again needed a carpenter. He offered the work to Biggs, who was able to scrape by on what the stockbroker paid him.

This new boy in town was so outgoing, attractive, and ready for a good time that his circle of friends grew quickly. It included foreigners and natives as well, even though he didn't speak a word of Portuguese, the language of Brazil, when he arrived. He soon became involved with a good-looking 27-year-old named Edith. Her sister didn't approve of the relationship since Biggs was married, and she tried without success to destroy it with macumba, a Brazilian form of voodoo. Biggs didn't like keeping secrets, and he told Edith his real name and why he was in Brazil. She kept quiet about his past, and for the time being Biggs was Mike Haynes to everybody else.

Back in Australia, Charmian was struggling with the unpleasant notoriety Biggs's flight had created. Once the true identity of the Cook family had become known, some of her neighbors began harassing her, throwing milk bottles at her house or letting the air out of her car tires. She and the boys moved to a different section of Melbourne, and she renamed herself Charmian Brent. But the news coverage had made her face so familiar all over Australia that when she

Lonely was Ned Kelly.
Lonely am I
In a crowd of other people.
Lonely is a wife without a husband.
Lonely is a lost child
In the Street.
Lonely is a parent without a child.
NICKEY BRENT.

went out she often heard strangers murmur to one another, "That's Biggs's wife." Reporters kept hounding her for interviews. More than ever, she was looking forward to joining her husband once he was settled. However, Biggs was making very little money and understood how complicated it would be to get his family into Brazil. He wrote Charmian that it would be best for her to remain in Australia for much longer than they had planned on; he even suggested that the children should finish their education there.

Then came disaster. On January 2, 1971, as she was driving home with her three boys after a seaside holiday, a driver ignored her right of way at an intersection and crashed into the passenger side of her car. Ten-year-old Nicky suffered terrible injuries and died before an ambulance could get him to a hospital. Charmian was devastated, and so was Ronald Biggs. When he got her letter, he was swept by the impulse to turn himself in and went immediately to the British consulate. At the last moment, he thought better of it and walked away.

In the months after Nicky's death Biggs wrote Charmian long, emotional letters. In one he assured her, "I love you my way; not always apparent, not always proclaimed, but it's there, very real, deep and eternal." He meant what he said, but in August thoughts of Charmian were partially eclipsed when he met 23-year-old Raimunda Nascimento de Castro, a waitress and sometime call girl he met in a nightclub. She had a volcanic temper and was capable of throwing knives to make a point when she and Biggs argued.

By this time Biggs had been in Rio a year and a half. He had friends, work, a place to live, yet he still felt uneasy and restless in this palmy paradise. He worried about his family — and he also worried about his true identity being discovered by Brazilian officials. Everyone in the country was required to carry identification papers, and the police often stopped people at random to check their documents. Biggs feared his turn would come, and in fact he had a number of close calls. On one occasion, for instance, he was driving through Rio with a friend when they happened on a checkpoint where the

Only hours before his death in a car wreck, 10-year-old Nicky Biggs steadies his upside-down brother Christopher, with little Farley posing beside them for their mother's camera. In a melancholy poem composed after his father had fled to South America *(top)*, Nicky makes Australian bandit and folk hero Ned Kelly the stand-in for Ronald Biggs. Nicky—or "Nickey," as he preferred spelling it—signed with the surname the family was going by at the time.

police were stopping every passing car. The officer put his hand out for the friend's papers, but he ignored Biggs. Another time two panhandlers became angry when Biggs didn't give them any money. They started to fight with him, and a policeman immediately showed up. Biggs was in a sweat, especially because his passport had expired. But the police officer dismissed him with a pleasant "Good day." Biggs joked to himself as he walked away, "Must be my honest face."

Not long after his dustup with the panhandlers Biggs had more reason than ever to worry about the document-crazy police. Mike Haynes wrote from Australia that he had decided to move back to England and needed his passport. He'd told the authorities that he'd lost his, but they told him to find it—they wouldn't issue him a new one. Biggs appreciated his friend's problem, and he sent the passport to Haynes. Biggs was now nobody at all, not even the imposter Mike Haynes.

By now he'd confided his secret to 20 or so people. "I had decided that to remain real friends with people they had to know all about you," he later explained. His revelation didn't excite great interest; the Great Train Robbery had been greeted as sensational news in many places around the world, but the crime seemed hardly to have registered in the consciousness of most Brazilians. Nevertheless, the police there were sure to know about him, and Biggs sometimes wondered whether it might be a relief if they caught him. He even began thinking seriously about turning himself in. At least he'd be free to be himself, even if he was behind bars.

One man who knew Biggs's story was Constantine Benckendorff, an art student from London who met the Great Train Robber during a visit to Rio in 1973. The two hit it off immediately, and Biggs discussed the possibility of surrender with his new friend. Parole was the key issue for Biggs, and he said to Benckendorff, "If it looks as if I might get away with completing ten years and then be set free to begin my life again, I think I could face it." The young man told Biggs he must be "potty" even to think of going back to prison, but he promised to size up the situation when he returned to London. Biggs was also thinking about selling his life story to a journalist. "When you go back to England," he said, "see if you can find a newspaper willing to buy the whole thing; you know, the story and me giving myself up." Because he still wasn't sure he wanted to surrender, his friend must take care to find a trustworthy jour-

nalist who wouldn't run to the law with the news that the long-sought Ronnie Biggs was hiding in Brazil.

Back home, Benckendorff found his man, reporter Colin Mackenzie of the *Daily Express,* a major London tabloid. Mackenzie arrived in Rio in January 1974 with Benckendorff and a photographer. Biggs's fee was to be a handsome £35,000, and he asked that £30,000 be sent to Charmian and the rest to Nascimento.

When Biggs arrived at Mackenzie's hotel for his first interview, he was still absorbing the news Nascimento had delivered that morning: She was pregnant. It saddened him to think of a baby that he might never see if he decided to turn himself in.

Mackenzie and Biggs had settled down with a tape recorder when there was a knock on the door. Benckendorff answered, and in walked a tall, nattily attired man. "Nice to see you again, Ronnie," he said. "Think you'll remember me. It's been a long time." It was Jack Slipper, Detective Chief Superintendent for Scotland Yard. He'd been part of the Yard's squad assigned to hunting down members of the Great Train Robbery gang.

Biggs thought he smelled a rat—Mackenzie. The reporter, he suspected, had gone to the police after learning of his whereabouts from Benckendorff. Whatever the case, it was a terrible blow. He'd hoped he'd get a break on his prison term if he gave himself up, and here were the cops before he'd decided what to do. For his part, Mackenzie would later insist that although he had acted in good faith, a higher-up at the *Daily Express* had tipped off the police without his knowledge.

Whatever the truth of the matter, Jack Slipper had made a big miscalculation. Brazil had never signed a reciprocal extradition treaty with Great Britain, but he thought local authorities would let him be on his way with his Great Train Robber in handcuffs, possibly as early as that same evening. However, the official with the authority to give Slipper the go-ahead, one Inspector Garcia, wasn't going to be rushed into a decision by a foreign policeman. Biggs was whisked off to jail, and Brazilian authorities began mulling over how to handle the affair. Jack Slipper had no choice but to cool his heels that day. There was no telling what would happen.

What happened was salvation by Nascimento. The other men sharing Biggs's cell wanted to know what he had done, and he quickly filled them in. One of the men, a taxi driver named Mario, advised him that if he had a Brazilian child,

Daily Express reporter Colin Mackenzie *(left),* in town from London to interview Biggs, relaxes with him on a balcony overlooking Rio de Janeiro. The city's famous landmark, the cone-shaped Sugarloaf Mountain, rises in the distance.

he would be exempted from extradition. Biggs told him about Nascimento and the news she'd delivered that morning. "But that is beautiful," Mario cried. "If you have a girlfriend pregnant, you have got it made. That is as good as having a baby." Biggs began to cheer up a little.

On the following day Nascimento came to visit him, and when she heard about Mario's legal advice, she went immediately to Inspector Garcia's office. She loved Biggs, she declared, and she intended to have his baby; she wouldn't think of having an abortion. The inspector summoned Biggs and directed him to tell his history beginning with his arrival in Brazil. By the time Biggs had told his tale, Garcia was determined to find a way for the English criminal to stay in Brazil. Quickly devising a public relations campaign, he arranged for a television crew to interview the couple. Before the camera rolled, he gave them some directorial advice:

"You must hold hands and look as if you really love each other. Smile at the camera and say you want to live in Brazil, to be together as a family when the baby is born. Tell the viewers you want to get married."

Several days later Jack Slipper got bad news: Biggs would remain in Brazil while the government deliberated his case. Having no notion when a decision would be reached, Slipper flew back to England empty-handed. Biggs was flown to the capital city of Brasilia, where foreign prisoners are jailed during extradition proceedings. A horde of reporters followed him to Brasilia, for he was almost as hot a story as he had been at the time of the Great Train Robbery 11 years before. To heighten the drama the Sydney *Daily Mirror* bought Charmian Biggs a plane ticket to Brazil and sent a reporter to cover her reunion with Ronnie in prison.

The couple hadn't seen each other for four years, but

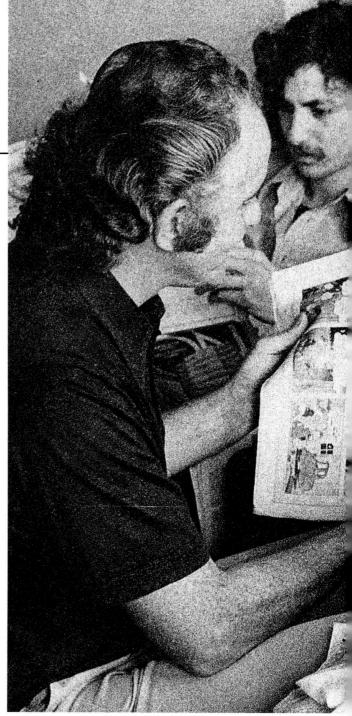

the fact that Biggs was going to be a father put a damper on the reunion. He put it delicately: Charmian was "not happy" about Nascimento's pregnancy. Colin Mackenzie was still on the scene, and when he suggested that the two women meet, Charmian agreed. "Like any woman, I wanted to see the opposition," she explained. "I also wanted to reassure her I didn't bear her any malice." The half-hour the women spent together was reportedly quite civil. They even exchanged gifts—a necklace for Charmian, a ring for the expectant mother. The next day Charmian was on her way home.

Following three months of diplomatic wrangling, the Ministry of Justice decided not to extradite Biggs. However, since he had entered Brazil under a false passport, the ministry refused him permission to remain and gave him 30 days in which to find another country that would be willing to take him in. Biggs's lawyer appealed the decision to the Supreme Court and won. The deportation order was suspended indefinitely. Biggs could stay where he was—as long as he had a little Brazilian citizen to support. In August, Raimunda Nascimento gave birth to Michael Fernand Biggs. The new father was uncommonly grateful for his son's safe delivery.

In May, Charmian had paid one more visit to Brazil, bringing Christopher and Farley with her. Her stay was punctuated by furious quarrels with Biggs, and by the time she went back to Australia it looked as though the marriage was washed up. The couple divorced in 1976, but the relationship wasn't over yet. Charmian went to Brazil in 1981 to attempt a reconciliation but went home to Australia calling Biggs a scrounger on "a giant ego trip."

Thus Ronald Arthur Biggs began life again, as himself. He could forget about those 28 years left to go on his sentence back in England. Biggs was not, however, free as a bird, for the Brazilian government imposed a number of restrictions on him when it suspended his deportation order. He had to report to the police twice a week, and he wasn't allowed to leave the state of Rio de Janeiro. Another limit put a cramp in his social life: He wasn't supposed to be in a bar or a nightclub after 10 p.m. Nor could he marry. But at least as far as his relationship with Nascimento was concerned, this restriction posed no problem. Soon after Michael's birth, she left Brazil for Switzerland, leaving Biggs to care for the baby. She worked as a striptease danc-

er and eventually married a Swiss man and settled there.

Biggs was also banned from holding a job and from giving interviews to the press, but he managed to get around the bans, perhaps because friendly officials looked the other way. As he knew already from his dealings with the *Daily Mirror,* fame could be lucrative. More deals followed, with newspapers, television companies, and authors wanting to publish his life story. He was game for all sorts of new ventures. In 1978 guitarist Steve Jones and drummer Paul Cook of the Sex Pistols rock group met Biggs during a visit to Rio and asked him to be lead singer for a recording.

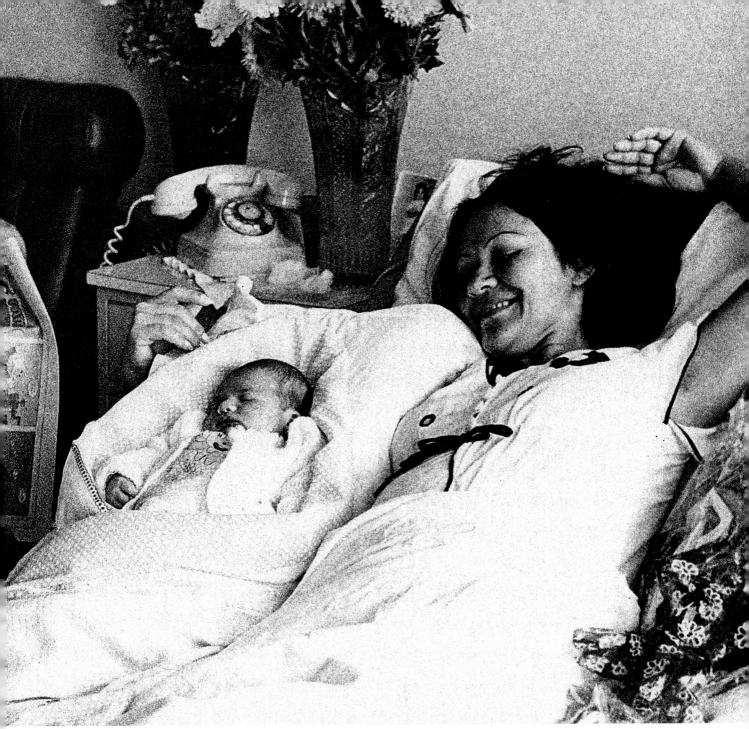

Among Biggs's lyrics were these lines from a song entitled "No One Is Innocent":

> God save the Sex Pistols
> They're a bunch of wholesome blokes.
> They just like wearing filthy clothes
> And swapping filthy jokes.

The record rose to number six on the pop charts in London and sold seven million copies.

Although he was forbidden to do so, Biggs did leave the state of Rio once. The trip wasn't his idea. One afternoon in early 1981, as Biggs was sitting in a barbecue restaurant, two men approached his table. One suddenly put a headlock on him, and the other punched him in the stomach. They carried him out to a van, blindfolded and gagged him, zipped him into a large canvas bag, drove to the Rio airport, and flew him aboard a rented Lear jet to the city of Belem, three hours away. There he was transferred to a 62-foot yacht, and four days later he and his abductors debarked on the Caribbean island of Barbados.

The motive for the kidnapping has never been clear. Two

of the kidnappers were partners in a London security firm. At a press conference they called to crow about their coup, they claimed they'd been paid by a prominent Briton who wanted to see Biggs brought to justice. Some journalists speculated that the abductors were trying to generate publicity for their security company, which specialized in bodyguard services, but the operation seemed extravagantly expensive for an advertising campaign. The kidnappers might also have hoped to sell rights to the story of their exploit for the handsome sort of sum that news of the ever-popular Ronald Biggs commanded. Rumors were floated that Scotland Yard was behind the kidnapping, but hardly anybody believed the agency would stoop so low, even in the case of one of England's most wanted criminals. The now-retired detective Jack Slipper expressed his disapproval of such tactics.

The *Nowcani II,* the yacht on which Biggs was shanghaied out of Brazil, developed engine trouble off Barbados and was rescued by the island's coast guard.

Barbados police officers escort Biggs from court after an extradition hearing. He spent five weeks in custody in Barbados before his lawyers defeated England's demand for his return.

Nevertheless, it looked as though Ronald Biggs was in grave danger, for Barbados had an extradition treaty with Britain. But Biggs got hold of something just as good—three sharp lawyers. They discovered that the treaty had not been voted on by the Barbados Parliament and was therefore invalid. The lucky Ronald Biggs went back to Brazil.

His escape from the clutches of kidnappers made him more famous than ever. Another Biggs was also winning his share of fame. During the legal battle over extradition from Barbados, six-year-old Michael went on Brazilian television to plead for his father's return. "I know that the Queen of England wants my dad," he said, "but I want him, too." A Brazilian executive for CBS Records watched the broadcast and was charmed by Michael's winning ways. He invited him to audition for a children's singing group, and soon Michael became one of Brazil's biggest recording stars. By 1986 the group had cut three gold and four platinum records. With some of the boy's earnings, his proud papa bought an interest in a Copacabana discotheque and a spacious apartment with a swimming pool.

In a 1984 interview Ronald Biggs succinctly stated the obvious: "I've been lucky." Indeed, fortune seems never to stop smiling on him, for in 1993 the Brazilian Supreme Court removed some of the restrictions he'd lived with for 19 years. He no longer was required to check in weekly with the police and was now officially permitted to give interviews to the press—a restriction that he had honored in the breach over and over, without getting in hot water. Biggs was also free to get a license for a gun, adopt a child, drink alcohol, and, if he wished, to marry. The court wouldn't grant him permission to work, but this hardly mattered— Biggs had gotten along very nicely for years in spite of his official lack of income.

Ronald Biggs published his autobiography in 1981, but for a man with so eventful a life it was soon dated. To keep his public abreast of his subsequent adventures, Biggs at the age of 64 was planning another volume of memoirs. Given the Great Train Robber's charmed life, it probably won't be the final installment. ◆

An attractive visitor to Rio poses with the 64-year-old Great Train Robber in 1993 as he cashes in on his notoriety by hawking T-shirts. When a purchase is made, Biggs inscribes a personalized greeting and signs his name.

I know someone who went to Brazil and met Ronnie Biggs... honest!

Τhe Devil has
taken over the Mor-
mon Church.

JOHN SINGER

4

True Believers

There wasn't much sound to speak of—just a muffled boom followed by a concussion that jolted Max and Patsy Lewis awake and knocked a picture off the wall of their home in Marion, Utah. Patsy looked at the clock by the bedside. It read 3 a.m. Max got up and went to the door, stepped out, and peered into the darkness. He saw nothing, shrugged, and went back to bed; maybe it had only been a strong gust of wind hitting the house. Other residents who were roused by the shock thought it might have been snow sliding off their roofs on this bitterly cold Saturday, January 16, 1988.

Shortly after 6 a.m. Max Lewis cranked up his tractor and drove over to plow out the local Mormon church, which he served as custodian. He saw something white fluttering on the wall of the stake center, as Mormons call their places of worship, and at first he thought that pranksters might have festooned the place with toilet paper. But then he realized that curtains were billowing from a shattered window. Lewis rushed inside. Three small fires were burning. He doused them with a hose—and as he looked around, he knew what had happened.

The stake center had been bombed by someone who meant to make an emphatic statement. Doors were blown off their hinges; furnishings and glass were reduced to splinters and shards. The chapel was virtually destroyed: Interior and exterior walls were cracked and the roof was torn open. At the point of explosion a crater three feet wide by two feet deep had been blasted from the concrete floor. Officers from half a dozen agencies converged on the little town. They figured that the bomber had used between 50 and 75 pounds of dynamite. Engineers estimated that it would cost the Mormon church a million dollars to repair the center, if it was worth salvaging at all.

No one had to wonder for very long about the identity of the bomber. A spearlike cedar pole was stuck into the snow on the grounds of the stake center. Affixed to the spear were nine hawk feathers, and burned into the wood, along with several arcane symbols that meant nothing to

investigators, were the initials "JS" and a date: "January 18, 1979." On that day, nine years before, police had shot and killed John Singer.

Singer, a 48-year-old zealot and Mormon excommunicant, had long been bitterly at odds with both religious and civil authorities on issues that ranged from the number of wives he had to how he wanted his seven children to be educated. He, his two wives, and the children had lived on a little farm in the hamlet of Marion, barely a mile away from the stake center and some 35 miles east of Salt Lake City. After its founder's death the clan stayed on and was now headed by Singer's 26-year-old son-in-law Addam Swapp. The Singer-Swapp family had changed little through the years, still fervently practicing Mormonism as they saw it, still polygamous, still fiercely independent of both churchly and civil rule—and all of them bleakly vengeful over the death of John Singer.

In the snow that had just blanketed the area on the night of the bombing, police found footprints leading from the Singer-Swapp compound to the bombed-out stake center. Another line of tracks led back from the center to the compound. It seemed obvious that Addam Swapp, as an act of both retribution and defiance, had desecrated this Church of Jesus Christ of Latter-day Saints. But he was not alone. Vickie Singer, the 45-year-old widow of the dead patriarch, spoke for Addam Swapp and them all.

"We are not going to make peace," she told reporters. "We will not surrender. We are going into battle. The talking is over with. Yes, there will be killing, death. We are not hateful people. We are not a vicious people, but we are sick to the core of this hellish, corrupt society and the powers that rule it.

"I am telling you now," the widow said, "that God will come out of his hiding place and will show forth his arm." And with that, the siege was on, the police grimly determined to uphold their authority, the Singer-Swapps steadfast in resisting it. The standoff would last for 13 desperate days and in the end would bring the death of one man,

Addam Swapp's symbolic declaration of war, a cedar pole festooned with hawk feathers, stands beside a fence bordering the grounds of the bombed-out Kamas Stake Center *(background)*. He left incriminating footprints between the stake center and his home.

the wounding of another, and the dissolution of a family whose members had asked nothing more of the world than to be left alone.

The bitter battle wouldn't have surprised early Mormon believers. Dispute and violence were central to the Mormon experience for generations after the new religion sprang forth in 1830 from the fertile mind of a 25-year-old New York State farm boy.

Prophet Joseph Smith, Jr., and his apostle, Brigham Young, preached of divine revelation, of direct, ongoing contact with God, not only for themselves but for every man, woman, and child who believed. The believers called themselves Latter-day Saints, or merely Saints, and they trusted in the Mormon preachment that God would restore relations between himself and the faithful to what they had been in the days of Jesus Christ: God—an intimate, active, one-on-one God—would lead his newly chosen people down the path of righteousness to salvation.

In the *Book of Mormon*—which scoffers regarded as a half-baked concoction of the King James Version of the Bible, contemporary archaeology, and Indian lore—Smith laid down the foundations of his faith. A second massive tome, *Doctrine and Covenants*, recorded every revelation delivered to Smith as "Prophet, Seer and Revelator." There were a lot of them, 138 sections involving all of life from church hierarchy (all worthy white males over the age of 12 were priests of God) to the desirability of plural marriage (Smith had at least 40 wives, Young 70 or more).

From its Saints the church demanded absolute obedience. It further required unstinting work on its behalf and a considerable outpouring of wealth; every Mormon family was expected to tithe, or donate at least 10 percent of its annual income to the church.

Mormon leaders, in the early years at least, were contemptuous of other religions. "Behold, there are save two churches only," proclaimed Smith in the *Book of Mormon.* "The one is the church of the Lamb of God, and the other is the church of the Devil." As a consequence of this disdain, members of the church tended to be clannish, rigidly disciplined, and fervidly missionary.

Their attitudes—and the reaction of nonbelievers to their frequent commercial success—thrust the Mormons into frequent, sometimes bloody, conflict with their neighbors. In the 1830s and 1840s, Mormons were driven from commu-

Drafted during the Korean War, Singer *(left)* was dissuaded from deserting the Marine Corps by his uncle, Gustav Weller.

John Singer, shown here as a teenager, left war-torn Germany for New York City in 1946 to live with an aunt and uncle.

nities they had established in New York, Ohio, Missouri, and Illinois. Joseph Smith was jailed, beaten, tarred, and finally, in 1844, killed by an angry mob. After a three-year struggle, Brigham Young took over as the savior, and in 1847 he led his followers across 1,400 miles of prairie and mountain in search of the Saints' promised land of Zion. They found it in the harsh Utah desert, where, by dint of incredible labor and uncommon shrewdness, they founded Salt Lake City and flourished.

Over the next decades, economic needs and the desire for statehood mellowed the church. In 1890, after a pragmatic revelation known as the Great Accommodation, then-Prophet Wilford Woodruff declared an end to Mormon polygamy; shortly thereafter, Utah was accepted into statehood. Eighty-eight years later, in the Second Great Accommodation, Prophet Spencer Kimball put forth a revelation accepting blacks into the priesthood. In between, the Saints adjusted to outside society in numerous other ways—and kept prospering until, by the 1990s, Mormondom counted something like 8,000,000 adherents worldwide. The vast majority submitted to their leaders without question. But not the fundamentalists, about 50,000 of whom remained in Utah and elsewhere in the American West, keeping to themselves, practicing polygamy, believing in sepa-

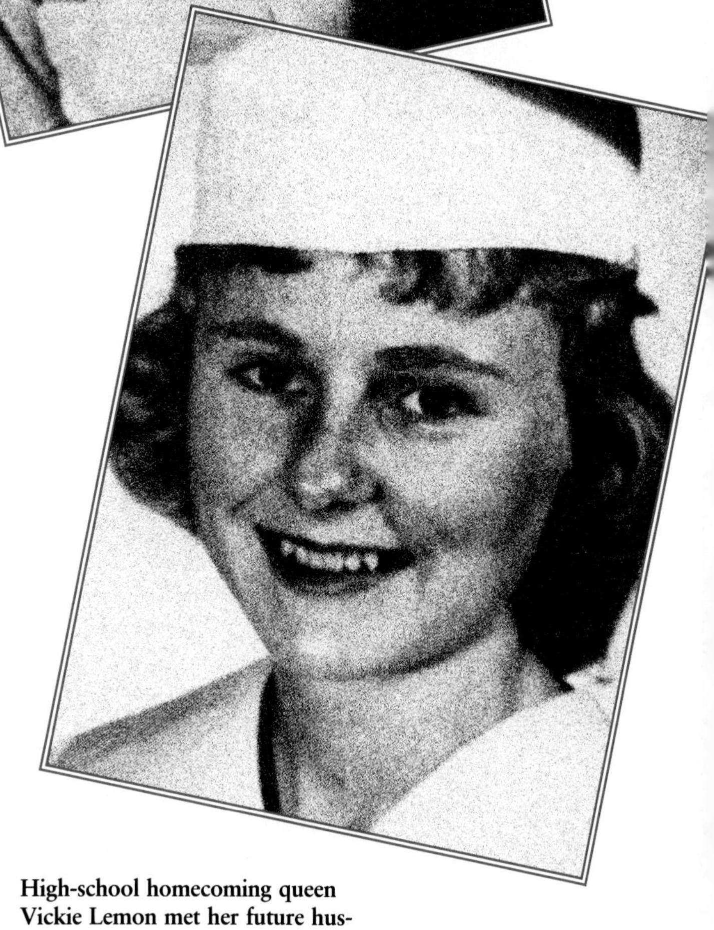

High-school homecoming queen Vickie Lemon met her future husband, John Singer, the summer after this graduation picture was taken.

ration of the races, and relying—as did Joseph Smith—on direct revelations from God to chart their lives. John Singer, Addam Swapp, and their kin counted themselves among these Mormons.

Rigidity of belief and an abhorrence of authority had been burned into John Singer's personality at an early age. He entered the world on January 6, 1931, born to German parents temporarily living in Brooklyn, New York. They were not a happy couple: Mother Charlotte was a resolute Mormon convert, father Hans an equally determined Nazi, who hurried home to Germany with his family in 1932 to glory in Adolf Hitler's promised Thousand-Year Reich. Bad to begin with, the shouting matches between the Singers grew worse as more children arrived: another son, Harald, and two daughters, Edeltraud and Heidi. They were Nazis and would never become Mormons, Hans said again and again. To drive home the point he enrolled the boys in an SS preparatory school as soon as they were old enough.

But the Mormonism was sticking and the Hitlerism was not. Within 18 months both lads were expelled by the SS for "rebellious behavior"—making stink bombs. By now the war was on, with Hans at the front, while Charlotte somehow endured with the children in Berlin—and spent her hours instilling in them an ironclad Mormonism.

John never saw his father again. Though Hans survived as a prisoner in France, Charlotte divorced him and he faded into unpleasant memory. Meanwhile, the 14-year-old boy was undergoing a religious experience that would fortify his faith forever. In the final days of the war, the family left Berlin, hoping to make their way south and west to Munich. On the way, John became separated from the others. One night, in the gutted, rubble-strewn maze of Leipzig, a German soldier took the lost youth in hand and for the next seven hours silently led Singer through the devastated city to the railroad station where he could board a train for Munich. The soldier then vanished into the predawn darkness.

It was clear to John Singer that his guide had been one of the *Book of Mormon*'s Nephites, immortal Israelites who had been dispatched by God to spread his word across the American continent.

The next year, 1946, John immigrated to the United States—as an American citizen by reason of his Brooklyn birthplace—and moved in with relatives in New York City. While waiting for his foreign-born family members to secure their papers, he attended high school, studied English (although a heavy German accent would never leave him), learned TV repair in shop class, and immersed himself in the Mormon church. At last, in 1949, Charlotte and the others arrived from Germany. They bought a 10-year-old Chevrolet and headed west to Utah and the land of Zion.

In many respects the Mormon homeland was in truth paradise, certainly compared with war-ravaged Germany. John's brother, Harald, acquired a bachelor's degree, then a master's and a fine job as a certified public accountant; the girls married well; everyone chipped in to supplement what Charlotte earned working as a maid. John himself made good money repairing TV sets, did a two-year stint in the Marines during the Korean War, then returned to pick up the TV business and help Charlotte's brother, Gustav Weller, run a 160-acre farm in the Kamas Valley. John worked so hard on the farm that within four years Uncle Gus gave him a two-and-a-half-acre piece of land as a homestead. And there John built a sturdy log house, felling trees in the nearby forest and lovingly fitting the timbers together with his own hands. He put in plumbing, electricity, and a big wood-burning stove for heat and cooking.

John also gleaned from his uncle a stern Mormonism, much closer, he believed, to the fundamental otherworldliness of Joseph Smith's teachings than the accommodations of modern Mormon leaders. In this, he and Uncle Gus were set apart from their neighbors.

At 30, John Singer was making it in life; he was strong, hardworking, family-oriented, decent in all respects. But he was not particularly well liked. The folks in the Kamas area thought him strange. Part of it was his thick accent, which made people uncomfortable about his youth in Nazi Germany. Then there was the buckskin clothing he sometimes wore. But what mainly annoyed people was the superintense—abrasive, they thought—way that John Singer went about his religion.

Even among Mormons he stood out, forever quoting the scriptures and finding fault with modern-day Mormonism. At sacrament meetings—one of several forms of worship—it annoyed Singer that some of the teachers were women, and that they were actually instructing men, the priests of Mormondom. It upset him further that these teachers were not studying the scriptures themselves, but merely parroting lessons prepared by church elders. When there were contradictions between the lessons and the scriptures—and John found a great many—he would politely but insistently raise his questions and urge that the worshipers study *Doctrine and Covenants* or, better yet, listen to the words of God, not the opinions of men.

Singer did nothing to further his popularity by likening strict obedience to church leaders to German slavishness toward Hitler. A higher moral law prevailed, he said.

The townsfolk's feelings about the maverick in their midst hardened in the summer of 1961—not over subtle theological issues, but because of Singer's personal life: He had started dating Vickie Lemon. They made an unlikely couple, this rough-hewn, scripture-spouting German and the bright, bubbly 18-year-old blonde Mormon girl who had just graduated from South Summit High School. Vickie impressed people as the sort of young woman likely to succeed at almost anything: She'd been homecoming queen and organizer of the Twirlerettes baton drill team in high school, and she was a talented dancer intent on studying ballet at the University of Utah.

Her parents were appalled when they learned that she was seeing a man 12 years her senior—and an oddball at that. But Vickie had powerful feelings for John Singer. She liked his strength, his confidence, his freedom of spirit and maturity, and she wanted to learn more from him about her religion. Vickie entered the university. However, her heart wasn't in it, and she dropped out after a year. As the romance blossomed between the teenager and her older suitor, Vickie's frantic mother threatened to throw herself under a train; her aunt tried to get her niece committed to a mental hospital. All to no avail. Demonstrating the same gritty stubbornness that characterized her future husband, Vickie steadily refused to give John up. The pair eloped to Elko, Nevada, where on September 9, 1963, they were married by a justice of the peace.

Neither one had known such fulfillment. The farm seemed to them an earthly heaven. The Singers raised chickens for eggs and meat, expanded the vegetable garden, and put in a berry patch. They canned and preserved and dug a root cellar for winter. Vickie taught John about cooking and sewing; he tutored her in plumbing, heating, and carpentry. Evenings they and Uncle Gus studied the scriptures together. John continued his TV repair business. They bought supplies in Kamas and sometimes attended social gatherings at the nearby stake center, but they were happiest alone on the little farm, secure from the woes and complexities of the world outside.

In the Mormon way, healthy, handsome children started arriving: Heidi in 1964, Suzanne a year later, next Timothy. Eventually there would be seven young Singers. The first three babies were delivered by doctors at the hospital in nearby Coalville; but then Vickie and John decided that natural childbirth was best, boned up on it, and successfully delivered Charlotte, Joseph, Benjamin, and Israel at home, without help. The Lord, Vickie said, would see her through.

Also in the Mormon way, the Singers strove for self-sufficiency. After Charlotte was born, they bought a couple of dairy cows, then a calf to raise for beef. The Singers laid in stocks of cloth, building materials, and an extra workshop of carpentry tools. Huge supplies of firewood and kerosene made electricity more a convenience than a necessity. The $200 or so that John earned from television repairs each month sufficed for food staples, gasoline, electricity, the telephone, and clothing. All else the Singers provided for themselves.

In time there would be a still larger family to provide for. Shortly after John and Vickie were wed, John had experienced a dream involving two women. He and Vickie both took this to be a revelation from God that they should practice the original Mormon custom of plural marriage. There was little question who the second wife would be. For several years, Uncle Gus had counseled Shirley Black, a pleasant, attractive woman a year older than John. Shirley's husband was a crude, abusive construction worker, and she was hungry for emotional support and sympathy. Gus furnished it at first, and later so did John and Vickie.

Within a few years Shirley herself had received a message from God "that I belong to John and Vickie, that someday I would be a member of their family. But I should be patient, for this event would not take place for several years."

Not all of John Singer's dreams were as pleasant as the one suggesting that he take another wife. Another dream, one that came around 1970, revealed to him, as he wrote in his journal, "that the Devil has taken over the Mormon Church." And so it seemed to John and Vickie from the constant disputes they encountered at meetings. The dissension became so unpleasant that the Singers withdrew from active membership and stopped paying the obligatory tithes. As a Mormon priest, John performed the sacraments himself and baptized the children when each reached the age of eight.

The church could not allow this breakaway behavior to go unanswered. In May 1972 John and Vickie were called to trial before the president of the Kamas Stake, his two counselors, and 12 high priests.

Did they fully accept the present-day teachings of the General Authorities of the Church of Jesus Christ of Latter-day Saints? the court asked.

Did they accept Joseph Fielding Smith, the current president, as "Prophet, Seer and Revelator of God"?

No, he could not, John responded to both questions.

Finally, they were asked if they accepted the 1890 manifesto banning plural marriages.

Again John's answer was no.

The Singers were asked to leave the room while the High Council conferred. When they were summoned to return, John and Vickie learned that they had been excommunicated from the Mormon church.

It was only a short step to the next level of conflict.

Less than a year after his excommunication, on March 29, 1973, John Singer walked into the South Summit Elementary School, where Heidi attended third grade, Suzanne second grade, and Timothy kindergarten. Singer made for the principal's office, a textbook Heidi had brought home clamped in his hand. The principal, Rex Walker, was one of the Mormon high priests who had excommunicated the Singers. He may have guessed something of what was coming.

Singer flipped open the textbook to a picture of George Washington, Martin Luther King, Jr., and Betsy Ross, with a caption describing the trio as great Americans. Singer objected to painting the black civil rights leader as a hero, the equal of Washington. Mormon scriptures discouraged intermingling of the races. Walker should know this full well, said Singer.

When the principal protested that it was the state of Utah that decided on textbooks and that he didn't find the picture offensive in any case, Singer angrily declared that he would have to remove his children from school and teach them himself.

Walker was astounded. He reminded Singer that Utah had a compulsory school attendance law requiring children to attend either public school or a qualified private school.

Singer promptly reminded Walker that the Constitution of the United States prevented the state from interfering with his religious beliefs. Then John Singer marched to the classrooms, collected his children, and took them home. Heidi and Suzanne were delighted; their classmates, aping parental attitudes, had made cruel fun of the Singer girls' religious upbringing and their long, pioneer-style dresses. Timothy was tickled, too; one little girl in kindergarten had kept trying to kiss him.

Yet everyone, even the youngest, would soon understand how serious things had become. The Martin Luther King issue, as Singer later confessed, was merely "a motive," a spark that touched off some preexisting kindling. John and Vickie had long been disturbed about modern-day education with its emphasis on book learning at the expense of practical skills necessary to survive the cataclysms that they believed would come. The permissiveness of schools, with smoking, liquor, dope, crime, and teenage pregnancies, was another big problem. No, the children belonged at home, free from such corrupting influences and taught by their loving parents.

There followed almost six years of struggle between the Singers and the state of Utah, its school system, its courts, and law enforcement agencies. Ordinarily the state was not rigid about enforcing its compulsory school law; it was, in fact, quite flexible, largely leaving the matter up to the local school boards. The South Summit Board of Education, which had jurisdiction in the Singer matter, was amenable to some compromise, as were the juvenile courts when they entered the case. The Singers on occasion also amended their position. But there were points beyond which neither side would go, and in the end no lasting compromise was possible.

Knowing the family's determination, the authorities reluctantly agreed that the children could be taught at home — provided that the Singers follow a prescribed curriculum and that the kids were tested regularly for achievement. Vickie and John strove conscientiously to comply with these conditions, and while the children fell slightly behind their school-enrolled peers, the program was deemed satisfactory. But the Singers were increasingly unhappy. John and Vickie, chafing under the school board's standards and struggling to balance the needs of education with those of their farm, began reducing and modifying the board's curriculum. By April 1975 the Singer children were so far behind that Anthony Powell, school psychologist for the South Summit district, told John that the youngsters really ought to be back in school.

That was not possible, said John. Vickie added that their children were interested in the Kingdom of God, not academic competition. The Lord, not the schools, would guide them though life, and the kids would progress at their own pace. Powell decided to let it go for a while.

In May Singer began building a one-room schoolhouse on the farm. He finished it in June, fixed up some old furniture for it, and installed a blackboard and a wood-burning stove. The children helped paint their schoolhouse a bright red. The building gave the family a renewed sense of independence. Vickie and John held classes all summer—but with little attention to standard hours or curriculum. After morning chores the kids studied academic basics for two or three hours, then in the afternoon learned the skills necessary to their life: gardening, animal care, painting, carpentry, cooking, canning, and cutting firewood.

Schooling suffered another setback that fall, when Vickie fell ill with tooth abscesses so severe that the infection afflicted her entire body. The Singers didn't believe in doctors but relied on their faith to heal them. It took five months, until February, before Vickie could teach the children again. And by then, she and John had resolved that they must free themselves from the school board yoke once and for all. When Tony Powell called on April 1, 1976, Vickie told him that there would be no further testing. She and John had decided to restore lost freedoms, she told Powell. The principal one was the freedom to educate their children according to their religious beliefs.

Powell took the news with resignation. The school board had no quarrel with religion, he replied, but this was a secular issue. He urged Vickie to look at it that way. Soon, they would have little choice but to do so.

On August 23, 1977, there began a series of hearings before a succession of judges, to determine whether John and Vickie Singer were guilty of child neglect under the Utah Code. In January of 1978 they were found guilty and received the maximum sentence of 60 days in jail and a fine of $299 each. The judge further ordered the Singer children placed in temporary custody of the state Division of Family Services. But he offered to suspend it all if the parents would agree to one simple demand: that they and the children be tested and evaluated so that the judge could make a final determination in the case. The Singers disputed the ultimatum vigorously, but by November University of Utah psychologist Victor B. Cline had finished his evaluation. He submitted a report that was at once heartwarming and heartrending.

"The Singers," wrote Cline, "have put together a remarkably happy and cohesive family. The husband and wife have a strong marriage with much love and affection and mutual support between the two." Moreover, continued the psychologist, "they are greatly committed to the task of raising obedient, loving, responsible and resourceful children and are doing a truly remarkable job of this."

John's IQ of 121 put him in the top eight percent among men of his age—"a tough, competent, resourceful, some-

John Singer and children pose before the log house that he built with his own hands *(left)*. From left to right are Joseph, Charlotte, Timothy and his little brother Israel, Suzanne, Benjamin, John Singer, and Heidi. The girls wear the long dresses that were prescribed for Mormon women until the 1920s. Above, family members relax in their sunny living-dining room.

John Singer *(left)* and Vickie
Singer *(above)* preside over lessons in the family's one-room

Vickie Singer *(left)* displays the long hair declared by the early Mormon church to be a source of divine strength. John Singer's second wife, Shirley Black, shown below with her youngest child, Julie Anna, also adhered to such fundamentalist beliefs.

times stubborn, shrewd self-made man," Cline concluded. "There is absolutely nothing suggestive of mental illness." Vickie proved to have an IQ of 108, putting her in the top 30 percent of her age group, and was "of sound mind, knows clearly what she is doing and is overall a remarkably resourceful and adequate woman." The children likewise, wrote Cline, were "happy, kind, affectionate. I found a remarkably powerful chemistry that bound them together with the parents totally committed to the unity of the family regardless of what sacrifices had to be made."

So why not leave them alone? The kids' IQs were the problem. They tested a "shocking" average 34 points below their parents, Cline found. And since IQ is largely inherited—and the children therefore were probably naturally bright—the only logical explanation had to be their isolation and inadequate education. In other words, they were being intellectually deprived. Cline strongly recommended "peaceful negotiations" in order to get the children "back into some kind of high-quality educational experience."

The court offered the Singers three choices: Return the children to public school, enroll them in a certified private school, or accept a tutor in their home. To John, the dispute had come full circle. After more months of fruitless negotiation in early 1978, the Singers rejected all three options.

They also rejected one final compromise that would have given them almost complete victory. This was arranged by the directors of a private school in Salt Lake City—acquaintances of the judge on the case—who offered to design a home study program that would preserve the values of the Singers while satisfying the state's demands. They reminded the judge, after visiting the Singers, that because of the skills being taught the children, it was a virtual certainty that none would ever become a welfare case. They also pointed out that, after years of well-publicized conflict, returning the children to public school would be like "leading lambs to the slaughter" owing to the prejudices of teachers and students.

The judge accepted the offer—but the Singers did not. Even this would compromise their principles. In the opinion of the well-meaning educators, the refusal would eventually make a martyr of John Singer.

In fact, Singer was already preparing for his martyrdom. In June of 1977 he had told his longtime acquaintance Sheriff Ron Robinson that he would rather die than go against his religious beliefs. Then, one morning that August, John

had carried his rifle and two pistols to Hoyt's Canyon on the farm. He used a natural pool there as a baptismal font—and it was there that he dedicated his weapons to the Lord, promising the Almighty that he would use them only to defend his family and their rights.

He took to wearing a gun, and he had not left the farm since December of 1977, when a warrant was issued for his arrest for ignoring a summons to appear in court after the Cline interviews.

Now, in mid-July of 1978, Singer flouted another of society's norms. With Vickie's assent and participation, John in his role as Mormon priest performed the ceremony sealing himself to Shirley Black in "celestial marriage." Shirley and the four youngest of her seven children immediately moved into a house John had built in the compound. It made no difference to the three adults that Shirley had not yet divorced her wife-beating husband. But to those outside the family, the action was seen as an act of defiance. It eroded much of Singer's public support and reinforced official determination to do something about the children.

The first attempt at forcible arrest was a farce. Sheriff Robinson knew that he couldn't handle John Singer by himself, and he had no heart for it anyway. He went for help to the Utah Department of Public Safety, the administrative umbrella for the Utah Highway Patrol, the Division of Narcotics and Liquor Law Enforcement, and three other agencies. Narcotics and Liquor got the job of going after Singer, and before long Director Robert Wadman had a plan.

The telephone came to life in the Singer house on the morning of October 18. The caller identified himself as Bob Wilson, a reporter for the *Los Angeles Times*. The media had long since learned of the human interest story out in Utah, and the Singer family had been cooperative with them all. Wilson offered John $600 for an exclusive story. Singer courteously declined any money but agreed to see Wilson and a couple of photographers the next afternoon. Wilson hoped that they could meet in private, he said. He had a couple of questions that were, well, delicate.

The *Times* men arrived at sunset the next day, driving up the lane in a black Lincoln Continental followed by a blue van. John came to meet them. The tall, thirtyish man climbing out of the Lincoln introduced himself as Bob Wilson. They shook hands, and Wilson led Singer to the van to meet his camera crew. A stocky man came forward. He was introduced as Grant Larsen. The man grasped John's hand.

Near Halloween, Shirley Black *(left)* and Vickie Singer demonstrate pumpkin carving as several of their children watch.

The trampoline John Singer installed near the goat pen *(rear)* was big enough to accommodate a crowd.

At that instant, they pounced. Larsen grabbed Singer's right wrist and started twisting it up behind him. From behind, Wilson hurled a forearm around Singer's neck and groped for his left wrist. The third man lunged for Singer's legs. All three started dragging him into the van.

Singer started yelling and fighting back with every ounce of the considerable strength in his wiry body. Looking out a window of the house, Suzanne saw her father struggling and screamed a warning to her mother. In a flash, Vickie was out the front door, followed by Shirley and the kids, all of them racing to Singer's rescue.

Somehow Singer managed to brace his left arm against the van. He got a leg free and pushed away from the vehicle, carrying his assailants with him down onto the ground. Larsen whipped out a pair of handcuffs. But Singer was too strong and too quick. With his free left hand he reached into his waistband and jerked out a .38-caliber pistol. He cocked the weapon and leveled it at his attackers. "Let go or I'll shoot," Singer shouted—just as two women and a gang of children slammed into the invaders, screaming, kicking, punching, and scratching.

The three law officers backed away, Larsen flashing his badge. With a warning from Singer, they piled into their vehicles and raced off down the lane.

When real reporters arrived an hour later, Singer was standing guard in the dark, a rifle in his hands. Vickie and Shirley wore pistols. Timmy held his BB gun; Heidi had her bow and a quiver full of arrows, while the younger kids had sheathed knives strapped to their waists.

It turned out that "Bob Wilson" was none other than Division of Narcotics boss Robert Wadman himself. Grant Larsen was his assistant director, and the third man, Bill Riggs, was an officer in the division. Four sheriff's cars had been waiting up the road to roar in once Singer was in custody. Their task was to arrest Vickie, haul the Singer children off to the Family Services detention center, and return the Black children to their father.

The police swore that they'd identified themselves and told Singer that he was under arrest the moment they grabbed him. He remembered no such thing. Whatever the facts, John Singer now faced three counts of aggravated assault for resisting arrest with a gun. Before long, the authorities would come after the Singers again. And most ominous, an order forbidding the use of deadly force in dealing with Singer was now lifted.

But the police were apprehensive. The media had lambasted them for impersonating journalists in the "*L.A. Times* caper," as it was instantly termed. They couldn't afford to make fools of themselves again. Wadman, Sheriff Robinson, and their colleagues considered cutting off the Singers' water, food, and electricity but discarded the idea because of the women and children. They thought about putting a tranquilizer into the water, about using a U.S. Army armored personnel carrier to charge the house and lobbing tear gas through the windows, about calling in a SWAT team from one of the cities—plans all rejected for fear of harming the women and children.

But there was pressure to do something—soon. Harald Singer petitioned Governor Scott Matheson to step in and help settle the case peacefully. He refused. Sheriff Robinson—a friend of Singer's and best man at the wedding of Shirley and Dean Black—was told to move promptly or face contempt-of-court charges himself.

According to the plan that finally evolved, the officers

Returning home from an out-of-state job to find that his children were living at the Singer farm, Dean Black *(far left)* demanded that Sheriff Ron Robinson *(left)* retrieve them.

10 o'clock Wadman and Sheriff Robinson met with Grant Larsen and a team of 10 carefully chosen officers: two Summit County deputy sheriffs, six narcotics agents, and a pair of highway patrolmen. Wadman handed out aerial photographs of the Singer compound and outlined the plan.

According to the surveillance log, Singer's daughter Heidi ordinarily picked up the family's mail at the box 200 yards down the lane from the compound. But in recent days Singer had taken to collecting the mail himself, walking out alone to the mailbox. The police may have wondered why Singer would place himself in such obvious jeopardy. The answer, as John had told Vickie, was that he feared the police might grab Heidi as a way of getting at him. At any rate, to the lawmen Singer's trek to the mailbox seemed to afford them the best chance they were likely to get to

would try to catch John Singer alone and confront him with a show of force so massive that he would have no choice but to surrender.

Intensive surveillance began on December 27. Sheriff Robinson rented an empty house with a view of the Singer compound, and a deputy made arrangements for a couple of snowmobiles. Three officers disguised in ski clothes and posing as vacationers arrived in a station wagon bearing out-of-state license plates. They set up an observation post by a window and glued themselves to binoculars. From time to time one or two men hit the snowmobiles to relieve the monotony and get the lay of the land. After 12 hours a relief shift arrived — and so it went, around-the-clock for 18 days. Every movement in the compound was dutifully noted, every visitor, every license plate logged and checked out. The Singers immediately saw through the disguises and stared right back through their own binoculars.

By January 17 the police felt that they had enough information to work up an arrest scenario. That morning at

take him without endangering the women and children.

In the course of their snowmobile excursions, the authorities had discovered an abandoned A-frame cabin not far from the compound. When Singer went out to get the mail, two-man teams riding snowmobiles could converge on him from both the rented house and the A-frame. As the plan developed, the police settled on five such teams, armed with .38-caliber revolvers and 12-gauge shotguns. That would make the odds 10 against one.

Grant Larsen, stationed in the A-frame with a walkie-talkie radio, would run the operation. Also in the A-frame would be a couple of snowmobile teams ready to roar down on Singer at Larsen's command. Three teams would wait in the house. Their leader would be Lieutenant Lewis Jolley, 32, a 10-year law enforcement veteran. Although Jolley was the Narcotics Division's weapons instructor, he had never fired his own weapon at a human.

Someone asked about medical help, just in case anybody got hurt. Wadman said that an ambulance anywhere in the vicinity could give away the game; the arresting officers would, however, have immediate access to the University of Utah's Lifeline helicopter unit, a service geared to transport gravely ill or wounded people to immediate aid. One final thing: Wadman instructed his men to use their weapons only in self-defense.

At least one of the men, Narcotics Division officer Ron Gunderson, thought the plan sounded dangerous and told his boss so in the hallway after Wadman had outlined the scheme. But Wadman was in a hurry and they didn't discuss Gunderson's objections. Gunderson's objection was simple: The operation's success hinged on the assumption that a reasonable man, when surrounded and confronted by a show of force, would submit. The problem was, he tried to explain, John Singer was not a reasonable man.

It snowed that night, a heavy storm that persisted the next day and grounded the Lifeline chopper. Wadman sent his men out anyway. Nobody, except maybe Gunderson, expected much trouble.

At 8:30 a.m. Singer and Shirley emerged from the house and took a short walk in the woods in back of the compound. John had a rifle with him. The police stayed put. The couple eventually went back inside.

At 12:15 p.m. Singer came out of the house with a snow blower. He was dressed in a blue, sheepskin-lined jacket and wearing a blue watch cap. He again had the rifle. He set it down at the gate by the lane, got the blower going, and cleared a parking place inside the gate, then opened the gate and started clearing the lane.

As Singer worked, watching police saw the mailman drive up. Singer stopped the snow blower and began trudging through the snow toward the mailbox.

Now was the time.

Larsen issued the order to begin as soon as Singer reached the mailbox. The two teams in the A-frame ran out and jumped onto their snowmobiles. So did the three teams under Lieutenant Jolley in the house up the road.

John Singer heard the racket of the engines, saw the snow-spouting machines, and saw the men with the shotguns. He yanked a pistol from his belt and started to run. Jolley's snowmobile bore down on him. Still running, Singer half-turned and waved the pistol in the lawmen's direction.

"Halt. Police. Drop your gun," shouted Jolley.

Singer kept going, turning, waving the pistol.

A second snowmobile with Gunderson aboard raced

A neighbor tries to comfort a weeping Edeltraud Lawrence, John Singer's sister, near the place where he was shot.

along behind Jolley. "Police officers. Drop your gun," hollered Gunderson.

Jolley's snowmobile was closing fast, only about 25 feet from the running man with the pistol. The lieutenant said later that he saw Singer raise the pistol and close one eye as if taking aim. Jolley sighted down the shotgun barrel and pulled the trigger.

The heavy load of double-O buckshot knocked John Singer flat on his face in the snow. He tried to lift himself but fell back.

Jolley and Gunderson were on him in an instant. They disarmed Singer and rolled him over. His eyes were open, staring. Blood gushed from his mouth and nose.

Watching from the house, 10-year-old Charlotte saw her father go down and screamed for Vickie. But John Singer's wife had already heard the shotgun blast. She took one look out the window and grabbed a rifle as she dashed out the door. Heidi, Shirley, and Timothy were right behind her. At the gate, Timothy picked up John's rifle and ran on.

The other officers had come up by now. A deputy sheriff who knew the Singers called out to the women and children and warned them to stop. Vickie and the children ceased running but kept walking out to the lane.

Before they got to where Singer lay, the police had lifted him into one of their pickup trucks and started off for Summit County Hospital, about 20 miles away in Coalville. When Vickie and the children reached the spot where he had fallen, they stared down at John's watch cap and a pool of blood slowly spreading in the snow.

In the pickup, officers radioed ahead to alert the hospital emergency room. It took them half an hour over snowy roads to reach Coalville. Nurses and doctors were waiting. But it was much too late. The examining surgeon worked over the riddled body for a minute or two. Then, at 1:15, he pronounced John Singer dead. As an autopsy later revealed, the massive 12-gauge load had slammed into Singer's back and right side. Six of the pellets destroyed his heart, aorta, and lungs.

John Singer's funeral took place on Monday, January 22, at the Larkin Mortuary in Salt Lake City. With tears streaming down his face, John's brother, Harald, delivered an impassioned eulogy before a crowd of 350 people. Harald spoke for nearly an hour, and he left no doubt whatever about whom he blamed for his brother's death. He accused the state of Utah of plain, cold-blooded murder. "Twelve days after his 48th birthday, he was felled by an assassin's bullet," cried Harald. "My brother, in my opinion, was murdered." At which a rumbling chorus of "Amen" filled the chapel.

While he lived, his neighbors felt free to criticize John Singer's eccentric behavior. But to independent and self-sufficient Mormons—even those who'd disliked Singer and disagreed with him—he did not deserve to die because of it. The circumstances of Singer's death struck a resonant chord. After all, the essence of their early history had pitted the Mormons—the outsiders, the oddballs—against entrenched powers. What was so different today?

Many of the news media echoed the sentiments expressed at Singer's funeral. Over the months the stubborn loner had often been characterized in the press as the heroic David beset by the Goliath of the state, a man who stood fearlessly with his family against the system. His death triggered a public outcry. And the indignation swelled when it was learned that Vickie Singer had been arrested right after her husband's death and separated from her distraught children. She thought the officers were taking her to see John, but she was clapped into Salt Lake County Jail instead, while her youngsters were handed over to the Division of Family Services.

The judge responsible for the widow's treatment quickly rethought the matter and reunited the family. But the outrage was such that practically everyone known to be connected with the case got threatening letters and phone calls. The state capitol was evacuated after a bomb scare. The governor kept his children home from school after receiving anonymous threats. Utah's attorney general started wearing a bulletproof vest and carrying a pistol for protection. Sheriff Ron Robinson had to get an unlisted phone to escape the dinning obscenities. Officials quickly sealed away the names of Lieutenant Lewis Jolley and the other arresting officers, ostensibly to protect them from public opinion; it took a lawsuit for Vickie Singer to learn who had killed her husband.

The outcry quickly grew so loud that the FBI mounted a month-long investigation of the killing, concluding by clearing Utah authorities of any illegality. But the image of malfeasance remained, and the local authorities aggravated their cause by botching the aftermath as badly as they'd botched the arrest. No one had bothered to mark or photograph the shooting scene, take measurements, or collect evidence; the shell casing from Jolley's shotgun never was found. The arrest teams just packed up their gear and left.

Perhaps shock, rather than ineptitude, explained the behavior of the officers, some of whom seemed deeply affected at the bloody outcome of the Singer stakeout. Lewis Jolley broke down and wept after shooting Singer, belying the public image that would form of him as trigger happy and heartless. Nevertheless, the actions of officialdom continued to suggest, at best, bumbling inefficiency: Four shotgun pellets were recovered from Singer's body by the medical examiner, but nobody could remember what happened to them. Deputy Sheriff Fred Eley admitted that "they just flat disappeared." There were public mutterings that a cover-up was afoot.

All the while, Vickie Singer was struggling to repair something of her life and the lives of her children. "Nighttime was the hardest," she later wrote in her journal. "The children would groan or make little whimpering noises in their disturbed sleep." She still dreaded that she might lose them over the education issue, and she knew that she had an agonizing decision to make. If she compromised with the law, she would break her covenant with God and violate a principle that her husband had been willing to die for; if she held fast, the state could take her youngsters away from her.

It was Harald who came to her rescue. He arranged for a private school in Salt Lake City to supervise Vickie's home schooling efforts. The school would train her, supply books, test the children, and report to the juvenile court. The one proviso was that the Summit County school district stay completely away from the education of the Singer children.

In May, the school advised the court of satisfactory progress in all respects. The arrangement was succeeding—though at great cost to Vickie Singer. She was managing the farm and teaching the children single-handedly; Shirley had moved out to be near her own children, who'd been awarded to their father. But the strain of work was the least of it for John Singer's widow. She felt, as she had all along, that the compromise still shackled her to an odious establishment. "Oh that we could be free and take the Holy Spirit as our guide in our schooling," she wrote in her journal. "How I loathe the injustice of this corrupt system."

But Vickie Singer had a tremendous revelation to sustain her: Her cherished John would return to life one day. He would be resurrected. She believed it absolutely.

The vision had come to her in early February, three weeks or so after John's death. Reading in the *Book of Mormon*, Vickie had come across a passage that promised: "But behold, the life of my servant shall be in my hand; therefore they shall not hurt him, although he shall be marred because of them. Yet I will heal him, for I will show them that my wisdom is greater than the cunning of the devil."

The grieving woman discovered a strong feeling "that this servant God spoke of is my beloved husband." She wrote: "Something marvelous is coming. I believe that John will come back! Something *great* is coming! Praise God for this beautiful hope." Lying in bed that night, Vickie Singer could sense her husband's presence. "It seems that John's spirit hugged me—I felt it," she wrote. "Oh, the Lord is good."

And before long, it seemed to Vickie Singer that the good Lord had sent her a sturdy staff to lean on while she waited for John. This pillar of support was Addam Swapp, a young Mormon, like herself a fundamental believer, who became her son-in-law in September of 1980.

Even those who learned to fear and hate him had to confess that Addam Swapp was a fine figure of a man—tall, lean, open-faced, with a square jaw, direct brown eyes, and a shock of thick, dark hair. His personality appeared to mirror his looks: He spoke earnestly, in a polite, pleasant baritone. He enjoyed a good laugh and maybe a little mischief. He was strong-minded and determined to assert his individuality, but overall he seemed gentle, modest, loyal, intelligent, and destined for a peaceable, successful career in whatever field he chose. Nothing in his background undermined that impression.

The first of eight children born to Ramon and Harriet Swapp, Addam began life on April 6, 1961—a significant date because Joseph Smith had officially founded the Mormon church on April 6, 1830. Addam spent his childhood and adolescence in Salt Lake City and Fairview, a small town 100 miles to the southwest. He was closely attached to his schoolteacher father and housewife mother, and to his siblings, particularly Jonathan, six years his junior. Young Addam did well enough through high school to earn a B-plus average, but he much preferred hunting and fishing with his father to scholastics. "I've always believed that sitting in classrooms for eight hours a day was wrong," he said later, and added in retrospect, "school was something that got me to see the wickedness of society."

The eternal verities taught by Joseph Smith played a large role in Addam Swapp's upbringing. Ramon Swapp taught his son the importance of prayer and of reading deeply in the scriptures, where the boy would find things that were not taught by the modern church. As Addam matured, he developed a powerful sense of oneness with founder Joseph Smith, so vulnerable and harassed in those early years of the new religion. Young Swapp felt an attraction to the underdog, and like Joseph Smith, he put his faith in the power of God. During moments of stress Addam always insisted that "the Lord will see us through." His father reminded him that faith alone might not put bread on the table, but Addam remained steadfast in his belief that faith was everything.

This fundamental Mormonism grew stronger when Addam entered the University of Utah in the fall of 1979. He intended to study mathematics, but he spent most of his time in the library, devouring Mormon history in the source documents of the early prophets. The persecutions seemed to him remarkably like those suffered by John Singer, whose slaying had filled him with revulsion. Addam went back into the papers and periodicals to learn all about Singer and was amazed at what he found. "I couldn't believe what I was reading," he recalled. "So much of what he said was what I knew to be true. It seemed like we agreed on almost everything."

The two men had never met, but the bond that young Swapp felt for Singer was both deep and complex. Watching the aftermath of Singer's killing on television, Addam had thought his heart would burst at the sight of 14-year-old Heidi, grief-stricken and weeping. "I'm going to marry that girl," he said to himself.

In the winter of 1980, Swapp paid a visit to the farm and got along wonderfully with Vickie—"I felt the spirit of her," he said—and started courting Heidi. The girl was not greatly impressed at first; it sometimes seemed that Addam made more of a fuss about John's books than he did about her. But Heidi gradually came around, and the two were married in September, when Heidi had just turned 16 and Addam was not quite 20. By now he believed, as Vickie did, that John Singer would be resurrected. Addam and Vickie expected the millennium to begin during their lifetime—and everything in the family's life was predicated on this belief.

Addam and Heidi moved into Shirley's yellow house in the Singer compound. By 1983 they had two children, a boy and a girl, and that year Addam followed in John's footsteps by taking another wife: Heidi's 14-year-old sister Charlotte. In 1986 Charlotte bore Addam a son; Heidi gave him three more children, two boys and a girl.

Father and wives were as fiercely determined as John and Vickie Singer had ever been to educate their youngsters at home, free of what they regarded as the state's corrupting influences. This time, doubtless remembering the Singer tragedy and its aftermath, the authorities were content to leave well enough alone when the first two children reached school age. But there were other confrontations in bitter profusion.

On April 21, 1980, Vickie Singer had stunned the state of Utah by filing a $110 million wrongful death suit against virtually every state employee who'd ever been involved with the Singers. These ranged from the head of the Summit County school district to the state attorney general, Highway Patrol superintendent, county attorney, and the as-yet-unnamed officers who had attempted to arrest John Singer. Representing Vickie was Gerry Spence, a flamboyant Wyoming attorney with a flair for oratory, a taste for buckskin jackets, and a national reputation for winning controversial cases that pitted the underdog against some formidable establishment opponent. Spence accused the state of violating Singer's constitutional rights in the matter of education, of gross negligence in planning and executing his arrest, and of conspiring to withhold information about the shooting.

The case dragged along for 28 months and never went to trial. All Vickie Singer got out of it was the identity of the officers who had tried to arrest her husband. The judge threw out the conspiracy charge for lack of evidence and ruled that no negligence was involved in the arrest: Singer had a duty to submit peaceably, the court said. When he refused and drew a gun, the officers had the right to use deadly force if they thought that their lives were in danger. As for Utah's compulsory education law, the judge concluded that it was "not so obviously unconstitutional" and decided that the defendants were within their rights in upholding the law. Spence took the case all the way to the U.S. Supreme Court, which in 1985 declined to intervene—and that was that.

Vickie Singer had greater success in a simultaneous battle to retain the homestead given to John by his uncle, Gus

Three generations of the Singer-Swapp clan sit for a portrait. From left in the back row are Timothy Singer, Heidi Singer Swapp and daughter Lillian, Addam Swapp and son Isaiah, Charlotte Singer Swapp with son John, Vickie Singer, and Hans Singer. In front are Joseph Singer *(far left)* and Israel Singer *(far right)*. Jonathan Swapp sits at center with Arazella, Hans, and Vanya Swapp, Addam and Heidi's children.

Weller. The old man had long since passed on, but his sons Jared and Sam claimed that since no deed had been transferred, the land legally belonged to them. The arguments flew back and forth until, on December 15, 1980, the Weller boys sent John's widow an eviction notice. She could pay back rent—and agree to pay in the future—or she could vacate the premises.

Vickie Singer was furious. John had worked the whole 160-acre farm for many years without receiving so much as a penny's worth of wages. In gratitude and payment, his uncle had conferred their two and a half acres by verbal covenant in 1957. John had scrupulously paid the taxes every year since, and relations with surrounding homesteads had never been a problem. "We are actually very good neighbors," said Addam Swapp. Witnesses testified to all of that, but it still took until April of 1982 before a judge ruled in Vickie's favor and forced the Wellers to issue her a deed.

Other aggravations piled on. The Wellers disputed her right to use an access lane from the nearby highway to the farm. There was a long and complicated squabble with the Wellers and the Marion Water Company over water resources; at one point, Jared Weller forcibly prevented Addam Swapp and 14-year-old Timothy Singer from opening up an irrigation ditch to the farm that had been closed off.

All the squabbling was extremely upsetting to Vickie Singer, and as time went on it also had a profound effect on her son-in-law. Something seemed to snap in Addam Swapp. Feeling his loved ones tormented constantly, his own powerful sense of rectitude aroused, Swapp began to lash out at all those whom he perceived as his enemies. Stealing out at night, Swapp spray-painted accusations of John Singer's murder on the Weller garage doors, and on those of Tony Powell, the school psychologist, and on a Halloween display in the yard of the school superintendent. But it was the letters, not the vandalism, that got him into serious trouble.

Addam Swapp had always been greatly taken by the written word. He carried on a voluminous correspondence with friends and relatives, wrote reams of poetry, transcribed every dream that came to him, along with what he perceived as revelations, the moral equivalent of scripture. And now he deluged his oppressors with a veritable flood of furiously accusatory and threatening letters.

On May 25, 1987, Swapp wrote to the Summit County commissioner and other prominent local citizens: "You people consented to and helped in the killing of John Singer. You are members of an evil society and an evil church with Satan at its head."

There were many other letters, and they grew progressively angrier and more inclusive. On September 14 a four-page handwritten missive went out to Mormon church leaders, school board members, judges, attorneys, and others, perhaps 20 people in all. Swapp accused them of "cold-blooded murder. You took an innocent man's life through careful planning and cunning." The killing, he wrote, was part of a satanic conspiracy ordered by the "hierarchy of the Mormon Church in Salt Lake City to get rid of that polygamist any way you can. When you had him shot down like a hardened criminal (in the back repeatedly), his blood poured upon the ground. It poured out on each one of your hands and heads. It is a blood you cannot wash off."

This blood, wrote Swapp in fury, "cries to the Lord for vengeance! The Lord's holy arm cannot be stayed any longer." The guilty were beyond redemption, Swapp raged, and would now "suffer the wrath of a just God."

Two weeks later, the Utah attorney general at the time of Singer's death received a letter from Addam: "You are a murderer! A member of the great Kingdom of Satan; a conspirator of blood!" said the frenzied script. "You cannot weasel out from under the sight of Almighty God—He sees all of your dark dealings. Your involvement with John's murder is known to Him. He knows your conspiracy with state officials."

Many recipients simply tossed their letters into the wastebasket. But others were alarmed and went to the police. On October 27, Fred Eley, who had replaced Ron Robinson as sheriff, drove out to the Singer-Swapp farm with a deputy.

Sheriff Eley had already spoken to Swapp about the vandalism and letters, and Addam had denied any personal threats. "God will take care of that," the sheriff recalled Swapp saying. Eley—who felt that Swapp, while possibly a fanatic and a hothead, was probably harmless—intended on the October trip merely to have another talk, a sort of take-it-easy-kid warning. But when he and the deputy walked past the No Trespassing signs, Swapp came out to meet them wearing a couple of revolvers. "Get off my land," he shouted. "You have three more steps. You murdered John Singer." Swapp unholstered both guns and pointed them at the lawmen.

That was a felony. Losing patience, the sheriff told Swapp that he would return with a warrant. Then he and the deputy left. "You better not come up here again," Swapp yelled after them, firing a pistol into the air for emphasis.

Sometime later a couple of shotgun-toting deputies hauled Addam's brother Jonathan out of a pickup truck at night, thinking that he was Addam. Charlotte Swapp was in the truck with her baby, John, and the lawmen apparently held a shotgun on her, too. The incident only angered the family further.

The flash point came shortly after the New Year. Although John Singer's bloodstained clothing, the photographs of his riddled body, and various videotapes, including those of his funeral, had played a role in Vickie Singer's wrongful death litigation, she hadn't shown much interest over the years in obtaining them. But somehow—no one seems to know for sure exactly how—the materials came into the family's possession in early January. On Wednesday, January 13, Heidi rented a video player in Kamas. That night the entire family sat sobbing as they relived John's funeral. Over the next few days, the final collision course was set.

The notion of bombing the Kamas Stake Center came to Addam Swapp as a revelation, he said, a direct contact with God. In part, Swapp would say later, the decision was a culmination of his outrage. "Look what's happening to this family. Look what these people are doing to us." A statement had to be made—one that would mark the way to John Singer's resurrection and a purging of evil from the Mormon church.

The bombing itself had a ritual precision. Swapp had 87 sticks of dynamite and 50 pounds of prill—an explosive mixture of ammonium nitrate fertilizer and fuel oil. He carefully bundled 81 sticks of dynamite into nine packets of nine sticks each, one for every year since Singer's death. He used three more sticks to detonate the prill. The remaining three sticks he reserved for another, unrevealed, symbolism. That much explosive properly placed against structural supports would have collapsed the building, but Swapp positioned it in the exact center of the church, where it would pulverize the contents rather than destroy the building. He wanted the explosion to effect a symbolic cleansing of the church. Then he measured out a length of fuse, lighted it, and returned home through the snow to stand outside in the 20-below-zero cold and watch through binoculars.

The building muffled the blast. But Swapp felt the heavy shock wave and saw flames shoot through the roof to a height of 200 feet "like a million devils were coming out of it," he said. At dawn he observed the fire engines, the arrival of the first police, and finally, the army of besiegers cordoning off the farm. Inside the main house with him were 14 people: Vickie and four of her sons, ranging in age from 12 to 21; Addam's 21-year-old brother, Jonathan; and the two Swapp wives and their six children, aged 10 months to six years.

All but the littlest child understood what was going on, and all were unshakably with Swapp. The compound had plenty of supplies, a small arsenal of weapons, and an abundance of ammunition. In the days ahead, Addam would rely heavily on his brother Jonathan and Vickie's 21-year-old son, Timothy. Three years before, Timothy had been crippled in a logging accident. He now got around in a wheelchair, but he was a tiger nonetheless—which in the end would lead to tragedy.

The operation against Addam Swapp was one of the most spectacular actions of its kind in Utah law enforcement history. The FBI arrived the next morning; the U.S. Bureau of Alcohol, Tobacco, and Firearms came into it because of the bomb; the Utah Department of Public Safety and the local jurisdictions had scores of men on the scene. In all, something like 150 law officers eventually converged on the Singer-Swapp compound, with 70 on duty at any given time. A command post was set up on the grounds of the stake center, with half a dozen heavy generators providing power for bunkhouse trailers, heaters, lights, cookstoves, radios, and other necessary paraphernalia. The authorities employed helicopters, fixed-wing aircraft, all manner of vehicles, ultimately including U.S. Army armored personnel carriers.

From the start, the commanders imposed one ironbound rule: No one, not under any circumstances, was ever to fire at the house. The children must not be endangered. No one ever violated this order.

At first, the police were hopeful that their massive show of force would bring Swapp to his senses and effect a swift surrender. But massive force had produced no such effect on John Singer nine years before, nor would it do so on Addam Swapp. If anything, it strengthened Addam's resolve to continue "the mighty work which God had begun."

Dressed in camouflage, a member of a SWAT team enters the Kamas Stake Center a few hours after it was bombed. Tearing a huge hole in the roof and splintering furniture in the chapel *(right),* the blast did more than $1 million worth of damage.

A federal agent watches a colleague descend from a platform set up for surveillance of the Singer-Swapp farm.

After the initial telephone conversation with reporters Saturday evening, during which Vickie proclaimed the family's defiance, Addam Swapp yanked out the phone to silence its incessant ringing. The next day, Sunday, authorities allowed Roger Bates, Swapp's cousin, to enter the compound. Returning, Bates relayed the word that the family had vowed not to leave the house until John Singer had risen from the dead. "They're just waiting for John to come home—to be resurrected," said Bates, adding, "They have weapons. If the police go up there and storm the place, there will be bloodshed." Someone asked him if Swapp and his kin had thought about being killed. "Yes, the family is prepared to die," answered Bates. "Whatever happens is all in the hands of the Lord."

It began to look like a long siege. "We're operating under the assumption that a direct confrontation will lead to violence," said Douglas Bodrero, Utah's Deputy Commissioner of Public Safety. The authorities announced that they intended to wait it out while they attempted to reestablish contact with the family. "All we want is communication— to resolve this thing peacefully," promised Bodrero's boss, John T. Nielsen.

The house remained ominously silent as Monday, January 18, rolled around. A plume of smoke curling up from the chimney of the main house was the only sign of life within the compound. This might be a very bad day, everybody knew, and tension among the authorities grew palpable when the hands of the clock moved toward noon. John Singer had been slain at 12:30 p.m. exactly nine years before. Lawmen wondered what Addam Swapp might do—maybe mark the moment with some sort of ceremony or possibly erupt into violence.

Police snapped alert when a couple of family members were spotted in the yard around the house. But they were only bringing in firewood, and the besiegers let out a whoosh of relief when the anniversary moment passed without incident.

Later that snowy afternoon, authorities tried again to make contact with the family. In the hope that they could reestablish communication with Swapp, the police brought in Roger Bates and sent him down the lane to the house, carrying new telephone equipment. Soon Bates returned with the gear; Swapp was not interested in talking. He was just waiting for the police to attack, said Bates—waiting for that and for John Singer's resurrection.

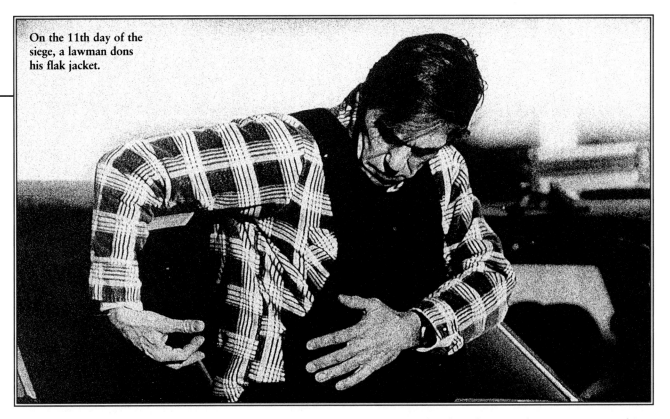

On the 11th day of the siege, a lawman dons his flak jacket.

By now state and federal warrants had been sworn out against Addam Swapp and Vickie Singer charging them with aggravated arson, possession of an infernal machine (the bomb), and various acts of criminal mischief—all felonies of one sort or another.

On Tuesday, the 19th, Addam Swapp reconnected the phone and held a brief, noncommittal conversation with an officer, which the authorities declared encouraging.

Then, for some reason, they decided to step up the pressure. In the afternoon, technicians erected a big bank of floodlights aimed at the house windows. When the lights went on that evening, the Swapps and Singers started shooting. And the pressure on the family increased: Down from the clouds roared a single-engine light airplane to buzz the compound repeatedly—"intelligence gathering," the authorities called it. Next, a SWAT team in white camouflage suits moved across the snow closer to the compound. Then an ambulance was brought up near the compound, "merely as an observation post," said Bodrero.

Four times Tuesday night and early Wednesday morning shots rang out from the house, perhaps 65 rounds in all. The fire seemed to be aimed at the lights. The police turned them off, then flashed them on again, and on and off all night long. They said that none of the lights had been damaged and no one injured. Strictly obeying orders, the police refrained from firing back at the house.

At 3:45 Wednesday afternoon the warrants arrived in a noisily whap-whapping helicopter that dropped the citations on the compound along with a demand to surrender. Watching through binoculars, the police saw a rifle-carrying family member dash out and retrieve the message canister. A police spokesman emphasized that the messages "expressed our concern for them, their families, and their children especially."

No response issued from the compound. To the media, cousin Roger Bates confirmed and embellished what he had told police earlier. "Addam wants a confrontation with law officials," said Bates. "He believes if there is one, John Singer will be resurrected—that he will stop the confrontation—making the way and preparing for the Second Coming." Added Bates, in a bit of bravado: "Try to serve a warrant against God and the people he's protecting."

On Thursday, there were brief moments of anticipation when surveillance teams noticed messages being flashed from the house, first with a mirror against the lowering sun at 4:15 p.m. and again with a lantern at 6:10 p.m. The messages were in a halting Morse code. But hope turned sour when experts deciphered the dots and dashes. "Cops not telling truth," they read. The family had obviously been following the media coverage on radio and TV and meant to get a message out to reporters.

Thus far the besiegers had made no move to interfere with

utilities going to the farm. But now they reconsidered. "As long as they can stay up there and watch the whole event on television and have all the amenities, and feel comfortable in their surroundings, there is little incentive to discuss a peaceful solution to the situation," asserted Bodrero. The next morning sharpshooters blew away connections to a transformer at the head of the lane, chopping off power to the compound.

It was now Friday, January 22. The siege was in its seventh day, and the frustration level soared. So did the pressure level. Down swooped the buzzing aircraft. Armed SWAT teams raced around the area on racketing snowmobiles. More floodlights rolled into position just at dusk.

The night became an exercise in psychological warfare, with the brilliant floodlights flashing on and off while blinding flares arced eerily into the sky. The airplane returned to swoop down through the darkness, adding its din to the scene. More shots, the flat cracks of high-

powered rifles, came from the house, at 5:32 a.m. and 5:36 a.m. Again, no one was hit.

On Saturday, the authorities found a pipe leading from a nearby spring to the house; they severed it, thereby cutting at least part of the family's water supply. They also upped the ante by installing public address loudspeakers at the edge of the compound. At 10 o'clock that night an earsplitting, high-pitched whine filled the air, so piercing that observers a mile away were rattled by it.

The early-morning hours of Sunday saw another sleep-robbing light show. A flare went up at 12:45 a.m. The floodlights burst on simultaneously, then blacked out at 3:35 a.m. Minutes later, red flares bloodied the sky—at 3:51, 3:56, and 4:01 a.m. The banks of floodlights blazed on again at 4:06 a.m. amid more buzzing aircraft and more snarling snowmobiles.

When the loudspeaker started up on Sunday night, Addam Swapp stood it for an hour and a half. Then he and two others came out of the house and fired into the public-address system. The speakers still whined away. Two hours lat-

Harriet Swapp displays a picket sign in an unsuccessful attempt to persuade officials to let her and her husband, Ramon, visit their besieged family.

In an attempt to keep the Singers and Swapps awake nights, floodlights like the one mounted on the military jeep above were beamed at the farmhouse windows. Drafted by authorities to try to negotiate an end to the standoff, Roger Bates *(below)*, Vickie Singer's son-in-law and a cousin of the Swapps, pauses to talk to a reporter as he leaves the farm.

A week into the siege, a phosphorous flare launched by FBI agents casts a brilliant, eerie light over the Singer-Swapp compound in the early-morning darkness.

er the trio raced out of the house and down the lane to the speakers. While lawmen watched through their night glasses, the three yanked the speakers off their mountings, ran back with them to the compound, and destroyed them with rifle fire. "Long live freedom, justice, and liberty," hollered a male voice.

Monday, January 25, marked the 10th day of standoff with no end in sight. The authorities added a flashing, high-intensity strobe light to their store of annoyances. But they were coming up short on fresh ideas, and everybody knew it, foremost among them Utah's governor, Norman H. Bangerter.

On Sunday night, Bangerter had met with Public Safety Commissioner Nielsen and Deputy Director Bodrero, after which Bodrero grimly told the media: "The governor is sensing we are running out of options. He's concerned this is deteriorating." Nevertheless, said Bodrero, "the governor is desirous we continue on a passive approach to bring this to a peaceful resolution."

Addam Swapp's parents, Ramon and Harriet, had of-

fered, even pleaded, to visit their son and act as mediators. The authorities refused. Not knowing Swapp's state of mind, not being able to communicate with him, they reasoned that for all they knew, he might have had a revelation to destroy his parents because they'd failed to join his cause.

But the officials did pick up on a similar offer made by Ogden Kraut, a longtime friend of the Singers, himself a polygamist and fundamentalist Mormon. He went up to the house Monday to see them and deliver cereal and milk for the children. Everybody was standing up to the ordeal just fine, he reported on his return. In fact, the kids were playing and making such a racket that the adults could scarcely carry on a conversation.

Kraut went back the next day, Tuesday, with a box of disposable diapers and some household medical supplies. He also carried with him a letter to "Dear Vickie and Addam" from Norman Bangerter. The governor wrote that he had "great compassion and understanding for families. The children are the real victims of this standoff and for their sake it should be ended immediately." Bangerter guar-

**With Addam in the lead, the Swapp
brothers carry rifles as they leave the
house to attend to farm chores.**

160

anteed that no harm would come to anyone and that he would use his influence "to see that the children remain with their natural mothers."

Kraut went up on Wednesday to bring back the replies. The response left lawmen grim. In two long letters, Vickie Singer and Addam Swapp flatly rejected any possibility of surrender. Swapp told the governor that he didn't acknowledge the government of the United States as having any jurisdiction over him whatsoever. He declared the farm and family to be a free nation and warned: "We will Defend ourselves in any manner we see fit. DO NOT COME AGAINST US. LEAVE THIS VALLEY IMMEDIATELY."

That night the harassments began anew as a plan to capture Addam Swapp was set in motion. Under cover of darkness FBI agents entered an unoccupied house—Roger and Suzanne Bates had once lived there—at the head of the lane leading to the compound. With them went Lieutenant Fred House, a state corrections officer and K-9 specialist. He brought two attack dogs. Meanwhile, other officers replaced the destroyed loudspeakers—and booby-trapped the

PA system with flash-bang grenades designed to temporarily blind anyone who triggered them. The idea was to incapacitate Swapp if and when he tried to remove the speakers. House would then loose his dogs at the blinded Swapp, and the FBI men would rush in to take him. The agents would be covered by two armored personnel carriers that would block any fire from the farmhouse.

The scheme almost worked. That night Swapp approached the speakers, but instead of trying to remove them, he took a shot that tipped them over. The grenades flashed, but not enough to disable him, and he ran back to the farmhouse. The federal men and the dog handler resumed their vigil in the former Bates house.

At 8:30 a.m. the capture team got another chance. The watching agents saw Addam and Jonathan, both carrying rifles, leave the farmhouse and walk down to the goat pen that stood between the main house and the lawmen's hiding place. It took only a few minutes to milk the goats. When the two brothers started back, Lieutenant House launched the dogs—and everything went terribly wrong.

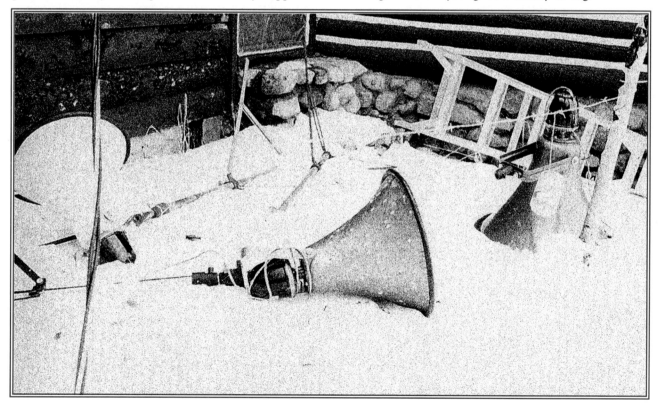

**Tormented by the earsplitting whine
directed at them, family members shot
these three loudspeakers and took
them back to the house.**

HEIDI'S HOUSE

CHARLOTTE'S HOUSE

SCHOOLHOUSE

TIMOTHY

MAIN HOUSE

GOAT PEN

POLICE LIEUTENANT
SHOT HERE

BATES HOUSE

In an aerial photograph of the
Singer-Swapp compound taken
during the siege, the window of
the main house from which Timothy Singer fired in Lieutenant Fred
House's direction is circled. The
circle at the Bates house indicates
the lieutenant's position when he
was hit by one of Tim's bullets.

The dogs started toward their targets but then hesitated. Fred House opened the door and, in K-9 fashion, urged them forward with voice and arm commands. Simultaneously, the crippled Timothy Singer, who was watching and giving cover from an open bedroom window, saw the dogs. He yelled: "They've got dogs! Get up here! Get up here! They've got dogs!" Timothy started firing his .30-caliber carbine as Addam and Jonathan raced for the safety of the farmhouse.

Memories play tricks in moments of extreme stress, and what happened next is a matter of dispute. Ever after, Timothy Singer maintained that he was shooting at the dogs to protect the Swapp brothers; the police accused him of shooting at the door where Lieutenant House was standing. In any event, one high-velocity .30-caliber slug hit 36-year-old Fred House in precisely the wrong place: a seam between protective plates on his flak jacket, penetrating his abdomen and severing his aorta before exiting his right side. House went down, mortally wounded.

The FBI asserted that Addam and Jonathan fired their rifles as they ran for home. The Swapp brothers denied it.

Whatever the case, after House was shot the two FBI agents rushed from their hiding place and aimed two shots with M-16 automatic rifles at the fleeing brothers. One bullet missed. The other caught Addam in the left forearm, passed through, entered his chest and lodged in his left lung near the heart. He stumbled, caught himself, and staggered on into the house after Jonathan.

Inside, pandemonium erupted, the men shouting, the women and children screaming and crying. "I've been hit!" gasped Addam. Then he pulled up his shirt and saw the gaping hole in his chest. He grabbed a towel and pressed it against the wound. He thought he might be dying. He thought of his family—the shooting, the danger. He threw open the door and lurched outside waving the bloody towel.

It was over.

Fred House was rushed by helicopter to the University of Utah hospital, where he was pronounced dead on arrival. Addam Swapp was luckier. After a three-hour operation, doctors at the hospital managed to save him, though they had to leave the bullet in his lung because it was

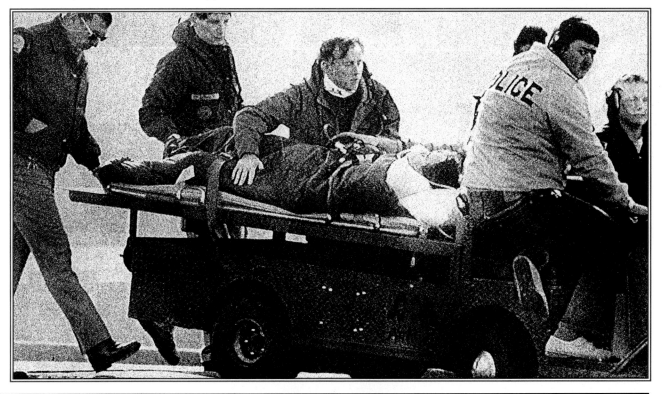

Critically wounded, Addam Swapp is rushed to a helicopter for transport to a hospital in Salt Lake City.

too risky to remove it. While Swapp recovered, police kept him chained to his hospital bed and under 24-hour guard.

Harriet and Ramon Swapp hurried to the scene and soon took temporary custody of the nine Swapp and Singer children under 18. All the adults—Vickie Singer, Heidi and Charlotte Swapp, Jonathan Swapp, and Timothy Singer—went to jail. It took until February before authorities released Swapp's two wives and they were reunited with their young children. But the others were remanded for trial on a long list of federal and state charges beginning with arson and ending with murder.

Searching the compound, authorities learned just how dangerous the family had become—and also how restrained it had been during the siege. Investigators found no fewer than 16 firearms ranging from sawed-off shotguns to pistols and automatic rifles, 8,300 rounds of ammunition, along with 22 sticks of dynamite and 44 blasting caps.

The 13-day federal trial added some interesting details about the last moments of the standoff. Not only had the K-9 dogs failed to attack the Swapp brothers; in their confusion and fear when their handler went down, the animals had raced back to the stakeout and assaulted the FBI agents. Moreover, an agent standing near Lieutenant House had come within a hair's breadth of death himself. Examining his flak vest, he found one of Timothy Singer's .30-caliber slugs lodged in the armor. At the time, he'd thought he'd been hit by a chunk of plaster.

There never was much question of guilt or innocence on most of the charges. Addam Swapp readily admitted bombing the Kamas stake center, and he, Vickie, and the two younger men remained defiant. Addam appeared in court wearing a John Singer-style buckskin jacket, lectured the judge on God's law, and at one point called a Salt Lake City radio talk show to plead his case over the airwaves.

On Monday, May 9, 1988, a federal jury of seven men and five women returned guilty verdicts against all four family members for arson and resisting arrest. In addition, Addam, Jonathan, and Timothy were found guilty of second-degree attempted murder for shooting at FBI agents during the standoff. A number of jurors had argued for acquittal on this last charge. "We didn't really think they had any intention to shoot anybody at all, because they had so many opportunities to do so," said one jury member. But the fact that they had shot at all made the question of opportunity irrelevant in the end.

The death of Lieutenant Fred House was Utah's business and the state trial began on December 5. Both Addam and Timothy, particularly, mourned the officer's death. An FBI agent testified that Swapp, when first told of the killing had groaned, "Oh, Tim, why did you do it? Oh, Tim, why did you have to shoot?" Timothy insisted that he was shooting in the general direction of the dogs. The idea of killing a human was "the sickest, sickest" thing he could imagine. "I was pretty mad, but I didn't want to kill anyone," he said. "I didn't fire at any people. I didn't see any people."

The jury must have felt some sympathy. In rendering their guilty verdict, the panel reduced the charges from second-degree murder to manslaughter for Timothy and Addam and to negligent homicide for Jonathan.

When Addam, Timothy, and Jonathan went to prison, each man knew that he faced a long sentence on both federal and state convictions. Five years later, the courts had not yet reached a final decision as to just how long those sentences would be.

Vickie Singer was released from jail on June 8, 1991, after serving three and a half years of her five-year sentence. She returned home to live quietly in Marion and later married a man she'd met—a fellow prisoner—in the prison sewing factory. "It seems that people are leaving her alone," says Addam, who still keeps in touch. Jonathan and Timothy also "are doing pretty well" as they serve their time, according to Swapp.

Addam himself has suffered a further blow. "My sweet Heidi left me," he says without rancor. "I still love her. I really respect her. But she went through a lot of hell. She's with another man now. She considers it as being remarried." Charlotte is still with him, and bringing up little John, teaching the boy herself in home school. Swapp is hopeful. "There is a saying going around the prison: If a woman will stay with you for five years, she'll stay with you forever."

Addam Swapp still fervently believes in the Kingdom of God as he sees it, still believes in the resurrection of John Singer, still believes in the Second Coming of Jesus Christ. Whatever has happened to him is God's will, he is certain. "God is Number One," he says. "He is the most important element in our lives, more important than family, wife, homes, lands, our good name, our reputations. He is everything." His own future, says Swapp quietly, "is in God's hands. Let Him take care of it. Right now, I just work on trying to love people." ◆

Handcuffed and in leg irons, Vickie Singer *(above, center)*, Charlotte Swapp *(left)*, and Heidi Swapp are escorted
back to jail after being arraigned in federal court. Dressed in buckskin jackets, Jonathan *(below, left)* and Addam Swapp look
relaxed and hopeful during their murder trial in state court. Addam's jacket, which bears religious symbols worked with
beads, was a joint birthday present from wives Charlotte and Heidi.

ADDAM SWAPP

For acts he carried out to avenge John Singer's
death, Addam Swapp *(right)* was given long
sentences in two trials.

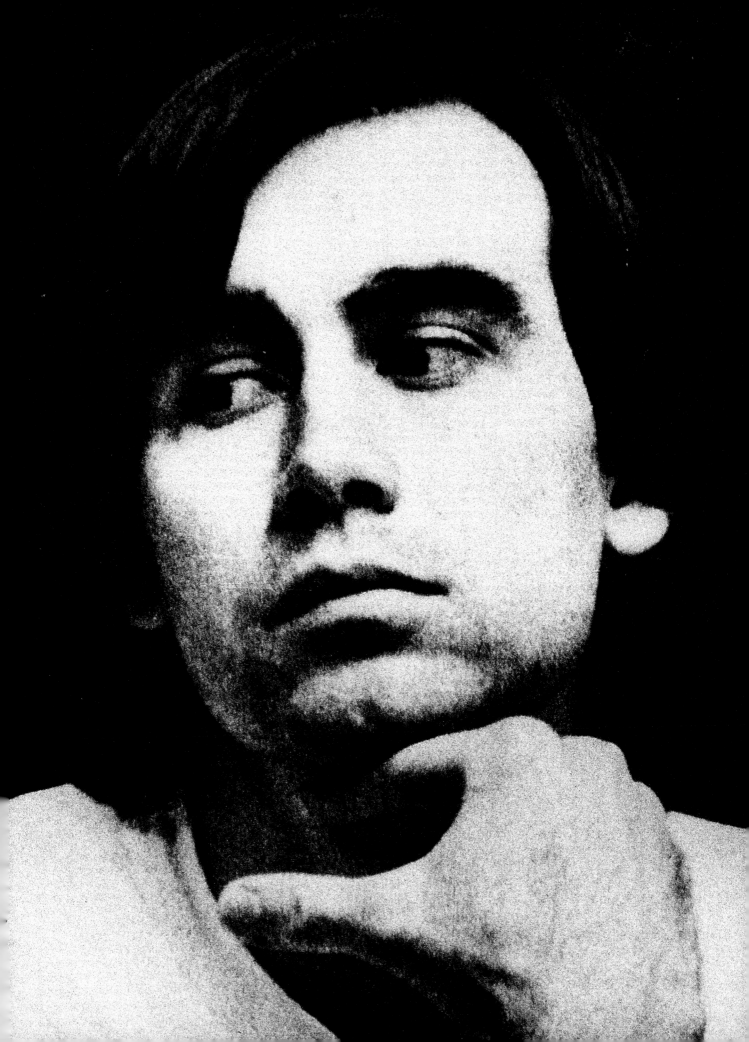

Acknowledgments

The editors thank the following for their valuable assistance:

Ronald Biggs, Rio de Janeiro; Sheri Elms, Boise, Idaho; Sergeant Rollo Green, Torrance, Calif.; Lieutenant John F. Hollihan, Boynton Beach, Fla.; Bill Murphy, North Miami, Fla.; Sheriff Tim Nettleton, Murphy, Idaho; Sergeant Arthur Newcomb, Palm Beach, Fla.; Dee Pogue, Boise, Idaho; Isabelle Sauvé-Astruc, Conservateur, Musée des Collections Historiques de la Préfecture de Police, Paris; Addam Swapp, Littleton, Colo.; Kenneth Whitaker, Jr., North Miami, Fla.

Bibliography

Books:

Bates, Tom, *Rads: The 1970 Bombing of the Army Math Research Center at the University of Wisconsin and Its Aftermath.* New York: Harper Collins, 1992.

Benford, Timothy B., and James P. Johnson, *Righteous Carnage: The List Murders.* New York: Charles Scribner's Sons, 1991.

Biggs, Ronald, *Ronnie Biggs: His Own Story.* London: Sphere Books, 1981.

Coates, James:
Armed and Dangerous: The Rise of the Survivalist Right. New York: Hill and Wang, 1987.
In Mormon Circles: Gentiles, Jack Mormons, and Latter-day Saints. Reading, Mass.: Addison-Wesley, 1991.

Cohen, Daniel, *The Encyclopedia of Unsolved Crimes.* New York: Dodd, Mead, 1988.

Corcoran, James, *Bitter Harvest.* New York: Viking, 1990.

Cromie, Robert, and Joseph Pinkston, *Dillinger: A Short and Violent Life.* New York: McGraw-Hill, 1962.

Dozhier, Parker, *Death in the Desert: The Story of Claude Dallas.* Sutton, Nebr.: Spearman, 1986.

Fleisher, David, and David M. Freedman, *Death of an American.* New York: Continuum, 1983.

Flynn, Kevin, and Gary Gerhardt, *The Silent Brotherhood: Inside America's Racist Underground.* New York: Free Press, Macmillan, 1989.

Fredericks, Dean, *John Dillinger.* New York: Pyramid Books, 1963.

Gibney, Bruce, *The Beauty Queen Killer.* New York: Windsor, 1984.

Gosling, John, and Dennis Craig, *The Great Train Robbery.* Indianapolis: Bobbs-Merrill, 1965.

Hoover, J. Edgar:
"The Ma Barker Gang." In *Murder in the 1930s,* edited by Colin Wilson. New York: Carroll & Graf, 1992.
Persons in Hiding. Boston: Little, Brown, 1938.

Horn, Huston, *The Pioneers* (The Old West series). New York: Time-Life Books, 1974.

Karpis, Alvin, with Bill Trent, *The Alvin Karpis Story.* New York: Coward, McCann & Geoghegan, 1971.

Kelly, Jack, *Mad Dog.* New York: Maxwell Macmillan, 1992.

Long, Jeff, *Outlaw: The True Story of Claude Dallas.* New York: William Morrow, 1985.

McDowell, Bart, *The American Cowboy in Life and Legend.* Washington, D.C.: National Geographic Society, 1972.

Mackenzie, Colin, *Biggs: The World's Most Wanted Man.* New York: William Morrow, 1975.

Martinez, Thomas, with John Guinther, *Brotherhood of Murder.* New York: McGraw-Hill, 1988.

Messick, Hank, and Burt Goldblatt, *Kidnapping: The Illustrated History.* New York: Dial Press, 1974.

Moore, Todd, *Dillinger: Book I.* Allston, Mass.: Primal, 1990.

Nash, Jay Robert:
Almanac of World Crime. New York: Bonanza Books, 1986.
Bloodletters and Badmen. New York: M. Evans, 1973.
Dillinger: Dead or Alive? Chicago: H. Regnery, 1970.
The Dillinger Dossier. Highland Park, Ill.: December Press, 1983.
Encyclopedia of World Crime. Wilmette, Ill.: CrimeBooks, 1989.

Jay Robert Nash's Crime Chronology. New York: Facts on File, 1984.

Newton, Michael, and Judy Ann Newton, *The FBI Most Wanted.* New York: Garland, 1989.

Olsen, Jack, *Give a Boy a Gun.* New York: Delacorte Press, 1985.

Purvis, Melvin, *American Agent.* Garden City, N.Y.: Doubleday, Doran, 1936.

Read, Piers Paul, *The Train Robbers.* Philadelphia: J. B. Lippincott, 1978.

Sabljak, Mark, and Martin H. Greenberg, *Most Wanted: A History of the FBI's Ten Most Wanted List.* New York: Bonanza Books, 1990.

Sharkey, Joe, *Death Sentence: The Inside Story of the John List Murders.* New York: Penguin Books, 1990.

Sifakis, Carl, *The Encyclopedia of American Crime.* New York: Facts on File, 1982.

Stutman, Robert M., and Richard Esposito, *Dead on Delivery: Inside the Drug Wars, Straight from the Street.* New York: Warner Books, 1992.

Toland, John, *The Dillinger Days.* New York: Random House, 1963.

Periodicals:

"Anders at St. Paul, Guarded by G-Men." *New York Times,* January 19, 1938.

"Await Ross Kidnap-Slayer Here: Terrified Youth Tossed $50,000 Aside on Signal." *Chicago Daily News,* January 18, 1938.

"Balaclava and the 40 Thieves." *Daily Sketch,* August 9, 1963.

Barden, J. C., "Gunfight Shatters Tranquility of Arkansas Hills." *New York Times,* July 3, 1983.

"Battles G-Men at Death Dugout." *Chicago Daily News,* January 22,

1938.

"The Biggest Blast." *Newsweek,* September 7, 1970.

"Biggs Biggest Scrounger, Says Ex-Wife." *Daily Times* (London), May 8, 1981.

Blythe, Paul, and Carolyn Davis, "Bereft Bonded by Hunt for Children, Answers." *West Palm Beach Post,* April 7, 1985.

Bonner, Hilary, "Pardon Me! I'm Just an Honest Crook." *Daily Mirror,* September 22, 1988.

"Britain Wins Biggs Extradition." *Daily Times* (London), April 18, 1981.

Buchanan, Edna:
"Aussie Racer Sought in Kidnaping of Model." *Miami Herald,* March 24, 1984.
"Boynton Suspect Still on the Lam." *Miami Herald,* April 5, 1984.
"Could Police Have Stopped Wilder Sooner?" *Miami Herald,* May 13, 1984.
"FBI: Wilder Stabbed Girl in N.Y." *Miami Herald,* April 13, 1984.
"FBI Gets TV View of Wilder." *Miami Herald,* April 7, 1984.
"Partner to Suspect: Surrender." *Miami Herald,* March 30, 1984.
"Race Driver May Be Link to Missing Models." *Miami Herald,* March 16, 1984.
"Suspect Knew Missing Model, Police Are Told." *Miami Herald,* March 29, 1984.

Buchanan, Edna, and Lisa Hoffman:
"Kidnap Suspect Put on FBI's Most Wanted List." *Miami Herald,* April 6, 1984.
"Was Lure of Cover-Girl Fame the Key to Disappearances?" *Miami Herald,* April 1, 1984.

Buchanan, Edna, and Richard Wallace, "Suicide Ruled Out in Wilder Death." *Miami Herald,* April 15, 1984.

Bucher, Jean, "Inside Addam Swapp." *Utah Holiday,* October 1988.

Campbell, Joel, Steve Fidel, and Chuck Gates, "Law Officers Tense on Anniversary of Singer's Death." *Deseret News,* January 18, 1988.

Carter, Mike, Christopher Smart, and Jim Woolf, "Letters from Swapp, Singer Leave Utah Lawmen Grim." *Salt Lake Tribune,* January 28, 1988.

Connelly, Michael, "Wilder Led Double Life in South Florida." *Palm Beach News/Sun-Sentinel,* April 15, 1984.

Cook, Christopher, "Walden Found Mission." *Beaumont Enterprise,* March 27, 1984.

Cummings, Valerie, "Body of Suspected Wilder Victim Found Near Utah-Arizona Border." *Miami Herald,* May 5, 1984.

"Dakota Dragnet." *Time,* February 28, 1983.

"Dallas to Go to Court Today." *Idaho Statesman,* June 8, 1987.

Davis, Carolyn, "Some Say System of Justice Let Dangerous Man Slip Away." *West Palm Beach Post,* April 7, 1985.

Davis, L. J., "Ballad of an American Terrorist." *Harper's,* July 1986.

Dean, John, "Dallas Taken to Owyhee." *Idaho Statesman,* April 25, 1982.

"Denver's Talk-Show Murder." *Newsweek,* July 2, 1984.

Etlinger, Charles, "Who Is This Man Named Dallas?" *Idaho Statesman,* May 9, 1982.

"FBI: Friends Helped Dallas Elude Lawmen." *Idaho Statesman,* March 10, 1987.

Finn, Philip, "Biggs a Prisoner of the High Sea Pirates." *Daily Mirror* (London), March 20, 1981.

Finnegan, James, "The Bloody Saga of Ma Barker and Alvin Karpis." *True Detective,* June 1960.

Fitzpatrick, Tim, "4 Singer-Swapp Clan Members Convicted." *Salt Lake Tribune,* May 10, 1988.

Fleischman, Joan, "Police Press Search for Missing Model." *Miami Herald,* February 29, 1984.

"Fred Barker and 'Ma' Die." *New York Times,* January 17, 1935.

Friend, Stuart, "£1,000,000 (Maybe Two!) Mail Train Robbery." *Evening News & Star,* August 8, 1963.

Garber, Andrew, and Jana Pewitt, "Hounds Lose Dallas' Scent at High-way." *Idaho Statesman,* April 2, 1986.

"G-Men Guard Killer on Plane from California." *Chicago Daily News,* January 18, 1938.

Gorrell, Mike, Jim Woolf, and Mike Carter, "Siege Ends in Burst of Bullets." *Salt Lake Tribune,* January 29, 1988.

Green, Michelle, and Meg Grant, "A Quarter Century after His Great Train Robbery, Ronald Biggs Isn't Railing against Life on the Lam." *People,* October 10, 1988.

Green, Timothy, "Ronnie Biggs Is Alive and Well and Living in Brazil." *Smithsonian,* November 1980.

Gregory, Frederick L., "Ronnie Biggs Ready to Celebrate 20 Illustrious Years on the Run." *Daily Post* (Rio de Janeiro), May 1/2, 1985.

Hamill, Pete, "Britain's Great Train Robbery." *Reader's Digest,* December 1964.

Heywood, Roger, "Surprise at Biggs Hearing." *Daily Times* (London), April 8, 1981.

Heywood, Roger, and Matheus Feldhuzen, "Biggs Toasts New Freedom." *Daily Times* (London), April 24, 1981.

"How Wilder's Terror Tore across Nation," *Miami News,* May 7, 1984.

Israelsen, Brent, "Siege of Singer Home Enters 5th Day; Lawmen Not at Scene Question Tactics." *Deseret News,* January 20, 1988.

"It's 307 Years: Great Train Robbery Sentences." *Evening News and Star,* April 16, 1964.

"Journey of Terror." *People,* April 30, 1984.

Jones, Robert F., "An Angry Rebel's Paradise Lost." *People,* September 22, 1986.

Jorgensen, Chris, "Standoff Persists at Singer Compound." *Salt Lake Tribune,* January 18, 1988.

Jorgensen, Chris, Mike Gorrell, and Jim Woolf, "Police Blast Noise at Singer Farm." *Salt Lake Tribune,* January 24, 1988.

"Karpis Captured in New Orleans by

Hoover Himself." *New York Times,* May 2, 1936.

"Karpis in St. Paul for Kidnap Trial." *New York Times,* May 3, 1936.

Kaye, Jeff, "Nevada Police Nab Wilder Look-Alike." *Miami Herald,* April 9, 1984.

"Kidnaper's Trial May Star Bellhop." *Chicago Daily News,* January 22, 1938.

"Kidnap Farce Costs Biggs His Freedom." *Guardian,* March 25, 1981.

King, Wayne, "A Farmer's Fatal Obsession with Jews and Taxes." *New York Times,* August 21, 1990.

Laughlin, Meg, "Room 30." *Miami Herald Tropic,* March 28, 1993.

"The Law Attacks the Order." *Newsweek,* April 29, 1985.

"Legal Hitch Gives Ronald Biggs Freedom." *The Times* (London), April 24, 1981.

Long, Jeff, "The Most Dangerous Game." *Rocky Mountain Magazine,* September/October 1981.

McQuiston, John T., "U.S. Seizes Woman in Inquiry." *New York Times,* May 25, 1989.

"The Madison Bombers." *Newsweek,* September 14, 1970.

"Man Dies as Bomb Rips Math Center." *New York Times,* August 25, 1970.

"Manhunt Ends with Colebrook Shooting." *News and Sentinel,* April 18, 1984.

Marks, Ellen:
"Hunt Leaves Pogue's Son Tired but Willing to Go On." *Idaho Statesman,* February 15, 1981.
"Searchers for Pogue Increase." *Idaho Statesman,* February 15, 1981.

Marriott, Michael, "The 'Perplexing' Killing of a Drug Agent." *New York Times,* March 2, 1989.

"Memorandum on a Mass Murder." *Newsweek,* April 9, 1990.

Misch, Laura, and Rick Rosenfeld, "Wilder Lookalike's Lament: Not Again." *Miami Herald,* April 14, 1984.

Morgan, Andy:
"Multiple-Killing Suspect Linked to

City Victim." *Saturday Oklahoman & Times,* April 7, 1984.
"Victims' Relatives Feel Anger, Relief." *Saturday Oklahoman & Times,* April 14, 1984.

Murphy, Tom, "Biggs Goes Ahead with Filming of Coffee Commercial for Aus." *Daily Post* (Rio de Janeiro), August 20, 1982.

Nichols, Hugh, "Wanted Again." *American West,* September/October 1986.

Omang, Joanne, "North Dakota Militant Eludes Lawmen." *Washington Post,* February 16, 1983.

"Order in Court." *Time,* September 23, 1985.

Palmer, Douglas D., "Singer Says the Talking's Over and Time for Holy War Has Come." *Deseret News,* January 17, 1988.

Palmer, Douglas D., JoAnn Jacobsen-Wells, and Lisa Riley Roche, "Singer Standoff Goes into 11th Day; Officials Worry about Children." *Deseret News,* January 26, 1988.

Pewitt, Jana:
"Dallas Manhunt Spreads to Three States." *Idaho Statesman,* April 1, 1986.
"Dallas Placed on FBI's List of Most Wanted." *Idaho Statesman,* May 17, 1986.

Pollack, Jill, and Donna Wares, "In Boynton, 11 Say Farewell to Wilder." *Miami Herald,* April 19, 1984.

Pooley, Eric, "A Federal Case." *New York Magazine,* March 27, 1989.

Prendergast, Alan, "The Law and Claude Dallas." *Rolling Stone,* December 9, 1982.

Priest, Dana, and Susan Kelleher. "A Double Life for 17 Years?" *Washington Post,* July 1, 1989.

Proctor, David, "Charisma Makes Killer a Hit on the Witness Stand." *Idaho Statesman,* September 6, 1987.

Raab, Selwyn:
"Slain Agent Also Helped Prison Inquiry." *New York Times,* March 10, 1989.
"Slain Suspect Had Hidden on East Side." *New York Times,* November

21, 1989.
"Raid Fails to Find Murder Suspect." *New York Times,* February 16, 1983.

Rawls, Wendell, Jr., "Man Dead in Gunfight Identified as Dakota Fugitive." *New York Times,* June 5, 1983.

"Retracing Wilder's Deadly Path," *Miami News,* May 5, 1984.

Rice, Robert, Lisa Riley Roche, and Brent Israelsen, "Power Cut in Effort to Drive Singers from Home." *Deseret News,* January 22, 1988.

Riley, Michael, "In Idaho: A Killer Becomes a Mythic Hero." *Time,* January 26, 1987.

Ringholz, Raye C., "Armageddon at Marion, Utah." *Utah Holiday,* January and February 1979.

"Rise of the Dynamite Radicals." *Time,* September 7, 1970.

Rocha, Jan, "Biggs Son to Ask for Royal Pardon." *Guardian* (London), September 10, 1988.

"Ronnie Rotten!" *Daily Mirror* (London), May 24, 1978.

"Ross's Body Found in Wisconsin Hunt; New Crime Solved." *New York Times,* January 21, 1938.

"Ross Slayer Goes into a Rage as U.S. Agents Arraign Him." *Chicago Daily News,* January 24, 1938.

"Ross Was Killed by Blow on Skull." *New York Times,* January 22, 1938.

"Scrutinize Anders in Mattson Killing." *New York Times,* January 20, 1938.

"Seven Get 30 Years Each." *Evening Standard,* April 16, 1964.

"Shootout in a Sleepy Hamlet." *Time,* June 13, 1983.

"Singer Home Cordoned Off after Blast at Church." *Deseret News,* January 17, 1988.

"Sketches of Four Suspects in the Wisconsin Bombing." *New York Times,* September 4, 1970.

"Slayer of Ross Guarded." *Chicago Daily News,* January 19, 1938.

Spiegel, Claire:
"The Story of the Victim Wilder Spared." *Miami Herald,* April 17, 1984.
"Suspected Killer Tied to Missing Girl." *Los Angeles Times,* April 12,

1984.

"Tina Marie Risico." *Los Angeles Times,* August 15, 1984.

"Wilder Slain; Torrance Girl Back Home Safely." *Los Angeles Times,* April 14, 1984.

"Standoff Ends as Shots Kill Lawman, Wound Swapp." *Deseret News,* January 28, 1988.

Starita, Joe, "Suicide Ruled Out in Wilder Death." *Miami Herald,* April 15, 1984.

Stein, George, "Wealthy Playboy Had It All—Including a Macabre Twist." *Miami Herald,* April 14, 1984.

Strauss, Gary, "Dallas Murder Trial." *Idaho Statesman,* September 26, 1982.

Stuebner, Stephen:
"Dallas: 'I Was Afraid' from First Day in Prison." *Idaho Statesman,* September 4, 1987.
"Dallas' Defense Puts Idaho Pen on Defensive." *Idaho Statesman,* September 3, 1987.
"Jury Acquits Dallas of Prison Escape." *Idaho Statesman,* September 5, 1987.
"Two Jurors: Dallas Had to Leave." *Idaho Statesman,* September 6, 1987.

Sullivan, Joseph F., "Music Played in 1971 as Police Found Bodies of 5." *New York Times,* April 4, 1990.

"Suspect Knew Missing Model Police Are Told." *Miami Herald,* March 29, 1984.

"Tax Nut Killed in Fiery Standoff." *New York Post,* June 4, 1983.

Tracy, Dawn, "He Was My Brother, My Dear Old Friend." *Salt Lake Tribune,* January 29, 1988.

"The Train Robber: 'I'd Do It Again.' " *Newsweek,* January 12, 1981.

"The Train-Robber Heist." *Newsweek,* April 6, 1981.

Tullett, Tom, Barry Stanley, and Edward Vale, "Yard Probe the Great Escape." *Daily Mirror* (London), July 9, 1965.

"Two Killed in Arkansas Fight Believed to Involve Fugitive." *New York Times,* June 4, 1983.

Vejnoska, Jill:
"Doctor: Stressed List Just Snapped." *Courier-News,* April 7, 1990.
"Doctor Recounts List's Getaway." *Courier-News,* April 11, 1990.
"Letter: List Shot Family, Prayed." *Courier-News,* March 29, 1990.
"List Family Secrets Revealed." *Courier-News,* April 5, 1990.
"Verdict Brings Mixed Reaction." *Idaho Statesman,* September 5, 1987.
"Violence on the Right." *Newsweek,* March 4, 1985.

Voboril, Mary, "The Mind of Christopher Wilder." *Miami Herald Tropic,* November 4, 1984.

Voboril, Mary, and David Marcus, "FBI Ties Wilder to Vegas." *Miami Herald,* April 18, 1984.

Warbis, Mark, "Murder Turned Myth." *Lewiston Tribune,* January 7, 1991.

"Wilder, Cornered, Kills Self." *Miami Herald,* April 14, 1984.

Woolf, Jim:
"Copter Drops Note Telling Singer Family to Give Up." *Salt Lake Tribune,* January 21, 1988.
"Signals Flash from Singer Ranch." *Salt Lake Tribune,* January 22, 1987.

Zinti, Robert T., "Dreams of a Bigot's Revolution." *Time,* February 18, 1985.

Zumbo, Jim, "Last Day of the Wardens." *Outdoor Life,* June 26, 1981.

Videos:

Hollenhurst, John, KSL-TV Interview February 6, 1987, with Addam Swapp and Vickie Singer.

Standoff in Marion, Utah. Utah Department of Public Safety.

Other Sources:

Federal Bureau of Investigation, "Barker-Karpis Gang." November 19, 1936 (revised April 1984).

Federal Bureau of Investigation Summary, John Henry Seadlund, September 28, 1938.

Index

Numerals in italics indicate an illustration of the subject.

Picture Credits

The sources for the illustrations that appear in this volume are listed below. Credits for the illustrations from left to right are separated by semicolons; from top to bottom they are separated by dashes.

Cover: William Albert Allard. **4, 5:** Rick Egan/*Salt Lake Tribune,* Salt Lake City, Utah. **6:** New South Wales Police Department. **8, 9:** Private collection. **12, 13:** Courtesy Manly Municipal Library, Sydney. **15:** Courtesy John F. Hanlon. **17:** Courtesy of the *Sun-Sentinel,* Fort Lauderdale, Fla. **18-20:** Courtesy John F. Hanlon. **21:** Private collection. **23:** Courtesy John F. Hanlon. **24, 25:** AP/Wide World Photos, New York; courtesy John F. Hanlon. **26:** Courtesy John F. Hanlon. **27:** H. B. Minor, hand-tinted by Philip Brooker. **30, 31:** Courtesy John F. Hanlon; inset, AP/Wide World Photos, New York. **32, 33:** Courtesy John F. Hanlon; inset, AP/Wide World Photos, New York. **34, 35:** Courtesy John F. Hanlon—AP/Wide World Photos, New York. **36, 37:** UPI/Bettmann, New York; inset, courtesy John F. Hanlon. **38:** Courtesy John F. Hanlon. **39:** UPI/Bettmann, New York. **40:** AP/Wide World Photos, New York. **41-43:** UPI/Bettmann, New York. **44, 45:** AP/Wide World Photos, New York. **46:** William Albert Allard. **49:** © Milan Chuckovich 1983. **51:** *Idaho Statesman* Photo, Boise State University Library, Boise, Idaho; inset, courtesy Sheriff Tim Nettleton. **52, 53:** William Albert Allard. **56, 57:** Courtesy Sheriff Tim Nettleton. **59:** AP/Wide World Photos, New York; Sheri Evans. **62, 63:** *Idaho Statesman* Photo, Boise State University Library, Boise, Idaho; inset, *Idaho Statesman,* Boise, Idaho. **65:** Courtesy Sheriff Tim Nettleton. **66-69:** *Idaho Statesman,* Boise, Idaho. **72, 73:** *Idaho Statesman,* Boise, Idaho (2); AP/Wide World Photos, New York. **75:** The Bettmann Archive, New York. **76:** UPI/Bettmann, New York. **77, 78:** AP/Wide World Photos, New York. **79:** The Bettmann Archive, New York. **80-82:** UPI/Bettmann, New York. **83:** AP/Wide World Photos, New York. **84-87:** UPI/Bettmann, New York. **88-91:** Courtesy Timothy Benford. **92, 93:** *People Weekly* © 1989/ Stanley Tretick; UPI/Bettmann, New York. **94, 95:** *The Bismarck Tribune,* Bismarck, N.Dak.; *The Herald Press,* Harvey, N.Dak. **96:** Lyn Alweis/*The Denver Post,* Denver, Colo. **97:** Zillah Craig. **98, 99:** United States Department of Justice, DEA, New York. **100:** Reuters/Bettmann, New York. **103:** W. B. Huber/Scope Features, London. **105:** Private collection. **106, 107:** Syndication International, London; inset, Popperfoto, Overstone, Northhamptonshire, England. **108, 109:** UPI/ Bettmann, New York. **111-113:** Topham Picture Source, Edenbridge, Kent, England. **115-119:** Private collection. **120, 121:** Sonai Rosenburg/Scope Features, London. **122, 123:** © Express Newspapers, London; Camera Press, London. **124, 125:** John Maier, Jr. **126:** AP/Wide World Photos, New York. **128, 129:** Utah State Historical Society, Salt Lake City, Utah. **130:** From *Death of an American: The Killing of John Singer,* by David Fleisher and David M. Freedman, The Continuum Publishing Company, New York, 1983. **134, 135:** Vinnie Fish—UPI/ Bettmann, New York. **136-143:** Vinnie Fish. **144:** From *Death of an American: The Killing of John Singer,* by David Fleisher and David M. Freedman, The Continuum Publishing Company, New York, 1983. **148, 149:** Utah State Historical Society, Salt Lake City, Utah. **152, 153:** UPI/Bettmann, New York; Utah State Historical Society, Salt Lake City, Utah. **154-156:** AP/ Wide World Photos, New York. **157:** AP/Wide World Photos, New York—Rick Egan/*Salt Lake Tribune,* Salt Lake City, Utah. **158, 159:** Lynn Johnson/*Salt Lake Tribune,* Salt Lake City, Utah. **160-162:** Utah State Historical Society, Salt Lake City, Utah. **163:** AP/Wide World Photos, New York. **165:** Gerald Silver/*Deseret News,* Salt Lake City, Utah—Lynn Johnson. **166, 167:** UPI/Bettmann, New York.

TRUE CRIME

SERIES EDITOR: Laura Foreman
Administrative Editor: Jane A. Martin
Art Director: Christopher Register
Picture Editors: Jane Jordan (principal),
  Jane A. Martin

Editorial Staff for *Most Wanted*
Text Editor: Sarah Brash
Writer: Robin Currie
Associate Editor/Research: Mark Lazen
Assistant Art Director: Brook Mowrey
Senior Copyeditors: Elizabeth Graham (principal),
  Colette Stockum
Picture Coordinator: Jennifer Iker
Editorial Assistant: Donna Fountain

Special Contributors: Douglas J. Brown, Elizabeth
L'Hommedieu King, Katharine N. Old, Catherine
Harper Parrott, Kathryn B. Pfeifer, Rosanne C.
Scott, Kathy Wismar (research); George Constable,
George G. Daniels, Jim Hicks, Jack McClintock,
Valerie Moolman, Anthony K. Pordes, Nancy E.
Shute, John Sullivan (text); John Drummond
(design); Mel Ingber (index).

Correspondents: Elisabeth Kraemer-Singh (Bonn);
Christine Hinze (London); John Dunn (Melbourne);
Christina Lieberman (New York); Maria Vincenza
Aloisi (Paris); John Maier (Rio de Janeiro); Ann
Natanson (Rome). Valuable assistance was also
provided by Elizabeth Brown, Katheryn White
(New York).

Library of Congress Cataloging in Publication Data
Most wanted/by the editors of Time-Life Books.
     p.   cm. — (True Crime)
  Includes bibliographical references and index.
  ISBN 0-7835-0020-3
  1. Criminals—Biography.
I. Time-Life Books. II. Series.
HV6245.M68 1993
364.1'092'2—dc20   93-24031
                                          CIP
ISBN 0-7835-0021-1 (lib. bdg.)

TIME LIFE BOOKS ®

Other Publications:
WEIGHT WATCHERS® SMART CHOICE
  RECIPE COLLECTION
THE AMERICAN INDIANS
THE ART OF WOODWORKING
LOST CIVILIZATIONS
ECHOES OF GLORY
THE NEW FACE OF WAR
HOW THINGS WORK
WINGS OF WAR
CREATIVE EVERYDAY COOKING
COLLECTOR'S LIBRARY OF THE UNKNOWN
CLASSICS OF WORLD WAR II
TIME-LIFE LIBRARY OF CURIOUS AND
  UNUSUAL FACTS
AMERICAN COUNTRY
VOYAGE THROUGH THE UNIVERSE
THE THIRD REICH
THE TIME-LIFE GARDENER'S GUIDE
MYSTERIES OF THE UNKNOWN
TIME FRAME
FIX IT YOURSELF
FITNESS, HEALTH & NUTRITION
SUCCESSFUL PARENTING
HEALTHY HOME COOKING
UNDERSTANDING COMPUTERS
LIBRARY OF NATIONS
THE ENCHANTED WORLD
THE KODAK LIBRARY OF CREATIVE
  PHOTOGRAPHY
GREAT MEALS IN MINUTES
THE CIVIL WAR
PLANET EARTH
COLLECTOR'S LIBRARY OF THE CIVIL WAR
THE EPIC OF FLIGHT
THE GOOD COOK
WORLD WAR II
HOME REPAIR AND IMPROVEMENT
THE OLD WEST

*For information on and a full description of any
of the Time-Life Books series listed above, please
call 1-800-621-7026 or write:*
Reader Information
Time-Life Customer Service
P.O. Box C-32068
Richmond, Virginia 23261-2068

This volume is one of a series that examines
the phenomenon of crime. Other books in the
series include:
Serial Killers
Mass Murderers
Mafia
Unsolved Crimes
Compulsion to Kill